ADVENTURES IN THE COUNTERCULTURE
FROM HIP HOP TO HIGH TIMES
BY STEVEN HAGER

HIGH TIMES BOOKS 2002

For Clay

Steve Hager

For Stacy and Brave

Adventures in the Counterculture: From Hip Hop to High Times
By Steven Hager

In "Appointment with the Apocalypse," material on the Danforth Report was based on research provided by Preston Peet, who received a co-byline on the article when the story was originally published in HIGH TIMES.

ISBN# 1-893010-14-7

Cover art by Steve Marcus
Book design by Frank Max
Copyedited by Gabe Kirchheimer
Managing Editor: Chesley Hicks
Special thanks to Aaron Melick and Jim Ski

High Times Books are distributed by Publisher's Group West
1700 4th St., Berkeley, CA 94710, 800-788-3123

Printed in the U.S.A.

First Edition March 2002

High Times Books
419 Park Avenue South, 16th Floor
New York, NY 10016
USA

HERITAGE OF STONE

Although John F. Kennedy was neither a saint nor a great intellectual, he was the youngest President ever elected, which may explain why he was so well attuned to the changing mood of America in the '60s. Americans had grown weary of Cold War hysteria. They wanted to relax and have fun. Like the majority of people across the planet, they wanted peace.

The President's primary obstacle in this quest was a massive, power-hungry bureaucracy which had emerged after WWII—a Frankenstein monster created by anti-Communist paranoia and inflated defense budgets. By 1960, the Pentagon was easily the world's largest corporation, with assets of over $60 billion. No one understood this monster better than President Dwight D. Eisenhower. On January 17, 1961, in his farewell address to the nation, Eisenhower spoke to the country, and to his successor, John Kennedy.

"The conjunction of an immense military establishment and a large arms industry is new in the American experience," said Eisenhower. "We must guard against the acquisition of unwarranted influence, whether sought or unsought, by the military-industrial complex."

At the beginning of his administration, Kennedy seems to have followed the advice of his military and intelligence officers. What else could such an inexperienced President have done? Signs of a serious rift, however, first appeared after the Bay of Pigs, a CIA-planned-and-executed invasion of Cuba which took place three months after Kennedy took office. The invasion was so bungled that Kennedy refused to send American troops to save the day and immediately afterward fired CIA Director Allen Dulles, Deputy Director General Charles Cabell and Deputy Director of Planning Richard Bissell.

Kennedy's next major crisis occurred on October 16, 1962, when he was shown aerial photos of missile bases in Cuba. The Joint Chiefs of Staff pressed for an immediate attack. Instead, Attorney General Robert Kennedy was sent to meet with Soviet Ambassador Anatoly Dobrynin. In his memoirs, Soviet Premier Nikita Krushchev quotes the younger

Kennedy as saying: "The President is in a grave situation... We are under pressure from our military to use force against Cuba... If the situation continues much longer, the President is not sure that the military will not overthrow him and seize power."

Military hopes for an invasion of Cuba evaporated as Krushchev and Kennedy worked out a nonviolent solution to the crisis. In return, Kennedy promised not to invade Cuba. Angered over the Bay of Pigs fiasco, the CIA refused to bend to Kennedy's will and continued their destabilization campaign against Castro, which included sabotage raids conducted by a secret army, as well as plots against Castro's life, which were undertaken with the help of well-known Mafia figures such as Johnny Roselli, Sam Giancana and Santos Trafficante. A bitter internal struggle developed around Kennedy's attempts to disband the CIA's paramilitary bases in Florida and Louisiana.

On August 5, 1963, the US, Great Britain and the Soviet Union signed a limited nuclear test ban treaty. Engineered by President Kennedy and long in negotiation, the treaty was a severe blow to the Cold Warriors in the Pentagon and the CIA. On September 20, 1963, Kennedy spoke hopefully of peace to the UN General Assembly. "Today we may have reached a pause in the Cold War," he said. "If both sides can now gain new confidence and experience in concrete collaborations of peace, then surely, this first small step can be the start of a long, fruitful journey."

"Years later, paging through its formerly classified records, talking to the National Security Council staff, it is difficult to avoid the impression that the President was learning the responsibility of power," writes John Prados in his book *Keepers of the Keys*, an analysis of the National Security Council. "Here was a smoother, calmer Kennedy, secretly working for rapprochement with Fidel Castro and a withdrawal from Vietnam."

Although Kennedy's Vietnam policy has not received widespread publicity, he turned resolutely against the war in June of 1963, when he ordered Defense Secretary Robert McNamara and Chairman of the Joint Chiefs of Staff General Maxwell Taylor to announce from the White House steps that all American forces would be withdrawn by 1965. At the time, 15,500 US "advisors" were stationed in South Vietnam, and total casualties suffered remained a relatively low 100.

On November 14, Kennedy signed an order to begin the withdrawal by removing 1,000 troops. In private, Kennedy let it be known the military was not going to railroad him into continuing the war. Many of the hard-line anti-Communists—including FBI Director J. Edgar Hoover—would have to be purged. Bobby Kennedy would be put in charge of dismantling the CIA. President Kennedy told Senator Mike Mansfield of his plans to tear the CIA "into a thousand pieces and scatter it to the wind." But these plans had to wait for Kennedy's reelection in 1964. And in order to win that election, he had to secure the South. Which is why Kennedy went to Texas later that month.

Could John Kennedy have stopped the war in Vietnam, as was his obvious intention? America will never know. His command to begin the Vietnam withdrawal was his last formal executive order. Just after noon on November 22, President Kennedy was murdered while driving through downtown Dallas, in full view of dozens of ardent supporters, and while surrounded by police and personal bodyguards. Thirty-nine years later, grave doubts still linger about who pulled the triggers, who ordered the assassination, and why our government has done so little to bring justice forth.

In 1963, no American wanted to believe that President Kennedy's death was a coup d'etat, planned by the military establishment and executed by the CIA. Today, such a claim can no longer be dismissed. Why has the national media done such an abysmal job of presenting the facts to the American people? Some light was shed by Oliver Stone's film *JFK*, a $30-million epic starring Kevin Costner, released to coincide with the 30th anniversary of Kennedy's death. As his focal point for the story, Stone chose former New Orleans District Attorney Jim Garrison, the only prosecutor to attempt to bring this case to court, and a man subjected to one of the most effective smear campaigns ever orchestrated by the US government. It is a frightening story of murder, corruption and cover-up. Even today, 35 years after he brought the case to court, a powerful media disinformation campaign against Garrison continues.

Born November 20, 1921, in Knoxville, Iowa, Earling Carothers Garrison—known as "Jim" to friends and family—was raised in New Orleans. At age 19, one year before Pearl Harbor, he joined the army. In 1942, he was sent to Europe, where he volunteered to fly spotter planes over the front lines. Following the war, he attended law school at Tulane, joined the FBI and served as a special agent in Seattle and Tacoma. After growing bored with his agency assignments, he returned to New Orleans to practice law. He served as an assistant district attorney from 1954 to 1958.

In 1961, Garrison decided to run for district attorney on a platform openly hostile to then-New Orleans Mayor Victor Schiro. To the surprise of many, he was elected without any major political backing. At 43, he had been district attorney for less than two years when Kennedy was killed. "I was an old-fashioned patriot," he writes in *On the Trail of the Assassins*, "a product of my family, my military experience, and my years in the legal profession. I could not imagine then that the government would ever deceive the citizens of this country."

A few hours after the assassination, Lee Harvey Oswald was arrested. Two days later, while in Dallas police custody, Oswald was murdered by nightclub owner Jack Ruby. Garrison learned that Oswald was from New Orleans, and arranged a Sunday afternoon meeting with his staff. With such an important case, it was their responsibility to investigate Oswald's local connections.

Within days, they learned that Oswald had recently been seen in the company of David Ferrie, a fervent anti-Communist and freelance pilot linked to the Bay of Pigs invasion. Evidence placed Ferrie in Texas on the day of the assassination. Also on that day, a friend of Ferrie's named Guy Bannister had pistol-whipped one Jack Martin during an argument. Martin confided to friends that Bannister and Ferrie were somehow involved in the assassination. Garrison had Ferrie picked up for questioning, and turned him over to the local FBI, who immediately released him. Within a few months, the Warren Commission released its report stating that Oswald was a "lone nut" murdered by a misguided patriot who wanted to spare Jackie Kennedy the ordeal of testifying. Like most Americans, Garrison accepted this conclusion.

Three years later, in the fall of '66, Garrison was happily married with three children and content with his job, when a chance conversation with Senator Russell Long changed his views on the Warren Commission forever.

"Those fellows on the Warren Commission were dead wrong," said Long. "There's no way in the world that one man could have shot up Jack Kennedy that way."

Intrigued, Garrison went back to his office and ordered the complete 26-volume report. "The mass of information was disorganized and confused," writes Garrison. "Worst of all, the conclusions in the report seemed to be based on an appallingly selective reading of the evidence, ignoring credible testimony from literally dozens of witnesses."

Garrison was equally disturbed by the background of the men chosen by President Johnson to serve on the commission. Why, for instance, was Allen Dulles, a man fired by Kennedy, on the panel? A master spy during WWII, Dulles had orchestrated surveillance of the Abwehr (Hitler's military intelligence agency). In the final days of the war, he'd supervised the secret surrender of the elite Nazi SS Corps., and he'd also played a major role in the subsequent incorporation of hundreds of Nazi war criminals, scientists and spies into the newly formed CIA. He was powerful, well-connected to Wall Street and had been director of the CIA for eight years. Certainly, he was no friend to John Kennedy. Serving with Dulles were Representative Gerald Ford, a man described by *Newsweek* as "the CIA's best friend in Congress," John McCloy, former assistant secretary of war and commissioner for occupied Germany immediately after the war, and Senator Richard Russell, chairman of the powerful Senate Armed Services Committee. Russell's home state of Georgia was peppered with military bases and military-industrial contracts. The balance of the commission was clearly in the hands of the military and CIA. The entire "investigation" was supervised by J. Edgar Hoover, who openly detested the Kennedy brothers.

Another interesting link turned up: The mayor of Dallas was Earle Cabell, brother of General Charles Cabell, who JFK had earlier fired from the CIA. Earle Cabell was in a position to control many important details involved in the case, including the Dallas police force.

Based on these general suspicions, Garrison launched a highly secret investigation around Lee Harvey Oswald's links to David Ferrie and Guy Bannister. Unfortunately, Bannister had died nine months after the assassination. An alcoholic and rabid right-winger, Bannister had been a former Naval intelligence operative and a star agent for the FBI. He was a member of the CIA-led John Birch Society and the Minutemen, and publisher of a racist newsletter. His office at 544 Camp Street was a well-known meeting place for anti-Castro Cubans.

Ferrie's background was even more bizarre. A former senior pilot for Eastern Airlines, Ferrie had been the head of the New Orleans Civil Air Patrol, an organization Oswald had joined as a teenager. Many of the boys in the Civil Air Patrol willingly had themselves hypnotized by Ferrie, supposedly to improve their skills and ability to withstand pain. Some of them attended homosexual orgies at Ferrie's house. When complaints concerning these parties were filed with the New Orleans police, Ferrie somehow had the investigations quashed, despite rampant evidence of sexual child abuse. Ferrie suffered from alopecia, an ailment that left him hairless. He wore bright red wigs and painted eyebrows. He founded his own religion, and kept hundreds of experimental rats in his house. He reportedly had flown dozens of solo missions for the CIA in Cuba and Latin America, and had links to Carlos Marcello, head of the Mob in Louisiana. Like Bannister, he was extremely right-wing. "I want to train killers," Ferrie had written to the commander of the US Air Force. "There is nothing I would enjoy better than blowing the hell out of every damn Russian, Communist, Red or what-have-you."

On the day of the assassination, Dean Andrews, a New Orleans attorney, had been asked to fly to Dallas to represent Oswald. When asked by the Warren Commission who had hired him, Andrews had replied Clay Bertrand. Bertrand, Garrison discovered, was a pseudonym used by Clay Shaw, director of the International Trade Mart. Shaw, a darling of New Orleans high society, was also well connected in international high-finance circles. He was also an associate of Bannister and Ferrie. Like many others connected with the assassination, Shaw was a former Army intelligence operative. The case against Shaw was circumstantial, but Garrison did have an eyewitness willing to testify that Shaw had met with Lee Harvey Oswald just prior to the assassination.

Just as Garrison was marshalling his case, some strange events took place. On February 17, 1967, the New Orleans *States-Item* published a story on Garrison's secret probe, indicating he had already spent over $8,000 of taxpayers' money investigating the Kennedy assassination. Soon thereafter, Garrison received an unusually strong letter of support from a Denver oil businessman named John Miller, hinting that Miller wanted to offer financial support to the investigation. When Miller arrived in New Orleans, he met with Garrison and one of his assistants. "You're too big for this job," said Miller. "I suggest you accept an appointment to the bench in federal district court, and move into a job worthy of your talents."

"And what would I have to do to get this judgeship?" asked Garrison.

"Stop your investigation," replied Miller calmly.

Garrison asked Miller to leave his office.

"Well, they offered you the carrot and you turned it down," said his assistant. "You know what's coming next, don't you?"

Suddenly, reporters from all over the country descended on New Orleans, including *Washington Post* contributor George Lardner, Jr. At midnight on February 22, 1967, Lardner claims to have conducted a four-hour interview with Ferrie. The following morning, Ferrie was found dead. Two unsigned, typewritten suicide notes were found. One letter made reference to a "messianic district attorney."

Three days later the coroner announced Ferrie had died of natural causes and placed the time of death well before the end of Lardner's supposed marathon interview. Lardner's possible complicity in the affair would never be called into question, while his highly influential articles in the *Washington Post* branded Garrison's investigation a "fraud." It was just the beginning of a long series of disruptive attacks in the media, and the first of many people connected with the case that would mysteriously turn up dead.

With Ferrie gone, Garrison had only one suspect left. He rushed his case to court, arresting Clay Shaw.

Ellen Ray, a documentary filmmaker from New York, came to New Orleans to film the story. "People were getting killed left and right," she recalls. "Garrison would subpoena a witness and two days later the witness would be killed by a parked car. I thought Garrison was a great American patriot. But things got a little too heavy when I started getting strange phone calls from men with Cuban accents." After several death threats, Ray became so terrified that instead of making a documentary on the trial, she fled the country.

Attorney General Ramsey Clark, a close friend of President Lyndon Johnson, announced from Washington that the federal government had already investigated and exonerated Clay Shaw. "Needless to say," writes Garrison, "this did not exactly make me look like District Attorney of the Year."

Meanwhile, all sorts of backpedaling was going on at the Justice Department. If Shaw had been investigated, why wasn't his name in the Warren Commission Report? "The Attorney General has since determined that this was erroneous," said a spokesman for Clark. "Nothing arose indicating a need to investigate Mr. Shaw."

Realizing he was in a political minefield, Garrison presented his case as cautiously as possible. A grand jury was convened that included Jay C. Albarado. "On March 14, three criminal-court judges heard Garrison's case in a preliminary hearing to determine if there was enough evidence against Shaw to hold him for trial," Albarado wrote many years later in a letter to the New Orleans *Times-Picayune*. "What did they conclude? That there was sufficient evidence. Garrison then presented his evidence to a 12-member grand jury. We ruled there was sufficient evidence to bring Shaw to trial. Were we duped by Garrison? I think not."

Thanks to all the unwanted publicity, Garrison's staff had swollen with volunteers eager to work on the case. The 6'6" Garrison, now dubbed the "Jolly Green Giant," had already become a hero to the many citizens and researchers who had serious doubts about the Warren Commission. Unfortunately, a few of these eager volunteers were later exposed as government informers. Shortly before the case went to trial, one of the infiltrators copied all of Garrison's files and turned them over to Shaw's defense team.

On September 4, 1967, Supreme Court Chief Justice Earl Warren announced that Garrison's case was worthless. The *New York Times* characterized the investigation as a "morbid frolic." *Newsweek* reported that the conspiracy was "a plot of Garrison's own making." *Life* magazine published the first of many reports linking Garrison with the Mafia. (Richard Billings, an editor at *Life*, had been one of the first journalists to gain access to Garrison's inner circle, under the guise of "wanting to help" the investigation.) Walter Sheridan, a former Naval intelligence operative and NBC investigator, appeared in New Orleans with a film crew. Their purpose? An exposé titled *The Case of Jim Garrison*, which was broadcast in June of '67. "It required only a few minutes to see that NBC had classified the case as criminal and had appointed itself as the prosecutor," writes Garrison.

Puzzled by the intensity of NBC's attack, Garrison went to the library and did some research on the company. He learned the network was a subsidiary of RCA, a bulwark of the military-industrial complex whose defense contracts had increased by more than a billion dollars from 1960 to 1967. Its chairman, retired General David Sarnoff, was a well-known proponent of the Cold War.

"Some long-cherished illusions about the great free press in our country underwent a painful reappraisal during this period," writes Garrison.

Clay Shaw was brought to trial on January 29, 1969. It took less than one month for Garrison to present his case.

Demonstrating the cover-up was the easy part. Although the overwhelming majority of eyewitnesses in Dealy Plaza testified that the fatal shot came not from the Texas School Book Depository—where Oswald worked—but from a grassy knoll overlooking the plaza, the FBI had encouraged many witnesses to alter their testimony to fit the "lone nut" theory. Those that didn't were simply ignored by the commission. The ballistic evidence was flawed and obviously tampered with. Even though the FBI had received several warnings of the assassination, they had ignored them. Security for the President was strangely lax. Although Oswald's killer, Jack Ruby, had ties to the CIA and Mafia, this evidence had been suppressed. Ruby was never allowed to testify before the commission. When interviewed in a Texas jail by Chief Justice Warren and Gerald Ford, he told them: "I would like to request that I go to Washington... I want to tell the truth, and I can't tell it here... Gentlemen, my life is in danger." Ruby never made it to Washington. He remained in jail and died mysteriously before Garrison could call him as a witness.

Even more disturbing was the treatment given the deceased President's corpse. Under Texas law, an autopsy should have been performed by a civilian pathologist in Dallas. Instead, the body was removed at gunpoint by the Secret Service and flown to a naval hospital in Maryland, where an incomplete autopsy was performed under the supervision of unnamed admirals and generals. The notes from this "autopsy" were quickly burned. Bullet holes were never tracked, the brain was not dissected and organs were not removed. The autopsy was a botched, tainted affair, performed under military supervision. (The medical aspects of the case were so weird, they would later form the basis for a best-selling book on the assassination, *Best Evidence* by David Lifton.)

The most important and lasting piece of evidence unveiled by Garrison was an 8mm film of the assassination taken by Abraham Zapruder, a film that only three members of the Warren Commission had seen, probably because it cast a long shadow of doubt across their conclusions. A good analysis of the film can be found in *Cover-Up* by J. Gary Shaw and Larry Harris:

"Had the Zapruder film of the JFK assassination been shown on national television Friday evening, November 22, 1963, the Oswald/lone assassin fabrication would have been unacceptable to a majority of Americans... The car proceeds down Elm and briefly disappears behind a sign. When it emerges the President has obviously been shot... Governor Connally turns completely to the right, looking into the back seat; he begins to turn back when his body stiffens on impact of a bullet. Very shortly after Connally is hit, the President's head explodes in a shower of blood and brain matter—he is driven violently backward at a speed estimated at 80-100 feet per second."

Although Time, Inc. could have made a small fortune distributing this film around the world, they instead secured the rights from Zapruder for $225,000, then held a few private screenings before locking the film in a vault. It was shown to one newsman, Dan Rather, who then described it on national television. Rather asserted that Kennedy's head went "forward with considerable force" after the fatal head shot (a statement that would have supported a hit from behind, from the direction of the School Book Depository). Several months later, Rather was promoted to White House Correspondent by CBS. As if to buttress this fabrication, the FBI reversed the order of the frames when printing them in the Warren Report. When researchers later drew this reversal to the FBI's attention, Hoover attributed the switch to a "printing error."

Although Garrison proved his conspiracy, the jury was not convinced of Clay Shaw's role in it. He was released after only two hours of deliberation.

The end of the Clay Shaw trial was just the beginning of a long nightmare for Garrison. On June 30, 1971, he was arrested by federal agents on corruption charges. Two years later, the case came to trial at the height of Garrison's reelection campaign. Although he won the case, he lost the election by 2,000 votes. However, the Jolly Green Giant remained widely respected in his home state, and was later elected to two terms on the second-highest court in Louisiana.

In 1967, the machinations of the CIA were unknown to most Americans. Today, thankfully, many brave men have left their comfortable careers in the agency and spoken out against CIA-sponsored terror around the world. One of these is Victor Marchetti, who was executive assistant to CIA director Richard Helms, and subsequently coauthored *The CIA and the Cult of Intelligence* with John D. Marks. In 1975 Marchetti confirmed that Clay Shaw and David Ferrie had been CIA operatives, and that the agency had secretly worked for Shaw's defense.

Over the years, many high-ranking officials have come forward to support Garrison's theory. "The big story in the Kennedy assassination is the cover-up," says retired Colonel L. Fletcher Prouty, Chief of Special Operations for the Joint Chiefs of Staff until 1964. Prouty was on assignment in New Zealand on the day of the assassination. After carrying a New Zealand newspaper article back to Washington, he checked the time of Oswald's arrest against the hour the paper had been printed and, with great horror, realized Oswald's biography had gone out on the international newswire before Oswald had been arrested by the Dallas police. Until his death in June, 2001, Prouty remained one of the most persuasive and persistent critics of the Warren Commission. His book, *The Secret Team: The CIA and its Allies in Control of the United States and the World*, is a frightening portrayal of the hidden rulers of America.

On March 6, 1975, the Zapruder film made its national television debut on ABC's *Good Night America*. As a result of this long-delayed national screening, enough public pressure was put on Congress to reopen the case. Unfortunately, this investigation became as carefully manipulated as the Warren Commission, eventually falling under the control of G. Robert Blakey, a man with close ties to the CIA. As could be expected, Blakey led the investigation away from the CIA and towards the Mob. Blakey's conclusion was that President Kennedy was killed as the result of a conspiracy, and that organized crime had the means, method and motive. "The Garrison investigation was a fraud," said Blakey. Richard Billings, the former *Life* editor, was a prominent member of Blakey's staff.

However, a number of highly-detailed books on the assassination later appeared, most of which support Garrison's thesis rather than Blakey's. The best of these include *Conspiracy* by Anthony Summers, *Crossfire* by Jim Marrs and *High Treason* by Robert Groden and Harrison Livingstone.

"Could the Mafia have whisked Kennedy's body past the Texas authorities and got it aboard Air Force One?" writes Garrison in *On the Trail of the Assassins*. "Could the Mafia have placed in charge of the President's autopsy an army general who was not a physician? Could the Mafia have arranged for President Kennedy's brain to disappear from the National Archives?"

Today, we know that the CIA frequently hired Mafia assassins to carry

out contracts. Undoubtedly some of these men were involved in the assassination and cover-up. Shortly before his disappearance, Teamster boss
Jimmy Hoffa said, "Jim Garrison's a smart man. Anyone who thinks he's a
kook is a kook himself." Was Hoffa silenced because he knew too much
about the plot? Just before their scheduled appearances before the House
investigation in the mid-seventies, Johnny Roselli and Sam Giancana were
brutally murdered in gangland fashion. Was this a message to other Mob
figures who had fragmentary information on the case?

In July 1988, *The Nation* published an FBI memorandum from Hoover
dated November 29, 1963. Obtained through the Freedom of Information
Act, the memo implicated "George Bush of the CIA" in the Kennedy
assassination cover-up. Although former President George Bush Sr.
denied any contact with the agency prior to his being named director in
1976, it is reasonable to assume that Zapata, the oil company Bush founded in 1960, was a CIA front.

Former President Richard Nixon is also implicated in the cover-up.
Nixon was in Dallas the day before the assassination, and his greatest fear
during the early days of Watergate was that the "Bay of Pigs thing"
would be uncovered. According to H.R. Haldeman in *The Ends of Power*,
"Bay of Pigs" was Nixon's code phrase for the Kennedy assassination.

As liaison between the CIA and Pentagon during the Bay of Pigs,
Fletcher Prouty was put in charge of ordering supplies for the invasion.
"The CIA had code-named the invasion 'Zapata,'" recalls Prouty. "Two
boats landed on the shores of Cuba. One was named Houston, the other
Barbara. They were Navy ships that had been repainted with new names.
I have no idea where the new names came from."

At the time, Bush was living in Houston. His oil company was called
Zapata, and his wife's name was Barbara.

If Garrison's investigation was not a fraud, it's reasonable to assume
that high-placed individuals in the conspiracy would either be dead or
would have obtained considerable power in the last 39 years. According
to an article in the March 4, 1991 issue *of U.S. News & World Report*, Nixon
and Bush remained close associates. "Nixon is in contact with Bush or his
senior staff every month," wrote Kenneth Walsh. "Nixon also speaks regularly on the phone with [National Security Adviser] Brent Scowcroft...
and Chief of Staff John Sununu."

In 1991, Len Colodny and Robert Gettlin published *Silent Coup*, an analysis of the real forces behind the Watergate scandal. According to the authors, Nixon fell prey to a military coup after refusing to work with the Pentagon. Is this book real, or, like so much of what has been published on the case, just another example of state-sponsored disinformation designed to muddy the investigative waters?

Mae Brussell in California and Carl Olgesby in Massachusetts were probably the first researchers to study the tracks of the Nazi spys, scientists and war criminals who made their way into the CIA, secretly protected and shielded through an operation supervised by Allen Dulles. Olgesby's hard-to-find book, *The Yankee-Cowboy War*, remains the best document on the links between the JFK assassination and the Watergate scandal. Later on, researchers began uncovering evidence that many prominent business-men and politicians, including Prescott Bush, the Harrimans and the Rockefellers, had maintained contacts with major corporations in Germany before and during the war. Some of these people may have even helped hide billions in Nazi profits. In the '80s, a researcher named Danny Casolaro would follow this research into a network he dubbed "The Octopus," a secret organization he felt was controlling illegal drug traffic, arms trading and money laundering around the world. In August, 1991, Casolaro lost his life in his quest to uncover the heads of this Octopus. Today most researchers would add child prostitution, child pornography, child slavery and the manufacture of Manchurian candidates through mind control to the list of crimes committed by this group.

One thing is for sure: a well-orchestrated disinformation campaign against Oliver Stone's movie predictably appeared long before Stone began editing his film. Longtime Kennedy researchers were not surprised to find the charge led by George Lardner, Jr., of the *Washington Post*, the last man to see David Ferrie alive.

"Oliver Stone is chasing fiction," wrote Lardner in the May 19, 1991 edition. "Garrison's investigation was a fraud." Later in the article he adds: "There was no abrupt change in Vietnam policy after JFK's death."

"That is one of the most preposterous things I've ever heard," says Zachary Sklar, editor of *On the Trail of the Assassins*, and co-screenwriter with Stone on *JFK*. "Kennedy was trying to get out of Vietnam, and Johnson led us into a war in which 58,000 Americans died. Lardner's arti-cle is a travesty."

"I wouldn't give Lardner the time of day," adds Gary Shaw. "I think he's bought and paid for."

Mark Lane, author of *Rush to Judgment*, one of the first books critical of the Warren Commission, agrees. "The CIA is bringing out the spooks who pose as journalists," said Lane. "The amazing thing about the Lardner piece is he's reviewing the film months before it's even completed."

Time magazine also slammed the film several months before its release. "Garrison is considered somewhere near the far-out fringe of conspiracy theories," wrote Richard Zoglin, a film critic who admits to knowing "very little" about the assassination. (For the 25th anniversary of the assassination in 1988, *Time* ran a cover story titled "Who Was the Real Target?" Inside was an excerpt from *The Great Expectations of John Connally*, a curious book that argued that Oswald really meant to kill Connally and only hit JFK by mistake. Someday this book may be viewed as a textbook example of CIA-sponsored disinformation.) Time, Inc., it will be remembered, is the same company that hid the Zapruder film for five years. When I requested slides from the film to accompany this article, the copyright holder sent me a three-page contract to sign. It included a prohibition against "any reference... that the Zapruder film was ever owned by Time, Inc...."

The American people have been bombarded with information about the Kennedy assassination, most of it critical of Stone and Garrison. It's important to understand that much of this criticism is written by intelligence assets working for the CIA. Even after the Cold War ended, the CIA budget continued to reach all-time highs; $30 billion of taxpayers' money buys a lot of propaganda.

How extensive is the CIA's infiltration of the national media? I called former agent Ralph McGeehee, author of *Deadly Deceits*, who has compiled a database on everything published about the agency. "In 1977, Carl Bernstein wrote an article in *Rolling Stone* that named over 400 journalists uncovered by the Church Committee who were working for the CIA," says McGeehee. If anything, their numbers have only increased.

When will the subversion of the national media end? When the American people demand it. If you want to help bring justice in this case, there's plenty you can do: Write your representatives in Congress. Tell them you want a law passed prohibiting journalists from working for the CIA. Although such a bill has been proposed many times, it never makes its way out of committee. Also tell them you want all the files relating to the assassination opened, unsealed and made available to the public.

Finally, stop accepting everything you hear on TV and read in the newspapers. Buy books on the assassination and cover-up and educate yourself. Only in this way can we keep hope alive that one day America will be the sweet land of liberty her founders intended.

THE KING OF CANNABIS

The house sits near the crest of a dike in a remote section of Holland near the German border. Built around 1880, it is a grand old structure with 15-foot ceilings, elaborate moldings and stained-glass windows. This is not your ordinary 19th-century mansion, however. Nevil, the man who lives here, breeds marijuana and sells the seeds for a living. Instead of wine cellars, his basement is filled with indoor grow rooms.

It is Thursday, November 6, 1986, and Nevil has just returned from his daily pilgrimage to a nearby post office. It is raining lightly and a cold breeze blows off the Rhine River. Although the sun made a brief appearance early in the day, massive, billowing clouds have since obliterated it.

As Nevil enters his house, he is assaulted by his watchdog, Elka. He climbs the stairs to his living room, flops on an old couch, and starts opening his mail. "Breeding is a matter of bending nature to your will," he says while drawing a toke on a joint of Skunk #1. "There's not a coffeeshop in Holland that can produce better weed than this. But I don't sell it. I give it away—or I throw it away."

In a few short years, Nevil has made an incredible transformation from penniless junkie to wealthy entrepreneur. Although he's an effective and efficient businessman, marijuana is his business, so things are run a bit differently around here. For example, resinous buds of exotic strains of cannabis are strewn haphazardly about the room, as are large chunks of hash and bags filled with seeds.

Nevil is a displaced Australian of Dutch heritage, and has a quiet, understated sense of humor. He lives in relative seclusion on his estate, breeding marijuana, playing pool, watching videos, waiting patiently for his many cannabis experiments to bear fruit. He has his doubts about the future of the marijuana business in the Netherlands, but these doubts disappear in a whiff of smoke whenever he samples a new, successful hybrid.

"In the beginning I was quite keen for people to come here and visit me, but I found it takes large amounts of my time," he says. "I have to sit around and smoke with them. Now it has to be someone worthwhile, someone who has a large project in mind. Most American growers are looking for the same thing: strong, overpowering, two-toke *indica* with huge yields. My number-one seller is Northern Lights."

After the mail has been sorted and delivered to the in-house accountant, Nevil visits the basement to inspect his prize plants. The doors to four grow rooms are wide open, disclosing the blinding glare of dozens of sodium and halide lights. Powerful exhaust fans circulate the air, and the smell of cannabis is overpowering. Three of the rooms are devoted to young seedlings, while the largest contains 40 flowering females in their spectacular resinous glory.

It's no secret that an explosion of indoor marijuana propagation has taken place in America: grow stores are sprouting across the nation and high-wattage grow lights are selling faster than Christmas trees in December. The reason for this sudden interest in indoor growing is no secret either: high-quality marijuana has been nearly impossible to find— unless, of course, one personally knows a grower. But any pot farmer will tell you good equipment does not guarantee a good harvest. The most important element, in fact, is good seeds. And until recently, good seeds have been as rare as a $15 ounce of Colombian Gold.

Thanks to Nevil, however, this sad situation has changed. Every day letters pour into his post office box, containing American dollars wrapped in carbon paper to avoid detection. The money is for seeds. Not ordinary pot seeds, but the best, most potent seeds on the market, seeds that will grow gargantuan buds dripping with resin, seeds that cost between $2 and $5 each.

Nevil's seed factory is perfectly legal. The Dutch government views Nevil as a legitimate, tax-paying businessman. Seed merchants are held in esteem in Holland, and even though Nevil is something of a small-fry by seed merchant standards, he is a protected national asset nonetheless. In 1985, his company supplied $500,000 worth of seeds to 15,000 American growers. If you smoke high-quality marijuana, chances are good the buds may have been grown with Nevil's stock.

There is a big difference between growing marijuana and breeding for quality. The best-known example of the long-term effects of breeding are the Cannabis *indica* plants that arrived in the United States in the '70s. For hundreds of years *indica* plants were bred by Afghani farmers for disease resistance, early flowering, large buds and wide leaves. The strain was developed for hash production, but it was also useful for American growers who had difficulty with *sativa* strains, most of which require longer growing cycles.

Ever since *indica* arrived in the USA, breeders have been creating hybrids that take advantage of *indica*'s hardiness and *sativa*'s clear, bell-like high. The results of these experiments first appeared at secret harvest festivals in California, Oregon and Washington. Then, in the early '80s, a legendary underground organization called the Sacred Seed Company began distributing these remarkable hybrids. Nevil's company, The Seed Bank, sells many strains originally developed by the Sacred Seed Company, including the famed Skunk #1, Early Girl and California Orange. More recently, however, some of the most mind-blowing strains have come out of the Pacific Northwest; Northern Lights, University, Big Bud and Hash Plant are adequate proof that Seattle and Portland now hold the breeding crown. Needless to say, Nevil's Seed Bank obtained cuttings and seeds of all these varieties as well.

Who is Nevil and how did he come to found this amazing company? As usual, the truth is wilder than anything *High Times* could invent.

The man who would be King of Cannabis is the son of Dutch migrants who settled in Perth, Australia in 1954. His father trained telephone technicians while his mother became a counselor for unwed mothers. They were adventurous, hardworking Catholics, and they raised their six children strictly, sending them to Catholic schools.

"I wasn't the most malleable child," admits Nevil. "From an early age I had an aversion to authority. I was the first-born, and I saw myself as a sort of pathbreaker for the rest of the children."

Despite his rebellious nature, Nevil was intelligent enough to jump two years ahead of his peers, a leap that resulted in his being the smallest in class. "I got beat up a lot," he admits. "A typical day would start with the teacher calling me up in front of the class to smell my breath. 'Yep,' she'd say, 'You've been smoking.' And I'd get six of the best straight away. And that was just to start the day! Usually a thing like that would put me into a bad mood, so the rest of the day wasn't much good either. It worked out I got the strap 900 times in one year, the school record."

Nevil was not your typical juvenile delinquent. At age seven, he began raising parakeets; two years later he joined the Parakeet Society of Western Australia. "My best friend across the road got some parakeets," he explains, "and I got extremely jealous. After he started breeding I became quite adamant I'd do the same."

He eventually became friends with one of Australia's leading parakeet breeders, Bob Graham. "I learned an awful lot from him," he says. "He was a quadriplegic and he was incredibly intelligent." Nevil learned Mendel's laws of breeding and began charting dominant, recessive and intermediate traits for his birds (something he would later do with cannabis plants). "I bought some of Graham's stock and got immediate results," he says. "When you breed parakeets, you breed to an ideal. It's like sculpting with genes."

When he was 15, Nevil was sent to a state school and forced to repeat his third year of high school. Consequently, he caught up with his classmates in size. "I got into a few fights," he says with a smile, "just to get back for all the times I'd been beaten up."

Although discipline at the school was considered harsh, it proved a cakewalk after Catholic school. "The first time I was brought before the headmaster to be punished, he made me hold out my hand and he tapped it twice with a cane," recalls Nevil. "I thought he was just aiming. I closed my eyes and waited for the real pain, but it never came. I was quite shocked. I thought, 'Well, now I can do anything I want.' I ignored the dress code and dressed how I pleased. That didn't go over well and I managed to get kicked out within three months."

He also discovered marijuana.

"I had an American friend who suggested we buy some," he says. "I remember thinking, 'Okay, I'm not scared.' We both pretended we'd done it before, when, in fact, neither of us had. After scoring from someone at school, we went back to a shed outside his house. I volunteered to roll joints, even though I'd never done it before. There were three of us and I rolled three joints, one for each of us," he laughs. "It seemed logical at the time, still does, actually, even though it was more normal to pass joints. But we didn't know any better. It was Indonesian weed and we got extremely ripped. I really liked the sense of time distortion—everything happened so slowly."

There was plenty of high-quality reefer going around Australia, and to insure a steady supply for himself, Nevil made the jump from smoker to dealer in a matter of weeks. Meanwhile, to satisfy his parents, he found a legitimate job.

"As long as I couldn't be the Pope, my mother wanted me to be a doctor or veterinarian," he says. "My father didn't see this as a possibility and just wanted me to get a job. Fortunately, I was offered work as a lab assistant at a local university, which was semi-professional, eh? And I was working, so they were both satisfied."

Nevil did well at the position. So well, in fact, that he was made acting head of the anatomy lab with responsibility for the operating room, animal room and office. He was given the only set of keys to the drug cabinet and placed in charge of ordering drugs when supplies ran low. For someone interested in sampling illicit chemicals, it seemed like the perfect job.

"Having heard horror stories about cannabis and how bad it was for you, I decided everyone in authority lied about drugs," says Nevil. "I knew cannabis wasn't harmful. I concluded the harmful effects of other drugs must be exaggerated as well. I started with barbiturates. I knew many people used them for sleeping tablets. Eventually, I tried morphine. I was quite good at giving injections. There's something very professional and doctor-like about giving yourself an injection. I had to inject rabbits and mice all the time, and if you can hit a vein in a rabbit's ear, you can get any human vein. I veined the first time I tried. Morphine made me feel good. I had friends who were already addicted to heroin and they encouraged me. Soon, I had a bag filled with tablets, pills and chemicals of all sorts from the lab." Unfortunately for Nevil, this situation was not destined to last. Within a few months, he was arrested for drug possession. And it didn't take long for the police to figure out where the drugs had come from.

The head of the anatomy department suggested Nevil be sent to a treatment center. His parents agreed and had their son committed to a university psychiatric ward for six weeks. "I wasn't addicted at the time," says Nevil. "I used far too large a variety of ingestibles to become addicted to any one thing. After I was released I had the option of working part-time at the university—to build up my position again. But I felt the stigma of being a known user. It was a bit unbearable. So I left and started hanging around with people who supplied smack. Even though I started shooting smack, I never sold it. I just sold weed."

One day Nevil woke up with a terrific backache. His hips and the base of his spine hurt terribly. He went to a doctor and was given some pain pills, which proved useless. The doctor couldn't find anything wrong.

Nevil went home and the pain still wouldn't go away.

"Then I realized, 'Shit, I'm addicted,' " he says. "It was quite a substantial shock even though I knew it had to come eventually." He enrolled in a methadone program, which proved to be an extremely dehumanizing experience. "They made me beg for drugs," he says. "I didn't like that. I was scoring weed in Melbourne and shipping it back in huge speakers, telling people I was in a band. I was making what seemed like a huge sum of money—$5,000 a week."

Unfortunately, Nevil gave a free sample to a girl who was later arrested by the police. The girl identified Nevil as her supplier and a long court case ensued, one that eventually reached the Australian version of the Supreme Court. Throughout the trial, Nevil was enrolled in a methadone program and under psychiatric supervision. "I got the feeling things were coming to a head," he says. "My drug problem seemed quite insurmountable and the case didn't look promising. So I flew to Thailand."

For several weeks Nevil lived in a cheap hotel in Bangkok, shooting heroin until his money ran out. He skipped out on the bill, moved to another hotel and began hawking his valuables to raise money. "I found a taxi driver who would take me to exclusive shops in the city," he says. "The driver would get a kickback from the store for delivering Europeans to the shop, whether they bought anything or not. After we left, the driver and I would split the kickback."

However, after they'd visited every shop in Bangkok (and were no longer welcome at any of them), Nevil telephoned his parents and asked for a plane ticket home. Unfortunately, the police had already appeared at his house with a warrant for his arrest. "It didn't seem prudent to return to Australia," says Nevil with typical understatement. His parents sent him a ticket to the Netherlands and the address of an uncle living in the countryside.

After Thailand, Nevil's habit was really out of control. Upon arriving in Holland, he immediately enrolled in a methadone program and discovered he required 24 tablets a day to stay straight. "I handled that for about six months," he says. "I was trying to cut down, trying to fit in. I had unemployment benefits, which is enough to survive in Holland. But I was feeling quite lonely." Six months later, he moved to Tillberg, the center of Holland's smack scene.

Obviously, Tillberg was not the sort of environment conducive to kicking heroin. Junkies had taken over the city, converting pubs and hotels into shooting galleries. "My first day in town, I went to a bar called the Lawyer's Purse," he says. "Smack was being sold up and down the counter. It was a madhouse. Apparently, the police didn't—or couldn't— do anything about it. It went on like that for quite some time. When the police would close one place down, everyone would move to another bar. It was a fairly rough town and I went through a time of hardship. I had no money except welfare. I had a raging habit. I was living in a town known for being tough and criminal. I cost the state large chunks of money as I went through all the available drug rehabilitation programs. After having made numerous failed attempts at stopping, I decided no one could help me. Which is true. No one can help a junkie. He can only help himself. So, I decided to kick heroin on my own. I convinced a doctor to give me 'ludes to sleep and a synthetic opiate, which probably didn't do anything. I stayed home and suffered for six weeks until I reached the point where I could handle alcohol. Then I started drinking every day, a half-bottle of Scotch in the morning, a half-bottle at night. I used the 'ludes to sleep, so that there was always a certain part of the day blocked out. Eventually, I got sick of hangovers and turned to grass. I decided it was probably the only acceptable drug."

In 1980, while still trying to kick his habit, Nevil stumbled across a copy of the *Marijuana Grower's Guide* by Mel Frank and Ed Rosenthal. "I'd grown some weed in the bush in Australia," he says. The book helped reawaken Nevil's interest in genetics. Why not combine his two favorite pursuits, breeding and getting high? Nevil applied for a loan to build an indoor growing chamber for marijuana. Only in Holland could such a request be taken seriously. "The drug program I was enrolled in gave grants to drug addicts to get them started doing something useful," he explains. "I told them I wanted to grow weed indoors. They weren't thrilled with the idea, but they gave me the money anyway." The unit employed eight five-foot fluorescent lights. "There was a vacant lot behind my apartment and I filled it with weed. I had Nigerian, Colombian and Mexican seeds. The Mexican was the best. I still have the strain. My dwarfs come from it." Although there wasn't much demand for home-grown weed in Holland, hash oil was a valuable commodity and could be sold easily. So Nevil became a professional hash-oil maker.

Nevil used petroleum ether, an extremely flammable liquid, for the distillation process. "I was heating it with thermostatically controlled electric plates," he says. Unfortunately, Nevil didn't realize the thermostat on the heater had to be placed in another room because the thermostat sparks when turned on. He had a sink filled with 40 liters of petroleum ether, as well as a can with another 10 liters on the floor. One day he turned on the thermostat and it sparked. The spark turned into a flame, which instantly turned into a raging fire.

With eyes closed, Nevil ran to the adjoining room and dove out the window, bouncing off a roof and rolling onto a sidewalk. "My first thought after hitting the ground was to save my dope," he says with a laugh. He ran back inside, grabbed whatever hash oil he could find, and buried it in the backyard. He went back again and collected whatever valuables he could find. "Then I went next door to tell the neighbors," he says. "They were shocked by my appearance. I didn't realize my hair was singed, my face was black, my clothes were torn. I was covered with burn blisters."

Twenty minutes later the police arrived followed by the fire brigade and an ambulance. At the hospital, the burn specialist told him he was lucky to be in such pain because it meant the burns weren't third-degree. He was given a shot of morphine to kill the pain. The next morning, Nevil refused further shots. "I knew I'd turn into a junkie again," he says.

Despite horror stories from his doctors about being scarred for life, Nevil was released two weeks later with no visible damage. There was one permanent change, however. Nevil decided not to make hash oil anymore.

Since Nevil had been reading *High Times*, he knew revolutionary new *indica* strains were appearing in the United States, even though none were available in Holland. If only he could grow weed the Dutch would consider palatable, then he'd be in business and could sell marijuana instead of hash oil. He searched through copies of *High Times* hoping to find an *indica* seed supplier. "I looked for hidden meanings in all the ads," he says. "Of course, it was just fantasy on my part. I knew how difficult it was to get good Nigerian and Indonesian seeds in America and I wanted to trade with someone."

Eventually, Nevil realized there was only one way to obtain good seeds, and that was to become a seed merchant himself. He hired a lawyer to investigate the legal implications and discovered it was possible to sell cannabis seeds in the Netherlands. Within a matter of months, he sent his first ad to *High Times*.

"I expected there were thousands of people just like me, and as soon as they saw the ad, I'd be in business," recalls Nevil. Business, however, was disappointingly slow for the first few months. Why? Probably because most readers found it hard to believe high-quality seeds could be obtained so easily. Nevil doesn't discuss his distribution system, but there is no doubt the seeds were getting through. Most of the money he received went back into improving his seed strains. Nevil went to great expense to obtain seeds, a commitment best illustrated by a secret trip to Mazar-I-Sharif in Afghanistan. According to the Moslem legend, one of Mohammad's sons died in the city. Consequently, it is a very holy place. It is also known for high-quality hashish. Although hash from the area had been readily available in Holland in the '70s, the Soviet invasion of the country greatly reduced exports. In 1985, an Afghan refugee told Nevil the fields around Mazar-I-Sharif were being destroyed. "That was all I needed to hear," says Nevil. "I caught the next plane to Pakistan to save the strain."

The story of this adventure first appeared in *Regardies* magazine and was written by former *High Times* reporter A. Craig Copetas. "After being smuggled into a refugee camp near Peshawar while lying on the floor of a car, Nevil made contact with a 30-year-old Muslim fanatic who had a throbbing vein that ran from between his eyes straight up his forehead," wrote Copetas. "The man took a lump of black hash out of his pocket and told Nevil that it had been processed by his uncle, a man known as Mr. Hashish....Surrounded by four men who were pointing machine guns at him, Nevil set about negotiating with Mr. Hashish, a Mujahedin commander, and finally persuaded him to send a squad of his men 280 miles into Soviet-occupied territory and come back with two kilos of healthy Mazari seeds."

"He thought I was ridiculous because I didn't want to buy hash or opium," recalls Nevil. "Nobody had ever come there before to buy seeds, and at first he had no idea what I was talking about. I stood there trying to explain genetics to this tribal hash leader in sign language. When he finally figured out what I wanted, he asked for too much money. I took a zero off his price and gave him ten percent up front. He called me a bandit, but I had the seeds four days later."

Nevil also went to great lengths to obtain *ruderalis* seeds, a little-known cannabis strain that grows primarily in Russia. Although some American growers had sold so-called *ruderalis* strains in the past, Nevil undertook the necessary trip to the Russian-Hungarian border to authenticate the plant. *Ruderalis* is not known for spectacular resin content, but it flowers automatically—regardless of photoperiod—which makes it a potentially useful hybrid, especially for outdoor growers. Nevil began crossing *ruderalis-indica* hybrids with his Mexican dwarfs. The result? An indoor/outdoor bonsai marijuana tree that matures within two months and never reaches a height over two feet. Such a plant would be difficult to detect from the air and it could take years before the DEA even figured out what it was. (After several years, Nevil abandoned his *ruderalis* experiments.)

"Since becoming a seed merchant, I've directed all my energies and money into finding people with superior strains of cannabis and getting seeds out of them," says Nevil. "And I can honestly say, I've never heard of a strain I wanted that I wasn't able to get—one way or another. Theoretically, there is someone out there growing better stuff than I am using my seeds. Why? Because tens of thousands of plants are being grown with my stock. Selection from tens of thousands gets phenomenal results, while I can only select from a few hundred. I'm not holding back anything. Any grower in America can experiment with the same stock."

HIP HOP

THE BRONX ON FIRE

In 1955, it seemed like everyone wanted to live in the Bronx. Second-generation immigrants from Manhattan's impoverished Lower East Side, blacks leaving the South, Puerto Ricans fresh from La Guardia airport, servicemen returning from overseas duty—they poured across the Harlem River in search of the American Dream, which would be lived out in an art deco apartment building overlooking the Grand Concourse, New York's finest boulevard and the Bronx equivalent of the Champs Elysees.

"The Bronx at that time was a paradise compared to [Harlem]," recalled Victor George Mair, who soon joined the migration northward. "Everything was so neat, so clean, so tidy, so orderly. I mean they were living in luxury."

Queens was dubbed "the borough of private houses," but the Bronx was known as "the borough of apartment buildings." Despite all the buildings, it wasn't easy to find a place to live. Rent controls enacted during World War II had kept the housing market tight and leases were usually kept in the family, handed down like priceless heirlooms. Most buildings, especially those on the Concourse, had long waiting lists.

It seemed impossible that within a few years this distinguished, orderly neighborhood could begin to suffer a precipitous decline that would not be slowed until more than 1,500 buildings were left abandoned. Lifelong Bronxites moved out in droves, entire neighborhoods were decimated by arson, and the once beautiful landscape of the South Bronx became so dominated by rubble-strewn lots that some visitors said it reminded them of Dresden after the war.

"It happened so slowly and to such an extent that I wasn't even aware of change until one day I decided to take a walk around the block and discovered we had no block," Mair told a historian from the Bronx Museum of the Arts. "Then I decided to take a walk around the neighborhood and found that we had no neighborhood."

The beginning of the end came in 1959, when Parks Commissioner Robert Moses began building an expressway through the heart of the Bronx. It was apparent that Moses cared little for the small, tight-knit communities that stood in his way. "When you operate in an overbuilt metropolis, you have to hack your way through with a meat ax," said Moses.

Marshall Berman vividly recalled the effects of Moses' ax in his book *All That Is Solid Melts Into Air*. "My friends and I would stand on the parapet of the Grand Concourse, where 174th Street had been, and survey the work's progress—the immense steam shovels and bulldozers and timber and steel beams, the hundreds of workers in the variously colored hard hats, the giant cranes reaching far above the Bronx's tallest roofs, the dynamite blasts and tremors, the wild, jagged crags of rock newly torn, the vistas of devastation stretching for miles to the east and west as far as the eye could see—and marvel to see our ordinary nice neighborhood transformed into sublime, spectacular ruins."

The middle-class Italian, German, Irish and Jewish neighborhoods disappeared overnight. Impoverished black and Hispanic families, who dominated the southern end of the borough, drifted north. Businesses and factories relocated. The open-air market on Bathgate Avenue was destroyed.

Along with the poor came their perennial problems: crime, drug addiction, unemployment. They also brought a smoldering sense of injustice, which exploded in nearby Harlem with a wave of "race riots" in 1965. Although there were no riots in the Bronx, it wasn't long before a Black Panther Information Center opened on Boston Road.

In 1968, Robert Moses completed his second grand project for the Bronx, a 15,382-unit co-op apartment complex, located on the northern edge of the borough and conveniently serviced by one of his expressways. Vacating their comfortable apartments, the Bronx middle class poured into Co-op City so fast one might have thought the hounds of hell were chasing them. With vacancy rates skyrocketing, reputable landlords panicked and quickly sold out to professional slumlords, who began buying, selling and trading buildings at a furious rate.

Coincidentally, 1968 marked another important development in the Bronx's history. During that summer a group of seven teenage boys began terrorizing the vicinity around the Bronxdale Project on Bruckner Boulevard in the Southeast Bronx. In itself, this might not seem significant, but it was the presence of this group that laid the groundwork for a surge of streetgang activity that overwhelmed the Bronx for the next six years.

At first, the group called itself the Savage Seven and were known primarily for beating up bus drivers and generally wreaking havoc near the Bronxdale Community Center. However, it wasn't long before other boys wanted to hang out with the Seven. The ranks swelled to several dozen and the name had to be changed. They chose "The Black Spades," which worked out nicely because they could take the spade emblem from a deck of cards, sew it on the back of a jean jacket and wear colors, just like the Hell's Angels. It wasn't long before a spray-painted Black Spade emblem began to appear in every hallway in the Bronxdale Project.

The Black Spades may have started out as kids aged 12 to 15, but collectively they assumed a power far beyond their age, a power that struck instant fear in the hearts of their elders. You couldn't pick a fight with one Spade without picking a fight with all of them. Together, they were invincible. They could swagger into any project in the Bronx and bully anybody.

The boys who lived in the Castle Hill Project in the North Bronx always hated the boys in the Bronxdale Project. It was one of those feuds that started shortly after the projects were built and never went away. Realizing it was time to get organized, the Castle Hill Project created a group called "Power," whose primary activity was getting into fights with members of the Black Spades. Wanting to do the Spades one better, they began creating divisions of Power in other projects.

Almost overnight, streetgangs appeared on every corner of the Bronx. Realizing they had a significant problem on their hands, the New York Police Department created the Bronx Youth Gang Task Force, a 92-member squad commanded by Deputy Inspector William Lakeman, who spent his first year on the job compiling dossiers on suspected gang leaders. By 1970, estimates of gang membership ran as high as 11,000. Reported assaults in the Bronx had risen from 998 in 1960 to 4,256 in 1969. Burglaries during the same period had increased from 1,765 to 29,276.

It wasn't long before the media became interested in the streetgangs, and, strangely enough, most of the early articles were somewhat positive, focusing on the gangs' attempts to wipe out heroin addiction in their neighborhoods. Howard Blum wrote in the *Amsterdam News*:

There are no junkies on Hoe Avenue in the South Bronx. The Royal Charmers ordered all junkies and dealers to leave their turf. Most left quickly. Those who stayed were beaten or killed. The Royal Charmers were brutal, but effective: there are no junkies on their turf.

On an August afternoon last summer a bedsheet was tied to two corner lampposts and stretched high across 173rd Street and Hoe Avenue in the Bronx like a campaign banner. The message on the sheet, written in large, childlike black letters, was direct: "No junkies allowed after 10 o'clock." The message was signed "R.C."

This message began a two-month period of vigilantism by the Royal Charmers. It was a campaign in which one dealer was pushed off a roof, his dead body found weeks later in an alley garbage can, two others were murdered, junkies were whipped through South Bronx streets, and one Royal Charmer was blinded, the victim of a shotgun blast in the face from a vengeful drug dealer.

Contrary to the myth created by this and other articles, streetgangs did not appear in the Bronx solely to rid the streets of junkies. Junkies just happened to be the first convenient target of newly formed gangs that wanted to flex a little muscle: They were easy to identify, they had no potential as gang members and they could be beaten up without arousing a cry of anguish from the community. Gang leaders were also smart enough to realize that heroin was one of the major reasons why the Bronx remained pacified throughout the '60s.

As the gang culture spread through the city, several hundred new gangs were formed. Most were dominated by four members: the president, the vice-president, the warlord (who attended pow-wows with rival gangs and declared war if necessary) and the masher, the best street fighter. The gangs had clubhouses where weekly meetings were held, and ritualistic initiation rites, the most common of which was called "Running the Mill," a rite of passage that required new members to run between two rows of members wielding chains, pipes and studded belts. Every gang had the same uniform: Levi jackets with insignias on the back, Lee jeans, Garrison belts and engineer boots. Lists of rules and regulations were drawn up and severely adhered to. It was easy to join and hard to quit.

The number of gangs in the Bronx kept growing through the summer of 1971, but this development went largely unnoticed until Adlai E. Stevenson High School reopened its doors in September. Located in the North Bronx, Stevenson was a new school in a predominately white neighborhood. During its second year the school started receiving busloads of blacks and Hispanics from the South Bronx, as well as a sizeable contingent of whites from middle-class neighborhoods in Throgs Neck and Pelham Bay.

Afrika Bambaataa, who would later become a leader of the largest gang in the city, was in the eighth grade when he was bused to Stevenson. He recalled the first two weeks of school in a theme he wrote for English class titled "Street Gangs Beware":

For the first week things seemed to go okay. There were no sign of a gang or gang activities in the school, not until a couple of Black Spades and Savage Nomads started flying colors in the second week. Then other gang members from a variety of streetgangs started wearing their colors. Suddenly, Stevenson officials found out that at least a member from every streetgang in the Bronx and parts of Manhattan went to Stevenson High School. Tension arose between the black and Hispanic against the whites. There was all kinds of trouble happening. A couple of white teenagers had a fight with a black who happened to be in the Black Spades. After school was over, the Black Spades led an army of students to the Korvettes Shopping Center where the white teenagers catch the #5 bus to Throgs Neck/Pelham Bay area. A rumble broke out... A white got thrown through a window and other whites and blacks and Hispanics got stabbed and stomped. After that day Stevenson was never the same peaceful high school again.

Several predominantly white gangs had been formed in the North Bronx, including the Aliens, the Golden Guineas and the War Pigs, but after the fight at Stevenson they merged into a single gang called Ministers Bronx. Violence in the school became an everyday occurrence. Many students refused to eat lunch in the cafeteria, where fights were likely to break out. All but a few of the bathrooms had to be locked permanently; those which remained open had guards posted at the doors.

Bambaataa joined the Black Spades in 1969, shortly after a division was founded at the Bronx River Project, where he lived with his mother. Although he became a devoted member, Bambaataa was far from a typical one. While the others were out playing basketball or hanging around street corners, Bambaataa was scouring record bins for obscure rhythm & blues recordings. Just as unusual was the name he chose for himself, inspired by the release of a feature film about the Zulus, a fierce warrior tribe in Africa. The original Bambaataa was a Zulu chief at the turn of the century. Translated into English, the word means "affectionate leader."

"Bam was never interested in sports. As long as I've known him, he's always been the music man," said Jay McGluery, who grew up at Bronx River with Bambaataa. "His mother was a nurse and she was constantly on the go, so we always went to his house to party. He had every record you could want to hear, including a lot of rock albums. James Brown and Sly and the Family Stone were his favorites."

In many snapshots from the period, Bambaataa looks young, lean and angry, his eyebrows fused in a permanent scowl of disapproval—just the sort of look designed to intimidate whitey. Despite the angry look, he tended to be quiet and philosophical, his guarded, reserved air frequently shattered by a laugh so friendly it infected everyone around him.

He was also more attuned to politics than many of his fellow gang members, some of whom understood only three basic concepts: "crush, kill and destroy." When he was 12, he had already begun hanging out at the Black Panther Information Center. His political leanings were encouraged by the appearance of "Say it Loud, I'm Black and I'm Proud" by James Brown and "Stand" by Sly and the Family Stone.

However, like many gang members, Bambaataa had a reckless, unpredictable streak. One time he and McGluery were playing war games and McGluery took refuge in one of the project's apartment buildings. Bambaataa poured gasoline on the sidewalk in front of the building, lit it, and announced he was holding everyone hostage. That same summer, he convinced his friends to buy bows and arrows so they could hunt rabbits on the banks of the Bronx River. "Bam was always a leader," said McGluery. "He was always full of crazy ideas."

During the early '70s, life at Bronx River changed dramatically. Since it was a stronghold for gang activity, the project was under constant police surveillance. Any teenager wearing engineer boots was likely to be stopped for a grilling, which usually started with the question, "Are you a Spade or a Skull?" (the two largest gangs in the area). It was not unusual for fistfights to break out between gang members and the police. Since the police were almost entirely white at the time, charges of police racism were rampant. Considering newspaper stories from the period indicate white gang members were seldom arrested, the charges may have had some foundation.

Although several rumbles were arranged between the Black Spades and the Ministers, they were usually aborted. The Spades couldn't board a bus headed uptown without it being surrounded by squad cars before it reached the Ministers' turf. Typically, the windows of the bus would fly open and a shower of chains, knives, bats and zip guns would hit the pavement. On June 27, 1973, a brief battle was broken up by police in front of P.S. 127 on Castle Hill Avenue, resulting in the arrest of 18 Black Spades.

Gang activity tended to quiet down during the winter only to resurface with even greater intensity each summer. Every year the gangs seemed to fall under the control of older, more demented individuals, many of whom were returning from stints in prison. By 1972, Running the Mill was being replaced by gang rape.

STREET GANG RAPES GIRL IN BRONX
(New York Post, *November 9, 1973*)
A 16-year-old cheerleader on her way home from practice at Evander Childs HS was abducted by members of a Bronx street gang and raped and beaten.

In another incident only hours earlier yesterday afternoon, a 15-year-old girl was abducted off the street, raped and beaten at gunpoint in a Brooklyn apartment, police said.

In the Bronx incident, the girl told police she was abducted around 4:45 P.M. by four youths in a car as she was walking near 212th St. and White Plains Road, four blocks from school.

She was blindfolded and taken to an apartment building in the Hunts Point section that police suspect was a clubhouse of the Black Spades, a Bronx street gang.

According to the account given police, the girl, whose name was withheld, was raped in the apartment by three youths and hit several times with bottles and chukka sticks—lengths of wood slung from rope or cord.

The girl said she was blindfolded again and driven to a deserted area at 151st St. and River Ave., where she was forced to commit sodomy with at least seven other youths.

Violence between gangs intensified as well. One feud between the Black Spades and the Seven Crowns lasted for 92 days, during which time the Bronx River Project was constantly peppered with gunfire from passing cars. Shootouts became so common that the residents started calling it "Lil' Vietnam."

"I was into streetgang violence," admitted Bambaataa. "That was all part of growing up in the Southeast Bronx." However, that's about all he'll say on the subject. "I don't really be speaking on that stuff because it's negative," he explained. "The Black Spades was also helping out in the community, raising money for sickle cell anemia and getting people to register to vote."

"He was not what I would call gung-ho," added McGluery, who became warlord of the Bronx River division before quitting to join the Marines. "Bam was more like a supervisor. There were so many different gangs and he knew at least five members in every one. Any time there was a conflict, he would try and straighten it out. He was into communications."

Gang activity probably peaked in 1973, when there were an estimated 315 gangs in the city, claiming 19,503 members. The Black Spades were by far the largest and most feared, with a division in almost every precinct. However, by 1974, the Black Spades began to disintegrate.

"Some gangs got into drugs," said Bambaataa. "Other gangs got wiped out by other gangs. Others got so big that members didn't want to be involved no more. Girls got tired of it first. They wanted to have children. Plus times was changin'. The seventies was coming more into music and dancing and going to clubs. The lifestyle was changing."

After many of the original Black Spades were killed, jailed or dropped out of the gang, Bambaataa took on an increasingly influential role. His affiliation continued until January 10, 1975, when his best friend, Soulski, was shot and killed by two policemen on Pelham Parkway. Bambaataa insisted that the shooting was nothing short of an assassination carried out during a police crackdown on gang activity. A copy of his friend's death certificate hangs in his bedroom. "He got shot in about nine different places," said Bambaataa. "The back, the stomach, the face. At first, I wanted to go to war with the police, but we couldn't really win. The *Amsterdam News* calmed everybody down and told us to fight through the system. It went to trial, but the cops never got convicted."

For over five years the Bronx had lived in constant terror of street-gangs. Then, in the summer of 1976, they unexpectedly failed to appear. Something better had come along to replace the gangs.

THE WAR OF WORDS

You know what it evolved from? The toughest guy on the block always had his name the biggest in the street. It told everybody it was his area, that he had the juice to do what he wanted and nobody could mess with him.

Tracy 168

To tell the truth, nobody really knows how graffiti evolved—we just know it's been around for a long time. During World War II, a welding inspector at the Bethlehem Steel shipyard in Quincy, Massachusetts named James J. Kilroy began writing "Kilroy was here" in crayon inside ships that were being built for the war. Many servicemen saw the markings and began spreading the message throughout Europe and the United States. Eventually, the phrase was combined with a cartoon of a long-nosed face peering over a wall.

In the '50s, streetgangs used graffiti for self-promotion and marking territorial boundaries. Gang graffiti had other uses, such as intimidation. When rival gangs walked into a new area and saw "Savage Skulls" written a hundred times—each with a different name underneath—it told them the Skulls were a powerful force to be reckoned with.

But then something changed. Around 1969, graffiti became more than a gang-related activity or thoughtless moment of vandalism. For hundreds of New York City teenagers it became a way of life with its own codes of behavior, secret gathering places, slang and aesthetic standards. No one knows who started it. We only know who made it famous: TAKI 183.

His real name was Demetrius and he came to New York from Greece. His family moved to Washington Heights, a working-class neighborhood at the northern edge of Manhattan. Demetrius was 15 when an older boy in the neighborhood told him about the gangs from the '50s. "They had an initiation where they would hang a new member by his ankles off the side of a bridge," said Demetrius. "While hanging upside down, the guy would paint his name on a pillar. I never saw it done, but the idea interested me."

Graffiti writing got a big technological boost in the '60s with the invention of the magic marker, which was easy to conceal and, like spray paint, left an indelible mark on just about any surface. In 1967, Demetrius noticed the name "JULIO 204" written on the street around his house. Julio, who lived a couple of blocks away on 204th Street, like to write his name and street number wherever he went. Demetrius lived on 183rd Street and his nickname was Taki. So he started writing TAKI 183.

He put his first "tag" on the side of an ice-cream truck during the summer of 1970. "I didn't have a job. I did it to pass time," he said later. Meanwhile, Julio was arrested for vandalism and forced into early retirement. When Taki returned to school, he got a part-time job as a messenger. While making deliveries, he found an art supply store on 53rd Street that sold extra-wide markers. "I think I was the first one to find that wide marker," he said. "My name got noticed because it was wider than everyone else's. But even more important, I was writing in a different area than most people. My name could have been on every street corner in Brooklyn and I wouldn't have gotten the exposure I got from writing on the East Side. A writer might come out of his office, see my name, and—maybe because it was a boring day—he would decide to write a story about me."

Taki graduated from high school and began working full time until he saved enough money to attend college. He continued writing, only now the interiors of subway cars had become his primary target. People have nothing to do in subway trains except read the advertising posters, he reasoned, so why not give them a little something extra to look at?

Unknowingly, Taki created a major controversy. "Pretty soon people were wondering, what is the squad of Taki-commandos?" wrote Richard Goldstein in *New York* magazine. "Rumors began: Is it the surveying crew for a new subway line, or is it a madman quoting stock averages, or is it a streetgang so obscure not even Leonard Bernstein knows them, or else is it some kind of arcane religious rite, like when I was a kid and people went around writing 'Beware of 1960' on the roofs?" The controversy was finally settled in July 1971, when an enterprising reporter from the *New York Times* tracked Taki down. The first newspaper article on graffiti appeared a few days later.

"TAKI 183" SPAWNS PEN PALS

Taki is a Manhattan teenager who writes his name and his street number everywhere he goes. He says it is something he just has to do.

His TAKI 183 appears in subway stations and inside subway cars all over the city, on walls along Broadway, at Kennedy International Airport, in New Jersey, Connecticut, upstate New York and other places.

He has spawned hundreds of imitators, including JOE 136, BARBARA 62, EEL 159, YANQUI 135 and LEO 136.

To remove such words, plus the obscenities and other graffiti in subway stations, it cost 80,000 man-hours, or about $300,000, in the last year, the Transit Authority estimates.

"I work, I pay taxes too and it doesn't harm anybody," Taki said in an interview, when told the cost of removing the graffiti.

And he asked: "Why do they go after the little guy? Why not the campaign organizations that put stickers all over the subways at election time?"

It was apparent that Taki had gained considerable status in his community for the graffiti. "He's the king," said one neighborhood youth. "He's got everybody doing it," said another. After the article appeared, Taki's status was no longer confined to his block, but stretched to every borough in the city, including the Bronx.

Actually, the Bronx had been writing similar graffiti long before the article on Taki appeared. However, it wasn't until the spring of 1971 that the fad began taking off. In March, two writers appeared on 163rd Street, SLY II and LEE 163rd. Lee drew immediate attention for his unusual tag, which stacked and fused the letters in his name into a corporate-style logo.

In October, Lee's cousin, Lonny Wood, began writing. "The previous year we'd given this party," said Lonny. "We were getting ready to give another one and I said, 'We'll call it Phase Two.' I don't know why, but I was stuck on the name. It had meaning for me. I started writing 'Phase 2.'" By this time, the unspoken graffiti code was already well established. Writers were supposed to be mysterious figures who never revealed their identities to outsiders (especially parents). They had to be light-fingered enough to steal markers and spray paint, and courageous enough to "run the train tracks" and participate in other daredevil stunts.

"We were like moles," said Tracy 168, one of the first writers to appear in the Bronx. "If anyone chased us, we ran into the nearest subway station and we'd be gone. Nobody would follow us down there." It took considerable nerve to jump off a subway platform and take off running down a dark, forbidding tunnel. The third rail, pulsing with 625 deadly volts, was just a stumble away. Somewhere behind the writer, moving at 40 miles an hour or faster, was a subway train, while perhaps a thousand feet in front was an abandoned station or lay-up track, where the writer could leave a tag, like a flag driven into a mountain peak. It was criminal, dangerous behavior, but the thrill was undeniable.

Phase 2 joined a large number of writers at DeWitt Clinton High School. One advantage to attending Clinton was the proximity of a Transit Authority storage yard across the street, where parked trains could be found any time of day or night. It wasn't unusual for Phase and the other writers to spend their lunch hour in the yard marking up trains. After school the writers would gather in a nearby coffee shop. Whenever a bus pulled up outside, dozens of writers came pouring out of the coffee shop waving markers. By the time the bus pulled away, it would be drenched in freshly scrawled signatures.

At first there were only a handful of writers in each neighborhood, and it didn't matter what a tag looked like. But after hundreds of writers appeared on the scene, it was necessary to embellish the tags to make them stand out. Two female writers, Barbara and Eva 62, enlarged their signatures and made them more colorful. Cay 161 drew a crown over his tag. Stay High 149 drew a stick figure with a halo lifted from *The Saint*, a popular television show. Stay High incorporated two smoking marijuana joints into his tag and became one of the most respected of the early writers by placing tags in extremely hard-to-reach places. He was also the first to master tags created with dual-color markers.

Graffiti began to draw the scrutiny of outsiders, most of whom assumed it was done out of anger and frustration. "It is part of the widespread vandalism, the mood to destroy, the brutalism that is everywhere," said Dr. Fredric Wertham. Mayor John Lindsay denounced the writers as "insecure cowards" and launched an all-out campaign to remove graffiti from public property.

Although the writers continued to hit buses, handball courts, schoolyards and other locations, the subway system was the primary target. "One thing that kept me writing on trains was seeing my name again," said Tracy. "You thought your tag would just disappear because there were so many trains. But then it would come back the next day, and you'd see somebody else's tag right next to yours. That was part of the communication thing. The train would shoot over to Brooklyn and somebody over there would see your style. But there was also more adventure on the trains. Daredevil stunts like jumping from trains to platforms would really get your adrenaline going. Competition was important too."

The writers soon moved from marking the insides of trains to marking the exteriors. It was decided the best place to have a tag was on the front of the train, where it would be the first thing seen as the train entered the station. But in 1972, Super Kool completely changed graffiti by spray-painting his name in super-wide pink and yellow letters. It took him about five times longer than a normal tag, and used almost an entire can of paint, but the results were worth it. His thick, colorful letters overpowered every other signature on the train. At first, the other writers couldn't figure out how Super Kool had gotten his letters so thick. It didn't seem possible with a regular can of spray paint, and, in fact, it wasn't. Super Kool had replaced the narrow-dispersion cap on his spray-paint can with a "fat cap," a wider-spraying cap from a can of oven cleaner.

"Everyone was damn negative about it at first," said Phase. "It took a whole can of paint for one signature! But then everybody picked up on it. I remember seeing some big block letters by Sentry. That's when I came out with my softie letters. People started calling it the bubble style."

The giant signatures became known as "masterpieces" and it suddenly became necessary to steal a lot of paint to execute them.

"Super Kool and his girlfriend were the first to rack up huge quantities," said Phase. "He always dressed very dapper and didn't look the part. Stealing went along with the graffiti style. I didn't get into it, but a lot of guys did. Not just paint, but leather coats, stereos. One time I led about twenty guys into a store. We went straight to the paint. Something came over me and I slapped all the cans off the shelf. It was crazy. There was so much confusion. The salesman tried to keep us in the store and guys had to throw blows to get out. The mounted police came. We ran around the corner and found we had four cans of paint between twenty guys. That wasn't the way to do it."

Like most writers in the Bronx, Phase was black. He was tall, skinny and almost always wore a hat jauntily perched on one side of his head—

a French cap made by Flechet was his favorite. He projected an almost explosive sense of urgency, his occasional stuttering heightening the impression that his physical being was struggling to keep pace with a hyperactive imagination. While talking, he frequently twisted and clenched his fingers, as if creating patterns for some bizarre new lettering style.

Style became the most important aspect of graffiti. It was still possible to gain respect and recognition merely by "getting one's name around" in large quantities, but it was more prestigious to create original lettering styles which were imitated by lesser writers, who were known as "toys." One had to be artistically competent to execute huge murals on the sides of trains. The less talented writers were forced out of the limelight. Meanwhile, the Transit Authority continued cracking down on graffiti and it became progressively more difficult and dangerous to enter the train yards. However, the danger only increased the writers' sense of satisfaction.

A writer named Topcat moved to New York from Philadelphia, where a separate graffiti subculture was flourishing. Topcat painted thin, elongated letters on platforms. He called it the "Philadelphia style," but after the letters were imitated by most of the writers on the Upper West Side, they were renamed "Broadway elegant."

Although most writers tended to be fairly independent, it wasn't long before they began gathering in loose-knit groups, which were closer to professional associations than gangs. Meetings were held at various "writers' corners" around the city, the two most prominent of which were located at a subway station at 149th Street and Grand Concourse in the Bronx, and on the corner of 188th and Audubon Avenue in Manhattan. Wherever they gathered, writers compared notes on various lettering styles and discussed methods for thwarting the Transit Police.

The Ex-Vandals, one of the earliest and most revered of the writing organizations, was founded at Erasmus High School in Brooklyn by president Dino Nod, whose tag could be found in every borough of the city. The name was short for "Experienced Vandals." In imitation of the street-gangs, the Ex-Vandals wore jean jackets with their name on the back. They were not a fighting gang, however. They preferred to spend their time developing highly elaborate, script-like tags. It was the beginning of the Brooklyn style, which eventually became so complex most people found it indecipherable.

Phase became president of the Bronx chapter of the Ex-Vandals until he helped found a separate group called "The Independent Writers," whose membership included prominent writers such as Super Kool and Stay High. The Independent Writers indicated their affiliation by writing "INDS" after their signatures.

Wanted, another important writing group, was founded by Tracy 168 in 1972. Tracy was a gutsy, streetwise white kid, tough enough to hang out with the Black Spades in his neighborhood. Unlike many of the other groups, Wanted had a permanent clubhouse, in the basement of an apartment complex on the corner of 166th Street and Woodycrest Avenue in the Bronx. In the mid-'70s, Wanted became one of the largest groups, with more than 70 members.

"The best year for graffiti was 1973," said Tracy. "Styles were coming out. We got into this thing with colors. First it was two colors, then three colors, then four. Then it was the biggest piece, the widest. Then it was top-to-bottom, whole car, whole train. We worked on clouds and flames. We got into lettering. Everybody was trying to develop their own techniques. When I would go into a yard, the first thing I'd do is look around and see who was good. That would be my objective. To burn the best writer in the yard. And I wouldn't leave until I did something better than him. I put a Yosemite Sam with two guns on a piece. That was the first cartoon character."

Although Phase wasn't painting as many trains as some other writers, he was inventing new styles on paper and handing them out to his friends. Many of his ideas found their way to the trains through Riff 170, who was considered a master colorist. "Riff revolutionized graffiti with a half-car, top-to-bottom," said Aaron 155, interviewed by Craig Castleman in *Getting Up*.

"It was a yellow 'Riff' with red, bloody drips coming down. And it had cracks painted on it. It took everybody out all over New York."

Other important writing groups included Magic Inc., Three Yard Boys, Vanguards, Ebony Dukes, Writers Corner 188, The Bad Artists, the Mad Bombers, the Death Squad, Mission Graffiti, the Rebels, Wild Style, Six Yard Boys and the Crazy 5. Many writers belonged to two or three at the same time.

Although Soul Artists was not a major group in the early '70s, it was founded by Mark Edmonds and Lennie McGurr, who would become well-known in the '80s. The two were best friends through grade school and organized Soul Artists in 1972, while working as gym instructors for the West Side YMCA. "At first we'd hit anything—buildings, cars, trucks," said Edmonds, who wrote "ALI." "Then after a while, we told the members that anyone signing the club initials S.A. to anything but trains would be thrown out. To join, people had to submit designs. We really wanted good artists and we would help each other develop techniques."

When Ali was 16, he earned a scholarship to study urban planning at Columbia University. He was black, handsome and possessed a quick wit. McGurr, who wrote "Futura 2000," was not a natural leader like Ali, but showed greater potential as an artist. He was adopted as a child and looked vaguely Puerto Rican. Futura graduated from a trade school specializing in the printing industry and took his tag from the name of a typeface. After he left school, he got a job at a McDonald's restaurant.

At 5 A.M. on the morning of October 8, 1973, Futura and Ali were standing on a train track north of the IRT station at 137th and Broadway. While they were painting a parked train, another train began moving slowly toward them. They crawled under the train they were painting to wait for the moving train to pass. Suddenly, the train they were sitting under also started up. They quickly crawled back onto the track.

"Ali had about twenty cans of paint with him in a sack," said Chris Pape, a former member of the Soul Artists. "One of the cans had a faulty nozzle that was spraying paint. A spark from the train ignited the cans just as Ali was diving back on the tracks. Ali jumped right over the explosion and was set on fire. Not only was he on fire, but he had no place to go. There was a train moving toward him, so he couldn't lie down and put himself out. Right here is where the story gets confusing. Does Futura put out the fire? Or does he run away? The way I think it happened is that Futura heard the explosion, but didn't know Ali was on fire. He went, 'Oh, shit!' and ran back to the platform. Then Futura saw Ali all burnt up, helped him out of the station and flagged a cab. The word on the street was that Futura had run out on Ali and betrayed him. I felt bad for him because there were a lot of former friends out to kill him. The boys from 105th Street—where Futura lived—were ready to curb-stomp him. To this day nobody really knows what happened."

While still in the hospital, Ali was interviewed by a reporter from the *New York Times*. "He is immobile, in pain, confused and contrite, and he wanted to tell his story and the story of the graffiti subculture in the hope of discouraging others from doing what he now says is 'crazy, stupid and too damn dangerous'... his best friend abandoned him and that memory adds to his pain," wrote Michael T. Kaufman.

The article created the impression that Futura had left Ali in the tunnel to die, a serious violation of the graffiti code. "I don't know why Ali said those things," said Futura several years later. "I took off my jacket, put out the fire and helped him to the hospital. But after that story came out, things got pretty heavy for me around the neighborhood." Futura had to get away, so he joined the Navy. Soul Artists disbanded. The accident caused a few writers to quit graffiti but it had little effect on most of the subculture.

Eventually, someone from the outside had to stumble across graffiti, realize that something more than mindless vandalism was going on, and try to refocus the energies and talents of the subculture into more legitimate enterprises. That person was Hugo Martinez, a sociology major at City College. In 1972 Martinez spent the summer working with street-gangs as part of a federally funded program at Queens College. When he returned to school that fall, his interest in youth groups continued. He heard about the graffiti subculture from a fellow student and set out for Washington Heights, a known hangout for writers. He met Freddie 173, who provided a tour of the neighborhood.

"The tour climaxed at 'Writer's Corner 188,' a wall at 188th Street and Audubon Avenue," wrote Martinez in the first graffiti-art catalog. "Freddie formally introduced me to the president and vice-president of the site, Stitch I and Snake I, along with CAT 87. They received me with silent suspicion and an air of being used to admiration, of expecting it. Stitch was wearing a black fishing hat, black leather buttoned-down jacket, dark gray beat-up pants and Pro-Keds. Snake wore a red corduroy jacket, Levis and Pro-Keds. They had founded Writer's Corner, converting the pink wall of the building into a tapestry of line and color. Here the best writers of Manhattan, the Bronx and Brooklyn would come to meet, sign in, exchange gossip and, if the feelings were right, go out and hit together. Here also toy (inexperienced, inadequate) writers could look upon their heroes and perhaps get their autographs. (Only the best writers of Manhattan were allowed to consider themselves privileged to add 'W.C. 188' to their signatures.)"

In October, Martinez arranged for 12 writers to come to City College for a graffiti-writing demonstration. He covered an entire 10-by-40-foot wall with wrapping paper and brought dozens of cans of spray paint. "They came armed with their own markers, ranging from 1/4-inch 'toy markers' to 2-inch 'Uni-wides,'" wrote Martinez. "Once they realized all the possibilities, all vestiges of street cool went out the window. They were ecstatic. The presence of so many masters together, all the spray paint and so much room to hit created a scene of controlled frenzy."

Later that month, Martinez founded United Graffiti Artists (UGA), a quasi-democratic organization designed to redirect the efforts of the elite writers. At first the group was entirely Puerto Rican—with the exception of one Greek. Since they respected the work of the Bronx writers, many Puerto Ricans wanted to admit writers like Phase 2, Super Kool and Lee 163rd. Martinez was widely accused of racism because he didn't allow blacks into UGA. "Three or four members did not want to accept blacks," Martinez said later. "I tried to manipulate votes and put pressure on certain individuals to bring them into the group." Within a few months the Bronx writers were admitted, but some felt they were being accorded second-class status. "I think he favored the Puerto Ricans," said Lee 163rd. "Sometimes he would hold meetings with them and we wouldn't find out until later."

One thing is certain: There was a tremendous amount of racial tension at UGA, which was unusual since most writers respected one another regardless of color. The tension eventually flared into a full-scale rumble at the new headquarters on Jumel Place and 168th Street. Henry 161 showed up one day accompanied by five members of the Young Galaxies, a local streetgang. They immediately began trashing the studio. "I got hit in the head with a stick," said Phase 2. "So did Hugo. I later found out certain writers felt threatened by us. Henry got kicked out of the group."

There were other problems, like the controversy between Snake I and Snake 131. Snake 131 was considered the original Snake and to prove it, he started writing "SNAKE I-131." It was too much for Snake I to bear. One day he showed up at Snake 131's house, accompanied by his friend Stitch, who packed a gun and was considered one of the toughest street fighters in the neighborhood. When Snake 131 opened the door, Stitch had only four terse words for him: "Drop the fucking one." Stitch and Snake I spun on their heels and left. From that day on, Snake 131 never wrote an extra one.

Martinez may not have been very effective at unifying the writers, but his appreciation for their work was obviously sincere. His analysis of the typical writer's economic background was perceptive. "All the masters were working-class offspring from working-class neighborhoods like Washington Heights, West Bronx and Flatbush," he wrote. "The hardcore poor of the Lower East Side, South Bronx and Brownsville—those from homes where neither parent works—did not create ambitious graffiti. The masters were 'good kids' whose parents worked for a living and participated in the American Dream of becoming middle-class. The bitterness and self-recrimination that permeate the poor were absent from their environments. Among the black families, it was not uncommon to find private houses, a car, color TV; in the Latino homes these articles were definite goals. High-school and even college education were fostered aspirations."

Martinez organized the first graffiti-art exhibition at City College's Eisner Hall in December 1972. Publicity for the show landed a commission from choreographer Twyla Tharp, who wanted graffiti-style backdrops for her production of "Deuce Coupe." The following year the Razor Gallery exhibited 20 giant canvases by UGA members. Media attention given to the show was overwhelming: Feature stories appeared in several newspapers, *Newsweek* provided a splashy two-page spread and droves of art critics appeared at the opening. However, praise for the work was hardly universal.

"The show-off ebullience of their work has, if anything, been heightened by the comforts of a studio situation," wrote Peter Schjeldahl in the *New York Times*. "It is too much to say, however, that any of them is yet a really accomplished artist. All are understandably weak in terms of structure; at best, their canvases tend to look like segments of something bigger rather than whole compositions. They really have trouble with small pictures, most of which resemble pepless, overelaborate doodles. But raw talent abounds."

Personality problems continued to plague the group. According to some members, Martinez attempted to manipulate the direction of the work, refusing to exhibit paintings that did not conform to his idea of "good" graffiti.

Charges of racism were still leveled at Martinez, who continued to hold segments of some meetings in Spanish. The writers were invited to come to
Chicago for an exhibit at the Museum of Science and Industry. When they
returned to New York, the membership seized control of the organization
and demoted Martinez from "director" to "advisor."

The 1975 art season opened in New York with a spectacular graffiti-art
exhibit at the Artist Space gallery in Soho. By this time Phase and Bama had
clearly emerged as the most talented artists in the $1,000-to-$3,000 price
range. However, the event failed to attract media attention comparable to
the previous shows. The group was losing its momentum. Whatever his
faults, Martinez was obviously an important motivating force behind
UGA. Without his guidance, the organization soon split apart and went
underground, leaving the galleries to return to the subway yards. It would
be five years before the subculture regained the prominence in the art
world that it had in 1975—and then it would be riding the coattails of the
sudden, unexpected commercial success of rap music.

HERCULORDS AT THE HEVALO

Since Clive Campbell's impressions of the United States had been formed
watching *Dennis the Menace* and *Bewitched* on his next-door neighbor's
television set in Kingston, Jamaica, it was easy to understand why he
thought the country was so clean, without a trace of garbage anywhere.
So it came as something of a shock when, at age 12, Clive landed at
Kennedy airport and took the bus to his mother's apartment on 168th
Street in the Bronx. It was 1967. Rather than clean suburban lawns, he
found a ghetto similar to the one in Kingston—only bigger.

Clive had a lot of trouble adjusting to the Bronx. His accent made him
sound like a hick and his favorite sports in Jamaica—soccer and bicycle
racing—weren't at all popular. Instead, everyone was playing basketball.
The first day Clive tried the sport, he got kicked by an angry teammate.
"I knew how to kick," he said, "so I kicked him right back. A fight started. Two members of the Five Percenters [a Black Muslim youth group]
came to my rescue. They weren't gonna let anybody dog me. I hung out
with them and started picking up the slang. Pretty soon, I was Ameri-
canized."

In 1970, Clive entered Alfred E. Smith High School, a trade school for auto mechanics. He began lifting weights and running on the track team. A friend nicknamed him Hercules for his well-developed body. "I resented the name," he said. "I broke it down to Herc. That sounded rare, so I kept it." That same year, Herc started hanging out at a disco called the Plaza Tunnel, which was located in the basement of the Plaza Hotel on 161st Street and the Grand Concourse. The deejay, John Brown, was the first to play records like "Give It Up or Turn It Loose" by James Brown and "Get Ready" by Rare Earth. Unfortunately, the Black Spades liked to drop by unexpectedly to steal girlfriends, rough up rival gang members and generally intimidate the crowd. When they arrived, Brown tried to pacify them by playing "Soul Power" by James Brown. They loved chanting "Spade Power! Spade Power!" along with the record.

"I was known as a graffiti writer," said Herc. "I wrote 'KOOL HERC.' I also ran the 880 relay on the track team, dressed well and danced. 'Get Ready' was my favorite song. But then the music stopped. I think the gangs stopped it. It got too dangerous for people to go to discos."

In 1973 Herc's sister Cindy celebrated her birthday by throwing a party in the recreation room of a housing project on Sedgwick Avenue. "She asked me to provide the music," said Herc, "so I went out and bought all the fresh, up-to-date records. I rigged a little hookup with two turntables. All our friends came to the party along with a lot of people from the neighborhood. I played songs like 'Give It Up or Turn It Loose.' People would walk for miles just to hear that record—because nobody could find it." The party was such a success that Herc continued deejaying at house parties and community centers. He collected a trunk full of dance 45s and invested in better equipment, including a mike with an echo chamber and strobe light. Later that year, he began charging a 25-cent entrance fee.

"I was twelve the first time I went to Herc's party," said Kevin, who became one of the original b-boys. "My brother Keith and I used to hang out with some girls around 165th Street and University Avenue and they kept saying: 'Y'all should come to Herc's! It's a party and he's jamming every week!' One night we decided to check it out. The thing I mostly remember was how loud the music was. The sound overtook you. The place was packed—a real sweatbox. Herc was on the mike. He'd say things like 'Rock the house' and call out the names of people at the party.

Wallace Dee, Johnny Cool, Chubby, the Amazing Bobo, James Bond, Sasa, Clark Kent, Trixie—those were the names you heard. Trixie had a big afro and he used to shake his head. It used to make him look so good! Wallace Dee had a move called the slingshot, which was a basic drop to the floor except he came up like he was shooting a slingshot. After that first time, we didn't want to go anywhere else. It was Kool Herc's, Kool Herc's, Kool Herc's. Every weekend. There was no such thing as b-boys when we arrived, but Herc gave us that tag. Just like he named his sound system the Herculords and he called me and my brother the Nigger Twins. He called his dancers the b-boys."

Despite their age, Keith and Kevin soon established themselves as the premier performers at Herc's parties. "When we danced, we always had a crowd around us," said Keith. "We wore Pro-Keds, double-knit pants, windbreakers and hats we called 'crushers.' One of us would always have the hat on backwards and we both had straws in our mouth." During the week, the twins spent hours working on new routines, inventing steps that would amaze the crowd. "James Brown had a lot to do with it," explained Kevin, "because he used to do splits and slide across the floor."

In 1975, Herc moved into a club on 180th and Jerome Avenue. Formerly known as Soulsville, it had just been renamed the Hevalo. With the gang situation cooling off, discos were just starting to reopen. Everybody wanted to get into dancing again. But while most deejays played the same disco hits one heard on the radio, the music at the Hevalo was harder, funkier. Herc knew how to bring the crowd up to a frenzied peak and hold them there for hours. During these times, he seldom played an entire song. Instead, he played the hottest segment of the song, which was often just a 30-second "break" section—when the drums, bass and rhythm guitar stripped the beat to its barest essence. Herc played break after break to create an endless peak of dance beats.

It wasn't long before the dancers at the Hevalo were known as "break" dancers. Rather than doing the Hustle or other disco steps, which required a male and female partner, break dancers performed solo. The dance was usually a competition between males to establish who had the suavest, most graceful moves. "Before we called it 'breaking,' it was known as 'going off' or 'burning,'" said Phase. "When we were kids we did dances like the Washing Machine, the Popcorn and the Mod Squad. The Busstop came out in 1974. Burning came out before the Busstop. It was all about taking a guy out, burning him. The big phrase was 'I'm gonna turn this party out.' I used to do shit with my feet that people didn't understand. I danced with three guys, Stak, Timbo and Sweet Duke. I think we brought a lot of shit out. This girl asked us: 'Where y'all learn to dance? You don't dance like nobody else.' Hand movements were really important, especially in a dance called the Salute. But I have to give credit to the Nigger Twins. Those boys were bad."

The freelance deejay, an independent entrepreneur armed with a portable sound system and extensive record collection, emerged as the new cultural hero in the Bronx around 1975. Previously, anyone wishing to gain notoriety either became a graffiti writer or an incomparable break dancer. However, by 1976, the most powerful, most revered figures were the deejays. Herc remained in a class by himself, primarily because of his McIntosh amplifier and twin Shure speaker columns, the combination he called "The Herculords." The awesome power of the Herculords was most evident whenever Herc played the parks. Even outdoors, the system was surprisingly clean, free of distortion and ear-shatteringly loud.

Herc also had the best records. While most other deejays played disco (Donna Summer and the Bee Gees were popular), Herc played hard-core funk with stripped-down drum beats. No record better epitomizes his style than "Apache," a song recorded by the Ventures in the early '60s and redone by The Incredible Bongo Band in 1974. "Apache" combined a melodramatic, Spaghetti-Western melody with wild bongo solos. The result was a bit corny, but it created a theatrical atmosphere perfect for a showdown between two break dancers. Since it was recorded by an obscure record company, "Apache" was not an easy record to find. To make matters even more difficult, Herc jealously guarded the names of the more obscure break records, even to the point of soaking them in his bathtub to remove the labels.

Other deejays began following Herc's style. At Stevenson High, Afrika Bambaataa formed a small group called the Zulus, who became an extension of the b-boy style, a gang into music and dance instead of violence. It wasn't long before the Zulus became a powerful force at Stevenson, so powerful, in fact, that the principal had Bambaataa transferred to a different school. On November 12, 1976, Bambaataa gave his first official party as a deejay at the Bronx Community Center.

At the time there were three main deejays playing "b-beat" music in the Bronx: Bambaataa in the southeast, Herc in the west, and, in the middle, an ambitious young deejay named Grandmaster Flash. However, there were also dozens of lesser-known deejays, all vying for recognition. The easiest and quickest way to establish a reputation as a deejay was to "battle" a known deejay. These battles were usually held in parks or community centers. Both deejays played at the same time. Whoever collected the most dancers around his system was declared the winner. However, with both systems cranked to maximum volume, the winner was often the deejay with the loudest sound. "There was a lot of confusion going on at the time," laughed Bambaataa. "If you outblasted the other deejay, he'd get mad, cut off his system and leave."

During one legendary battle against Disco King Mario, Bambaataa opened his show with the theme song from the *Andy Griffith Show*, taped off his television set. He mixed the ditty with a rocking drum beat, followed it with the *Munsters'* theme song and quickly changed gears with "I Got the Feeling" by James Brown. His knack for coming up with unexpected cuts and "bugging out" the audience earned him the title "Master of Records."

During the summer of 1976, young b-boys cruised through the Bronx on bicycles, looking for block parties. "Where they jamming?" they'd ask anyone in the street. "Flash is jamming at Twenty-Three Park!" would come the reply, and before long several hundred kids, many of them stoned on angel dust, marijuana or beer, would come pouring into the park where Joseph Sadler and Gene Livingston had their system wired to the base of a streetlight. The audience knew the two deejays only by their stage names: Grandmaster Flash and Mean Gene.

Flash, an electronics wizard from Samuel Gompers Vocational High School, had been deejaying house parties for two years. In 1976, he began attracting widespread attention for his outdoor parties, which were usually held in a park at 169th Street and Boston Road.

"You had to be entertaining to throw block parties," said Flash. "It was always a rough crowd and there was never any security. If the crowd wasn't entertained, the situation could get very dangerous. I would go to the Hevalo sometimes to check Herc out, but Herc used to embarrass me quite a bit. He'd say 'Grandmaster Flash in the house,' over the mike, and then he'd cut off the highs and lows on his system and just play the midrange. 'Flash,' he'd say, 'in order to be a qualified disc jockey, there is one thing you must have... highs.' Then Herc would crank up his highs and the high hat would be sizzling. 'And most of all, Flash,' he'd say, 'you must have... bass.' Well, when Herc's bass came in the whole place would be shaking. I'd get so embarrassed that I'd have to leave. My system couldn't compare."

However, if Flash couldn't compete with Herc's system, he was determined to find another way to establish himself as the premier deejay in the Bronx. He began visiting Manhattan discos, where deejays like Pete Jones were playing music for an older, more sophisticated audience. Although he disliked the music, Flash noticed that Jones knew more about mixing records than Herc. "It wasn't no hit-or-miss thing," said Flash. "Herc would drop the needle and cut the record in and hope he was in the right spot, but Pete knew how to pre-cue his records."

One night Jones relented and let Flash temporarily take over the controls of his system. "Once I put on the headphones, I knew the secret," said Flash. "A simple toggle switch let me hear what was on each turntable. At school, we called it a SPDT—single pole, double throw—switch. I didn't have one on my mixer, so I took some Crazy Glue and glued one on. I ran wires to my turntables and to a small amp, just powerful enough to drive a set of headphones. When Gene came back I told him: 'Gene, I got something here! I found a way to lock these beats up and keep the shit going!'"

Although Herc was the first deejay to buy two copies of the same record so he could keep repeating the same break indefinitely, it was Flash who devised the method for repeating break sections while keeping a steady beat. Rather than find the section by chance, Flash began pre-cueing through headphones. He spent hours sitting in his room practicing his mixing technique. By playing short, rapid-fire cuts from a variety of records, he invented the art of musical collage. "Mean Gene never seemed to get the hang of it," said Flash, "but his baby brother, Theodore, used to skip school and hang out with me. That's when I discovered the clock theory and Theodore caught on to it right away." In order to make a mix using five or six different records, Flash had to be able to locate precise moments on each record in a matter of seconds. The problem was that every groove looked pretty much the same. How could you find the right spot fast enough? The solution, Flash discovered, was to "read" the record like a clock, using the record label as the dial.

Ray Chandler, an independent concert promoter, approached Flash in

1976 and tried to convince him to open a regular night spot. Because most of his fans were junior-high-school age, Flash was dubious. Why pay to see him when lots of other deejays were playing the parks for free? However, after Chandler found a tiny club on Boston Road, Flash agreed to give it a try. The club didn't have a name, but the front door was painted black, so they called it The Black Door.

"It had two rooms with a long hallway between them," said Flash. "Each room was about the size of a living room. First thing we did was have a lot of flyers made up. Phase and Buddy Esquire were the main flyer makers. Those guys were great. Chandler hired a crew to pass the flyers out at schools. We'd open at eleven o'clock and by midnight, the place was so packed you couldn't buy your way in. The doors wouldn't open back up until six or seven in the morning."

By this time, Flash had converted several members of his crew into "emcees," who were supposed to keep the crowd dancing by talking over a microphone. Most of the attention, however, was still centered on the dancers. "Everybody was doing the Freak," said Flash. "That was a dance that made it permissible for the male to damn near have sexual intercourse with the female. It was a fast dance and you would bounce around with the girl jammed against you. And she'd be doing it right back to you. With some girls, it was even permissible to have a guy in the front and one in back, like a sandwich! If you weren't on the dance floor when that shit was jumping off, you missed out. It got super frantic. I would blow my tweeters and they'd sound like gunshots. You think that would disturb the dancers? Hell no. I had to program a calm hour after the frantic hour just to bring the crowd back to a normal state of mind. Lots of stick-up kids were coming to the club and they were the type to go up to somebody and demand his gold chain. If you weren't ready to fight, you'd have to hand it over. There was this one record—'Listen to Me' by Baby Huey. Something happened every time I played it. We called it 'the trouble record.' The stick-up kids would start looking for somebody the minute they heard it. We were having problems until Chandler hired a former division of the Black Spades to act as security. They had changed their names to the Casanova Crew and we didn't have any more problems after the Casanovas started taking care of security."

Within a few months, Flash's popularity was soaring and he had to move to a bigger club. Despite his success, he continued improving and updating his technique. In 1977 he invented back-spinning, which allowed him to repeat phrases and beats from a record by rapidly spinning it backwards. For example, he would take a phrase like "Let's dance" and repeat it seven or eight times—without losing the beat. "We conquered quite a bit of territory," said Flash. "High-school kids were getting into the music and we knocked off all the high schools. But the pinnacle of our dream was to play the Audubon Ballroom."

Meanwhile, Theodore and his brother Gene had formed their own deejay crew with "Grand Wizard" Theodore as the star. Although only 13 at the time, Theodore was one of the few deejays who could compete with Flash. While Flash was perfecting the back-spin, Theodore was working on a technical innovation of his own, which he debuted at the Third Avenue Ballroom in 1978.

While practicing at home, Theodore noticed he could create sound effects by spinning the record back and forth while keeping the needle in the groove. It wasn't always a pleasant sound—in fact, it could be highly irritating—but if controlled properly, it could also be explosively percussive. Many deejays were already familiar with the sound because they heard it in their headphones every time they pre-cued a record. Theodore wanted to try the sound in public, but he wasn't sure how the audience would react. "The Third Avenue Ballroom was packed," said Theodore, "and I figured I might as well give it a try. So, I put on two copies of 'Sex Machine' and started scratching up one. The crowd loved it... they went wild."

"Scratching" was soon imitated and improved by other deejays, including Flash, Breakout, A.J., Jazzy Jay and Charlie Chase. In a few years, Whiz Kid and Grandmaster DST would use the technique to create unbelievably smooth, synthesizer-like effects. However, in 1978, the focus began shifting away from the deejays and onto their emcees, who were busy creating a new, aggressive style of talking on the mike, which would soon be known around the world as "rapping." Before long, few kids wanted to be deejays anymore. Instead, they all wanted to be rappers.

A NEW RAP LANGUAGE

It was a hot, sweltering night in the Bronx, but waves of thunderclouds were gathering over Westchester County and it looked as though rain might be arriving to cool off the city. Although the rain never came, a lightning storm did, and at 8:30 P.M. several bolts struck the power transmission lines at the Indian Point nuclear power plant, causing a short circuit. Like falling dominoes, relay circuits stretching south into the city began shutting off. Lights went blank, elevators stopped, subway cars rolled to a halt. Within 20 minutes it became the worst New York City blackout since November, 1965.

Unlike the previous blackout, however, which had been remarkably trouble-free, the blackout of July 14, 1977, was almost immediately marred by reports of looting, arson and robbery, most of which came from the ghetto areas of Bedford-Stuyvesant, Brownsville, Harlem and the South Bronx. By 10 P.M. gangs of youths were congregating in front of the major stores. "Let's do it, let's do it," they'd say, trying to work up the nerve to break a window. A steel door guarding the Ace Pontiac Showroom on Jerome Avenue was smashed and 50 cars were driven off the lot. When police answered an emergency call from a supermarket on 138th Street, they were bombarded by bricks and bottles. "They couldn't understand why we were arresting them," said Officer Gary Parlefsky of the 30th Precinct to a *New York Times* reporter. "They were angry with us. They said: 'I'm on welfare. I'm taking what I need. Why are you bothering me?'" Fires, many undoubtedly set by arsonists, illuminated the streets, which were lined with looters carrying TV sets, stereos, groceries, clothing and anything else they could cart away. Within 24 hours, more than 3,000 people were arrested and 100 policemen were injured. The state troopers were rushed in to restore order. "The blackout just totaled the whole damn neighborhood," said Phase 2. "The businesses never came up out of it."

Until the blackout, few people realized the extent of the anger and frustration in the South Bronx, emotions that had been subdued but not eliminated by social programs like welfare, methadone treatment and food stamps. It is not surprising that these hostile feelings were also reflected in the new style of rapping formulated that same summer. Although it is difficult to trace the origins of rap, the genre is firmly embedded in black American culture and stretches back farther than even most rappers realize.

In 1976, Dennis Wepman, Ronald Newman and Murray Binderman

published a landmark study on black prison culture entitled *The Life: The Lore and Folk Poetry of the Black Hustler*. The book documented "toasting," a form of poetic storytelling prevalent in prisons throughout the '50s and '60s. "Toasts are a form of poetry recited by certain blacks—really a performance medium," wrote the authors. "They are like jokes: no one knows who creates them, and everyone has his own versions.... Most recitation sessions are somewhat structured: a reciter performs to a silent, appreciative audience. Good tellers may be highly valued and much in demand.... In Attica, Doe Eye, a young burglar from Harlem, could characterize the people of the toasts so exactly that, when he was speaking from his cell, one might have thought he had a group in there with him."

Probably the oldest and most famous toast, "The Signifying Monkey," had hundreds of different versions by 1976. Other famous toasts included "Duriella du Fontaine" and "King Heroin," a version of which was recorded by James Brown in 1972. Some toasts were moralistic fables, others related how a man in prison had been betrayed by a girlfriend. Almost all attempted to glorify the life of the petty criminal. The toast which follows was probably composed in 1964.

The Hustler
The name of the game is beat the lame
Take a woman and make her live in shame.

It makes no difference how she scream or holler,
'Cause dope is my heaven and my God the almighty dollar.

I, the Hustler, swear by God
I would kill Pope Paul if pressed too hard.

I would squash out Bobby and do Jackie harm
And for one goddamn dollar would break her arm.

I, the Hustler, kick ass morning, noon and night.
I would challenge Cassius and Liston to a fight.

I would climb in the ring with nothing but two P-38s.
And send either one that moved through the pearly gates.

I, the Hustler, can make Astaire dance and Sinatra croon,
And I would make the Supreme Court eat shit from a spoon.

During the '50s, black radio jocks entertained and amused audiences with prison-style raps. In 1955, the most popular of these radio personalities was Douglas "Jocko" Henderson, whose "1280 Rocket" show on WOV anticipated a hip hop fascination with themes from outer space. Jocko often opened his show with lines like: "From way up here in the stratosphere, we gotta holler mighty loud and clear, ee-tiddy-o and a ho, and I'm back on the scene with the record machine, saying oo-pap-doo and how do you do!" His witty, bantering style was updated and refined by New York club deejays like Frankie Crocker, who later became a radio jock on WBLS.

It is worth noting that Jamaican music also has a history of toasting: poems written in Jamaican slang were spoken to the beat of reggae records by deejays with enormous portable sound systems. Because of this, many critics have drawn parallels between the development of rap and reggae, a connection that is denied by Kool Herc. "Jamaican toasting?" said Herc. "Naw, naw. No connection there. I couldn't play reggae in the Bronx. People wouldn't accept it. The inspiration for rap is James Brown and the album *Hustler's Convention*."

Released in 1973, *Hustler's Convention* was written and performed by Jalal Uridin, leader of a group of black militant ex-cons known as the Last Poets. The group was discovered in the late '60s by record producer Alan Douglas, who saw them on a local television show. "I called the station, found out who it was and through some sources I made a contact. I went to 138th Street and Lenox Avenue one afternoon and they recited for me on the street corner," said Douglas. "I made a deal with them. The deal was, they would come to the recording studio, put this on tape, and if we all like each other when it was over, I'd put the record out. And if they didn't, they could take the master home with them."

The group's first record, which contained such raps as "Run Nigger," "Niggers Are Scared of Revolution" and "When the Revolution Comes," reportedly sold more than 800,000 copies despite its aggressively radical overtones, which annihilated any hope of radio play. Under the pseudonym "Lightin' Rod," Jalal went on to record *Hustler's Convention*, a solo album also produced by Douglas. It consisted of 12 prison toasts (with raps like "Four Bitches is What I Got," "Coppin' Some Fronts for the Set" and "Sentenced to the Chair") recited to musical compositions by Brother Gene Dinwiddie and Kool & The Gang. Although the record did not sell as well as the Last Poets' initial effort, it had enormous popularity in the Bronx.

With *Hustler's Convention* as inspiration, Kool Herc began composing prison-style rhymes using expressions like "my mellow" and "it's the joint." Herc discovered an echo chamber could provide dramatic flourishes at just the right moments. "Yes, yes, y'all," Herc would say. "It's the serious, serio-so jointski. You're listening to the sound system. The Herculords... culords... lords. And I just want to say to all my b-boys... boys... oys. Rock on. Time to get down to the A.M. But please remember—respect my system and I'll respect you and yours. As I scan the place, I see the very familiar face... of my mellow. Wallace Dee in the house. Wallace Dee, freak for me."

"I first went to the Hevalo when I was thirteen," said Sisco Kid. "This dude around my block said, 'Hang with me,' and he took me. Everybody was lined up around the block. They had a gangster look and were older than me. I said, 'Oh shit, this is crazy.' It was very dark inside, but there was an excitement in the air, like anything could jump off. You'd see some dude dancing and he'd be wearing alligator shoes. You'd say, 'Check out this dude!' Then Herc came on the mike and he was so tough. You'd get transfixed by his shit. He had this def voice that almost sounded like a southern drawl. You thought, 'This is cool, I want to be like this.'"

"People got ideas from *Hustler's Convention*," said Theodore. "But it was hard to get on the mike and say a rhyme. Nobody really had any rhymes. Mostly it was 'You're listening to the sound of so-and-so deejay and next week we'll be at such-and-such park.' Then Flash wrote this rhyme. 'You dip, dive and socialize. We're trying to make you realize. That we are qualified to rectify that burning... desire... to boogie.' At this point he didn't have any emcees. He asked Melle Mel, 'Will you say this rhyme?' Mel said, 'No, let Cowboy say it.' Cowboy said, 'No, let Mel say it.' It went back and forth like that. Flash wanted that rhyme said so bad he finally grabbed the mike and said, 'I'll say it.' And that's how it happened."

"Vocal entertainment became necessary to keep the crowd under control," said Flash. "When people first came to the park, they'd start danc-ing. But then everyone would gather around and watch the deejay. A block party could turn into a seminar. That was dangerous. You needed vocal entertainment to keep everyone dancing. I tried so many people. I used to leave the mike on the other side of the table so anybody who wanted could pick it up. A lot of people failed the test. The first to pass was Cowboy. Then Mel. Then Mel's brother Creole."

Since Cowboy had a deep voice similar to that of a radio disk jockey, his early rapping style more closely emulated disco deejays like Holly-wood, a Manhattan-based deejay who employed a slick, radio-jock sound. Mel and Creole, on the other hand, created a more percussive style of rap similar to the staccato exhortations used by James Brown on such hip hop classics as "Give It Up or Turn It Loose," a song in which key phrases were shouted to the beat. "Clap your hands!" screamed Brown. "Stomp your feet! In the jungle, brother! Clap! Clap! Ain't it funky now? Need to feel it!" Although Brown's vocals could not really be called rap, they provided the perfect accompaniment for dance records: They encouraged the audience to participate more fully in the music, they emphasized rhythm and raw emotion over melody, and each syllable was spoken directly on the beat—something that had not been attempted with toasting, which put its emphasis on vocal ingenuity and lyrical con-tent rather than rhythm. (Douglas attributes the difference to a change in musical styles. "The Last Poets were jazz-heads," he explained, "while today's rappers are into disco, rock and rhythm and blues. The words fall differently and you get a different feeling. The Poets didn't care if one could dance to the rap. The point was a story was going down that was memorable.")

Relying on an inventive use of slang, the percussive effect of short words and unexpected internal rhymes, Mel and Creole began compos-ing elaborate rap routines, intricately weaving their voices through a musical track mixed by Flash. They would trade solos, chant and sing harmony. The result was dazzling. It was a vocal style that effectively merged the aggressive rhythms of James Brown with the language and imagery of *Hustler's Convention*. They were immediately imitated by every other emcee in the Bronx.

To the hip hop, hip hop, don't stop.

Don't stop that body rock.

Just get with the beat, get ready to clap.
'Cause Melle Mel, is starting to rap

Ever since the time of the very first party.
I felt I could make myself some money.

It was up in my heart from the very start.
I could super sell, at the top of the charts.

Rappin' on the mike, makin' cold cold cash.
With a jock spinnin' for me called Deejay Flash.

To complement the new rap routines, Flash experimented with a recently invented electronic drum machine. The shock value alone made the machine a useful theatrical device. The turntables would be empty, Flash would step back from his set, and yet somehow the beats would continue with mechanical precision. "It bugged them out," said Flash, laughing. "Then we started featuring ourselves as Grandmaster Flash and the Three Emcees... with THE BEAT BOX. People would show up at the party just to see what the beat box was."

Failing to keep up with recent developments in hip hop, Kool Herc was having trouble maintaining his position, and, in fact, was undergoing a rapid decline in popularity, a development he attributed to his being stabbed at one of his own parties. "The party hadn't even started," said Herc. "Three guys came to the door and my people wouldn't let them in. They said they was looking for the owner. A discrepancy started. By this time, I'm finished dressing and I walk over and say, 'What's happening?' Boom, boom, boom. I got stabbed three times, once in the hand and twice in the side. The guy with the knife was drunk. Somebody stabbed him up but I'm sorry to say he lived. I took a piece of ice, put it on my side, and walked to the hospital. After that, the door was open for Flash. How do you think people feel about coming to a party when the host gets stabbed? Then my place burned down. Papa couldn't find no good ranch, so his herd scattered."

For over two years rap had developed in almost complete isolation from the rest of the world. Until 1980, hip hop music and rap were transmitted primarily through live cassette recordings which were noisily displayed via ghetto blasters, portable tape players carried by every self-respecting hip hopper. Tapes were circulated around New York, in prisons, in nearby states, and could even be found on army bases overseas. However, the first rap record using the South Bronx style was made not by a local group but by the Fatback Band, who recorded "King Tim II" in 1979. Several months later, Sylvia Robinson, a singer who recorded "Pillow Talk" and "Love is Strange" in the '70s, decided to make a rap record. One day she walked into a pizza shop near her home in New Jersey and heard a live tape being played by a man named Hank, who was the doorman at a rap club in the Bronx. The tape featured Grandmaster Caz and the Mighty Force Emcees.

"The way rap evolved is from people trying to outdo each other," said Grandmaster Caz. "You'd go to Herc's party and hear him say something. Then you'd go home and change it around to where it was your saying. I knew the entire *Hustler's Convention* by heart. That was rap, but we didn't know it at the time. Then everybody started saying nursery rhymes. Then Flash started the whole thing of having real groups. Then people started coming to parties just to see the emcees. I used to go to this club called the Sparkle and I told Hank about my group. I told him we needed a manager. So he went to work for us, helping us out on the financial end and stuff. He was also working at the pizza shop and that's where he met Sylvia. She heard him playing one of our tapes. So he told me about it. Later, I asked him, 'Whatsup?' and he said, 'Sylvia already has two rappers and she wants one more. And she asked me to do it.' So I said, 'Well, okay, I understand that.' If it was me, I would have done the same thing. And he said, 'Well, I want to use some of your rhymes.' I threw my rhyme book on the table and said, 'Take what you want.'"

Before long Robinson created the Sugarhill Gang, a group composed of Hank, Wonder Mike and Master Gee. Their first record, "Rapper's Delight," unexpectedly sold two million copies, launched a new independent record company and created a vast audience for rap music around the country. It also unleashed a mad scramble of emcee groups looking for record contracts. The song's success was due more to its novelty and its musical track, which was lifted from Chic's "Good Times," than to its rapping, which was weak and unimaginative by Bronx standards.

"I never thought about how big it might come out," said Caz. "I never thought Hank would become a millionaire and forget about me. When the record came out, I was going to high school at Roosevelt and every car that passed had it on the radio. Every box on the street had it on. Everybody knew those rhymes were mine and half were coming up to me, 'Yo, I heard you on the radio!' The other half was saying, 'You're not gettin' no money for that!' I never saw Hank again. It was like he was afraid to approach me."

(Caz later joined the Cold Crush Brothers and signed a contract with Tuff City, a subsidiary of CBS.)

When emcee groups realized they were the primary reason why many people were coming to hip hop parties, they demanded more money from their deejays, which led to arguments and eventual breakups. At the time, Bambaataa was working with a number of groups, including Soul Sonic Force, Cosmic Force and the Jazzy Five. However, he freely admits the most "treacherous" battles were taking place between Flash and the Furious Five versus Breakout and the Funky Four. "Flash was on top," said Bambaataa, "but they was battling for that number-one spot. Both groups was doin' flips on stage and settin' off smoke bombs." Theodore and his brother Gene formed a group called the L-Brothers, later known as the Fantastic Freaks. "Waterbed" Kev, one of their rappers, began wearing studded belts and chains, a style soon imitated by almost every other group. (Within three years, this "S&M look" would be picked up by thousands of teenagers around the city.)

In 1979, Special K, a Bronx rapper and member of the Undefeated Four, was attending Townes High School on 33rd Street in Manhattan. "I was not known as just a rapper," said Special K, "I was known as a Bronx rapper 'cause Manhattan rappers had more of a disco style with much more slang. My brother used to go to Stevenson High and he knew Breakout and Bambaataa. He was a break dancer—a member of the Zulu Masters. When rap came out, it wasn't about having a record deal or doing shows, it was about writing rhymes. It was a habit. I would write while walking down the hallway at school. At Townes I met the Treacherous Three, which was Spoonie Gee, L.A. Sunshine and Kool Mo Dee. One time they invited me to come down to one of their parties. First we was having battles, but then they started talking about getting together. I considered it and went back to the Bronx. Then, I found out Spoonie Gee had made a record, so I said, 'Ohh no, let me shoot on back down and see whatsup.'"

"'Rapper's Delight' changed everything," said Kool Mo Dee. "Spoonie's uncle Bobby Robinson [no relation to Sylvia Robinson] had a little record company called Enjoy, and Spoonie wanted to make a record. At first his uncle didn't pay him no mind, but after 'Rapper's Delight' came out, Spoonie's uncle got interested. He asked Spoonie who the best rappers were and Spoonie said the Funky Four and Flash. Then Spoonie made a record where he talked about how good he was in bed. That was his gimmick. Everybody had a gimmick. L.A. Sunshine's gimmick was his voice sounded like Hollywood, so we called him Baby Hollywood. My gimmick was using big words like 'establishment,' 'repent,' stuff like that. Spoonie had a whole book of rhymes on different ways to have sex. He got a lot of attention 'cause the girls like to hear that stuff. We asked Spoonie, 'Why didn't you take us down to the studio with you?' He said, 'I didn't think it was no big thing.' So Spoonie started doing shows by himself, only sometimes he'd get lonely and ask me to come with him. Spoonie had an ego at that time 'cause he had the most juice from his record. During that summer I made up fast rapping, a new style of talking very fast. We got to make a record with Spoonie as the Treacherous Three. That's when Special K became a member of the group."

The records sold better than Robinson expected, and it wasn't long before Grandmaster Flash, the Funky Four and Spoonie Gee were lured away to the more successful Sugar Hill label, leaving Robinson with the Treacherous Three. "We had a good relationship with Bobby," said Mo Dee. "He was very funny. The money was comin' in fast. We would never get checks, but when we saw Bobby he would feed us money. We was getting a lot of attention." "Yeah, but he flaked when it came to royalties," added Special K. "We made three more records on Enjoy and then Bobby sold us to Sugar Hill."

During the spring of 1981, the Treacherous Three released two records in rapid succession: "The Body Rock" and "Put the Boogie in the Body." The former featured a peppy, well-coordinated rap routine, a slow, slinky beat dominated by a synthesizer bass line and some shrieking, post-psychedelic guitar riffs. It was an infectious dance record and became an instant street classic. Even more effective, however, was the group's next release, "Put the Boogie in the Body," which remains one of the highest-energy raps every recorded. After opening with a series of shouts, the song builds in intensity for six minutes before ending in a fade-out of garbled nonsense words. Since the instrumental track is spare and minimal, the emotional force of this song is carried entirely by the rappers. Shortly before the record's release, The Treacherous Three established themselves as one of the premier rap groups in the city.

"A lot of people thought rap was going to fade out," said Special K. "They thought it was a fad and looked at rappers as being unintelligent, high-school dropouts. But it seemed like every time rap got ready to die, something new came along to add a new dimension—to boost it along."

BUT IS IT ART?

Moody, intense, often uncommunicative, Lee Quinones was never mistaken for just another graffiti writer. A short Puerto Rican with a prominent scar across the bridge of his nose, Quinones usually wore a car mechanic's overalls with a Plymouth insignia sewn over the breast pocket. In 1975, he snuck into a subway yard to paint his first whole-car mural. Half of the car was dominated by a large, brightly colored "LEE" outline, the obligatory element in every graffiti masterpiece, but the other half portrayed two derelicts standing in front of a burning building.

Instead of "throwing-up" large numbers of quickly executed pieces, Quinones concentrated exclusively on well-painted, whole-car murals. When it came to graffiti, he seemed zealous, resolute and driven by forces he could not express through any means except his paintings.

Although the graffiti subculture had quieted down after the breakup of UGA, it reached a new peak of activity in 1976, when whole-car murals began appearing in ever-increasing numbers. Because of his growing reputation, Quinones was approached by four writers interested in forming a new group called the Fabulous Five (formerly the name of a Manhattan streetgang).

Slug was the leader," said Quinones. "He used to be a Black Spade and he was very smart, very philosophical. The others were Doc and Mono, who had been members of a gang called the Puerto Rican Brothers, and Slave, who was a tall, skinny writer from Brooklyn." The Fabulous Five quickly

" established themselves as the premier writing group in the city. They robbed paint stores, drank beer, stayed up until dawn and spent endless weeks doing nothing but painting trains. One winter they pulled off the ultimate graffiti masterpiece—a 10-car train with a mural on every car. However, in the world of subway graffiti, kings were easily deposed. Each year a new generation of writers appeared and the younger ones tended to be more ambitious and energetic than their older counterparts, who moved into more profitable, less dangerous occupations. By 1978, Quinones was the only member of the Fabulous Five still painting graffiti.

Many writers dropped out in 1977, when the Transit Authority erected its "final solution" to the graffiti problem in a Coney Island train yard. At an annual cost of $400,000, the T.A. began operating a giant car wash which sprayed vast amounts of petroleum hydroxide on the sides of graffitied trains. The solvent spray was followed by a vigorous buffing. At first the writers called it "the Orange Crush," after Agent Orange, a defoliant used in Vietnam. Later it was simply known as "the buff." Fumes emanating from the cleaning station were so deadly that a nearby school closed after students complained of respiratory problems. The school later reopened after city officials assured the community that the health complaints had nothing to do with the graffiti removal operation. However, even T.A. workers admitted they couldn't stand downwind from the station without getting nauseous. Meanwhile, the solvent was seeping into the underfloorings of the trains, causing considerable corrosion and damaging electrical parts.

A few writers were sure the buff meant the end of graffiti: Phase wrote a rap elegy titled "After the Buff," and Tracy designed a cartoon with the inscription "Graffiti R.I.P." However, the buff never really eliminated graffiti. Instead, it mixed the spray paint into a single, grayish mud-like color. Writers soon learned to use better-quality paints and to spray murals with a protective covering of clear enamel. They couldn't defeat the buff entirely, but the T.A. had to run a train through the station several times before the murals were obliterated.

Quinones had a better solution. In 1979, he began painting handball courts around the Lower East Side. The concept of murals on handball courts had originated with Tracy several years earlier. However, Quinones was the first writer to become known primarily for painting them. Like his work on the trains, Quinones's court murals mingled cartoon imagery with a strong moral sensibility. One mural pleaded for an end to the arms race, while another portrayed a 10-foot-tall Howard the Duck (a character from Marvel Comics) emerging from a trash can, with the inscription: "If art like this is a crime, let God forgive me."

One day, while sitting in class at Seward High School, Quinones was approached by a tall black man wearing dark sunglasses. "I want to talk to you, man," said the stranger. Before he could say another word, the teacher removed him from the class. "When class was over, the dude was still waiting for me outside," said Quinones. "I was expecting a fight. But it turned out he just wanted to talk about what was happening on the trains. I didn't know if he was a policeman or what—so I gave him the brush-off." However, the man, whose name was Fred Brathwaite, kept returning to see Quinones. "He said he knew a way to make money with graffiti. I started thinking about what he was proposing and said, 'Well, let's give it a try.'"

A few weeks later, Brathwaite appeared with a clipping from the *Village Voice*. In the February 12, 1979, "Scenes" column was a photo of Brathwaite standing in front of one of Lee's murals. A brief article by Howard Smith followed.

"We call ourselves the Fabulous Five and we're the best at what we do—graffiti. Just recently we decided to start selling our services for $5 per square foot, and already we've got several commissions. All we need is for more folks to give us a chance. I mean, we're really incredible at redoing storefronts, old grimy walls, sides of trucks, boring building lobbies, interiors, exteriors. You name it; pay us; we'll paint it..."

"Are you kidding?" [Smith] interrupted. "Most people I know in the city are trying to get rid of you spray-can freaks."

Standing in front of me, his mouth open in shock, was Frederick Brathwaite, leader of the Fabulous Five. He puffed himself up in his spiffy suit and tie, and pounced back: "It's that kind of attitude I have to fight. I think it's time everyone realized graffiti is the purest form of New York art. What else has evolved from the streets? Lee, Doc, Slave, Mono and I are just taking it off the trains and bringin' it above ground... As you can see, we've obviously been influenced by Warhol, Crumb, and Lichtenstein..."

The article included a telephone number and address where Brathwaite could be reached for possible commissions.

Martinez may have been the first outsider to market graffiti, but he lacked a flair for the promotional intricacies of the art world. Brathwaite, on the other hand, was an insider to the subculture who realized the importance of connecting graffiti with the hip downtown art scene—especially with Andy Warhol, an artist many writers had probably never heard of, much less used as an influence. "Fred was a hustler," said Quinones. "He knew it was about time for graffiti to get going again."

Brathwaite received several calls after the article appeared, but the most important came from Claudio Bruni, an Italian art dealer who maintained a New York residence. Bruni told Brathwaite he could arrange a show if he had some work on canvas. Brathwaite and Quinones immediately went to work. "Claudio came and bought five paintings outright," said Quinones. "Fred had been painting on canvas, but the paintings Claudio wanted were all mine. At first, I wasn't really interested in the money. I just wanted to preserve my work. But the money started coming in after Claudio arranged a show in Rome. We flew over for the opening. They had a party and all the chic people came." Bruni had no trouble selling the work at $1,000 a canvas.

Brathwaite wasn't the only writer who sensed graffiti might be making a commercial comeback. Mark Edmonds (Ali), who had miraculously recovered from his subway accident without a single facial scar, reformed Soul Artists after receiving a grant from an arts organization. Ali wrote a letter to Futura 2000, who had served out his enlistment and was living in Georgia with a Navy buddy, urging him to return to New York. Although Futura did return, several months passed before he would enter a subway yard. The two friends did not discuss the accident and their relationship remained somewhat strained.

Three other contacts with the legitimate art world took place during this period. Stefan Eins, an artist and gallery owner who was operating a gallery on Mercer Street in Soho, decided to move his business to the South Bronx. "I wanted a stronger challenge," explained Eins. "If you continue to show the artists you know, you wind up following the same direction in the same social climate. It was very sobering to be in the Bronx. I couldn't fall into any art world patterns." Through his new gallery, Fashion Moda, Eins began cultivating a relationship with the local graffiti artists.

Sam Esses, a burly, outspoken collector from Park Avenue, became aware of a growing European interest in graffiti though conversations with the Italian dealer Bruni. When he discovered that his daughter knew some writers, he decided to make contact. "I don't know why, but I decided to rent a studio to see if I could preserve some of the work that was being created on the trains," said Esses. "I found an empty space on the Upper East Side and stocked it with supplies." Word soon spread through the graffiti grapevine, and the best writers from all over the city materialized on Esses's doorstep. Dozens of large canvases were completed and Esses set about finding a gallery to show the work. Although the exhibit was not held for two years, the "workshop" encouraged many writers to continue working on canvas.

A sculptor named Henry Chalfant, who had been taking pictures of graffiti for several years, decided to meet some writers. He visited the writer's bench at 149th Street and the Grand Concourse, where he showed his photos to several kids, who insisted on introducing Chalfant to Crash, a promising young writer and protégé of Kase 2, the reigning style master of the Bronx. Around the same time, Chalfant approached Ivan Karp of the O.K. Harris Gallery, who agreed to exhibit the photos in the fall.

In 1980, documentary filmmaker Manny Kirchheimer released *Stations of the Elevated*, a poetic and extremely well-photographed ode to late '70s graffiti. Juxtaposing the raw energy of graffiti art, especially the masterpieces of the Fabulous Five, against sterile corporate architecture and Madison Avenue advertising billboards, Kirchheimer was successful in documenting the importance of mobility to the art form. Like great hulking monsters, the trains slowly awaken from their slumber, roll out of their stations, rise to their elevated platforms overlooking the city and then flash their brightly colored murals for the enjoyment of all below.

During the summer of 1980, many observers of the art scene sensed something new was in the air. Although critics had been discussing the "death" of painting for almost a decade, the art market was booming, primarily due to the emergence of a cadre of upper-middle-class collectors, many of whom were looking for undiscovered artists to decorate the walls of their Upper East Side co-ops. Impoverished young painters denied access to the major galleries rushed to fill the demand. Minimalism, the foremost movement of the '70s, was exhausted, and it was obvious that a new "movement" was needed. The term "new wave" was coined to describe the con-

nection between art and current developments in rock music. Another popular term, "neo-expressionism," described the return to recognizable
imagery that was taking place simultaneously in several European countries as well as the United States.

In June, the young, aspiring artists and the graffiti writers got together for the first time in the Times Square Show, which opened in an abandoned massage parlor on 41st Street. The meeting proved extremely ben-
eficial for both groups. Organized by Collaborative Projects (Colab), an
independent, democratic collection of struggling young artists, the Times
Square Show was a chaotic display of aggressive erotica, graffiti, "punk"
art and political manifestos. Stairways were strewn with broken glass,
walls were splashed with paint and life-size rat sculptures were placed
strategically throughout the building's five floors in an effort to create a
proper environment for the work of more than 150 sculptors, painters,
photographers, filmmakers and conceptual artists. Patrons of the local
porno movie houses wandered in, as did prostitutes, pimps, winos,
newspaper reporters and art collectors. Samo, a conceptual graffiti artist,
wrote "FREE SEX" over the doorway, a statement that was hastily painted over by one of the show's organizers. Keith Haring, a recent dropout
from the School of Visual Arts (SVA), was among the many exhibitors
inside.

Haring, who had a round, boyish face, closely cropped hair, a receding
hairline and small blue eyes, had been keeping an eye on subway graffiti since he moved to New York from Kutztown, Pennsylvania, in 1978.
"The name 'Lee' really stuck out," he said. "I learned a lot about art by
looking at his work." Although he had made a few tentative forays into
graffiti art (composing William Burroughs-style "cut-ups" of fake newspaper headlines and posting them on the street, along with a few other
short-lived projects), it wasn't until the Times Square Show that Haring
met his first graffiti artist: Fred Brathwaite, who by that time had changed
his name to Fab Five Freddy.

"Fred had two paintings in the show," said Haring. "But I didn't know
who he was. I was standing next to him and I pointed at the paintings
and said, 'This is Fab Five Freddy. He had a show in Italy.' Then I talked
about graffiti. Fred said, "Uhuh,' like he didn't know what I was talking
about. He had a sketchbook in his hand and I asked to look at it. When I
opened the book, I realized who he was and that I'd just put my foot in

my mouth."

After the Times Square Show, Haring began producing the graffiti that eventually made him famous. When the city began covering unrenewed subway poster ads with black tar paper, he began drawing on this black paper with chalk. He developed an elaborate vocabulary of images which included crawling babies, barking dogs, spaceships, telephones, TV sets and atomic explosions. The images were instantly recognizable yet seemed to be involved in a mysterious, indecipherable narrative.

"We'd be walking down the street and Keith would just stop and do a drawing," said his friend and fellow artist Kenny Scharf. "They took about three minutes. He was fanatical about it. There were chalk drawings everywhere. He did so many it was unbelievable. A big crowd would usually form around him. Some people would say nice things. Everybody knew his work."

Unlike most graffiti, Haring's work was almost universally admired. Although the drawings could be easily rubbed off, they were seldom touched. One of his early efforts, executed on the door of a Times Square newspaper stand, remained intact for two months before being covered by a handbill. "The power of graffiti tags is that they come straight out of the head and onto the wall," said Haring. "There's no turning back. You've got to be completely on while it's happening. The real thing is the act of doing it. It's really hard to achieve complete control with no inhibitions. You see it in Chinese calligraphy. All my drawings were done in one shot. Some people have the mistaken idea that I drew in the subway, saw that it worked and then started doing work for the galleries. It didn't happen like that. I've always been drawing. The subways was just another place to put the work. And I didn't put anything in the streets until I'd looked at graffiti for several years. There's an unwritten code about what belongs in the street. It's a big responsibility, it's a big step to put your work there. In some ways, it's hard to argue whether you have the right, but at some point you make the decision, partly so that people who would otherwise never see the work will be confronted with it. When I arrived in New York, it was obvious the art world really had nothing to do with what was happening in the streets. It was off on its own intellectual tangent."

Haring began attending weekly meetings of the Soul Artists, which were held at Ali's house. He met Futura, Zephyr, SE3, Daze and other

S.A. members. At the time, Soul Artists meetings were drawing some of the more prominent writers around town, including Dondi, who led a group in Brooklyn known as the Crazy Inside Artists (CIA), and Quinones, who attended a few meetings without actually joining. An independent filmmaker named Charlie Ahearn showed up and announced his plans to direct a feature film on the subculture.

In December 1980, Richard Goldstein, author of the first pro-graffiti story in *New York* magazine back in 1973, wrote an extensive article on the new graffiti writers in the *Village Voice*. The article was especially important because it linked graffiti and rap music for the first time. "The big lie is that graffiti is confined to 'antisocial' elements," wrote Goldstein. "Increasingly, it is the best and the brightest who write on subway walls, tenement halls. Unlike the newspaper that has called for their demise, these bands are racially integrated, which gives writers access to the same cross-cultural energy that animates rock 'n' roll. In fact, the graffiti sensibility has a musical equivalent in 'rap records'—another rigid, indecipherable form that can sustain great complexity."

Although Goldstein's awareness of rap music was probably limited (most of his readers undoubtedly didn't even know what the term meant), his assumption that rap sprang from the same cultural conditions as graffiti was certainly correct. Goldstein went on to discuss Haring, a completely unknown artist at the time, and several other artists who were currently being influenced by the graffiti aesthetic, including Samo (Jean-Michel Basquiat) and John Fekner. Even more important was the accompanying two-page photo spread in blazing color, showing six whole-car designs by Dondi, Lee, Blade, Seen, Futura and Kell. Taken by Henry Chalfant, the photos introduced many New Yorkers to the glory of a freshly painted (and unbuffed) graffiti mural for the first time.

Just as new wave music inspired artists like Robert Longo and Laurie Anderson in the 1980 art season, the commercial success of rap music furthered graffiti art. Mention of graffiti writers began appearing in the music press, and several prominent writers went on to record rap records, including Phase 2, Futura and Brathwaite. When Kurtis Blow released "The Breaks," Futura went to the yards to pay homage to the record. The result was a full-car mural which looked like a relic from a nuclear holocaust. He painted the car to look blistered, as if it had been driven through a terrible fire. In the center he put a jagged hole big enough to drive a Volkswagen through. Since 1973, writers had been painting cracks in their letters, but Futura was the first to crack an entire car. A network of blue-and-violet circles appeared to drift across the car's surface, and, in contrast to these amorphous shapes, he added four constructivist-style symbols. Goldstein accused him of imitating Kandinsky, an artist whose work Futura had never seen.

In February, 1981, a sprawling exhibit titled "New York/New Wave" opened at P.S. 1, an alternative space in Long Island City, Queens. Curated by Diego Cortez, it was the first attempt to document the crossover between art and music that had taken place during the previous two years. Drawings, photographs and video works by such rock stars as David Byrne, Alan Vega and Brian Eno were placed alongside documentary photographs taken at rock clubs and scores of neo-expressionist paintings by undiscovered artists. An entire wall was filled with massive murals by members of the Soul Artists. Many people came away feeling the graffiti writers had stolen the show.

Brathwaite, now known as Freddy Love, became a sort of unofficial spokesman for hip hop. A raconteur of considerable skill, he entertained reporters with stories about his early days in Brooklyn and educated them in the inner workings of the subculture. He introduced the South Bronx scene to such downtown hipsters as Diego Cortez, rock critic Glenn O'Brien and underground film star Patti Astor, who had a reputation as the blond bombshell of the Lower East Side. "I met Patti at a birthday party for Stephanie Marlemé held at Duncan Smith's house," said Brathwaite. "I'd just seen her movie *Underground USA* and she was my favorite movie star. So I asked her for her autograph." Astor signed a scrap of paper and kissed it, leaving a perfect lipstick imprint.

A month later, when Haring was hired to operate a gallery space above the rock disco the Mudd Club, the Soul Artists were approached for an exhibit. Curated by Futura and Brathwaite, "Beyond Words" drew one of the largest and rowdiest art crowds of the season. Brathwaite arranged for Afrika Bambaataa to perform at the opening. It was his first contact with the hip downtown scene and Bambaataa was enormously impressed by the audience, especially when they gave his record *Zulu Nation Throwdown* an appreciative response. "I didn't even like the record that much," said Bambaataa, "but downtown everybody thought it was a classic. After that, I started liking it too."

Patti Astor, also in attendance at the exhibition, immediately fell in love with hip hop. An ex-revolutionary from the '60s and Barnard College dropout, Astor had studied acting at the Lee Strasberg Institute before landing the leading role in Amos Poe's *Unmade Beds*, a $5,000, 16mm remake of Godard's *Breathless*. "It was all very existential, I assure you," said Astor, laughing. "It was shown at the Deauville Film Festival and the cast flew over for the party, but I'm not sure the French got it." With her girlish, giggly voice, Jayne Mansfield figure and classic face, Astor had no trouble landing roles in a slew of underground films like *Rome '78*, *Long Island Four* and *Underground USA*. However, none achieved anything close to commercial success. When Astor discovered that her old friend Charlie Ahearn was making a film on hip hop titled *Wild Style*, she began pressuring him for a part.

In May, Astor and Ahearn bumped into each other at a rapper's convention in Harlem. "Patti was wearing a silver jumpsuit and she was probably the only white woman there," said Ahearn. "She was really throwing out her stardom vibes. People were staring at her like she was made of gold. I still wasn't sure I wanted her in the film. I was thinking it over. A week later I made up my mind. Of course, she turned out to be the perfect choice. The character she played in the film was the same character she was playing that night at the rap convention."

Astor was cast as a reporter who traveled to the South Bronx, discovered the graffiti scene and brought it back to the established art world, a role she would eventually play in real life. During the filming, she supported herself by working for her friend Bill Stelling, who ran a roommate referral service. One day Stelling mentioned that he had a studio in the East Village he wanted to convert into an art gallery. "I was picking up all this inside knowledge about graffiti from the movie," said Astor. She was convinced graffiti could be sold to serious art collectors, so she helped Stelling organize the Fun Gallery. Although it was never intended strictly as a graffiti gallery, several writers were given shows during the first year, including Brathwaite, Futura, Dondi and Quinones. Haring and Scharf, two painters who were being influenced by graffiti, were also given shows. At first the graffiti-based paintings didn't sell well, but Astor knew she was onto something when European art dealer Bruno Bischofberger rolled in from Zurich for Brathwaite's opening.

"I didn't even know who he was," said Astor. "He had a babe on each arm and he pulled out these index cards that were crammed with info. He asked who the most important graffiti artists were. Later I found out he's the second-biggest collector in the world after Count Panza. I immediately decided I wanted to be like Bruno."

Unfortunately, many writers found it difficult, if not impossible, to make the transition from guerrilla outlaw to studio painter. Graffiti murals depended largely on size, color and constant movement, and the work lost much of its impact when put on small, static canvases. To make matters worse, a number of entrepreneurs began selling graffiti paintings as if they were charming folk-art trinkets. The Fun Gallery became a notable exception to this trend, since Astor encouraged the writers to consider themselves serious artists. She provided a refreshing alternative to the sometimes pompous Soho art scene, where openings tended to be stodgy, boring and predictable. Openings at the Fun, on the other hand, were filled with wild energy and an eclectic mix of downtown celebrities, b-boys and art collectors.

It wasn't long before a few writers, notably Quinones and Futura, began working with imagery that translated well onto canvas. But the big break came in November 1982, when a cover story by Rene Ricard appeared in *Artforum*. For the past three years, Ricard had been cultivating a reputation for being at the cutting edge of the art scene, having successfully predicted the rise of such painters as Julian Schnabel and Jean-Michel Basquiat. Many collectors were watching Ricard closely to see if he would tell them what the "next thing" would be. They weren't disappointed. Ricard, who had appeared with Astor in *Underground USA*, wrote:

Patti Astor is a beautiful example of what John Ashbery would call 'An Exhilarating Mess' in operation. She isn't a business-woman: she's currently starring in Charlie Ahearn's movie Wild Style, *and the opening of the gallery coincided with (or caused) a definite shift in the social pattern of the last two years. The underground movie scene played itself out. The rock scene, sperm of the great club period in the second half of the '70s, has run to water, losing the music war and now, except for a few skin-head arsenals, barely exists. Painting became big news... When Futura 2000 or Dondi White walk into a club it sparks the same sparks usually reserved for rock or movie stars. Economics have influenced this power shift; new bands don't make the kind of money that very young painters do. The winning musicians are DJs, and they play wheels of steel, not guitars...*

In Lee Quinones' June 1982 exhibit at the old Fun (it moved during the summer) was a painting as radical and as difficult as it was pretty and decorative. It depicts a bird on a cliff in front of a nuclear sunset. It is spray-painted on tin in what could be termed 'Van Style.' The bird, the dove of peace, is like a cartoon character that we are already familiar with. It has the same recognition impact as a Donald Duck, but a Donald Duck who has failed and who, without melodrama, confronts the viewer with embarrassed helplessness. Everything about this picture defies currently approved tradition. It is extremely sentimental. It looks like a poster. It has no brushstrokes. Like all of Quinones' work this painting is the product of a personal and introspective sensibility that has earned him the reputation of a seer and prophet.

In the small, insular New York art scene, *Artforum* wields a tremendous amount of clout, and soon after Ricard's article appeared, the Fun Gallery no longer had trouble attracting collectors. In fact, Astor's biggest problem was holding on to her artists. Quinones joined the Barbara Gladstone Gallery on 57th Street, while Haring and Scharf, both heavily courted by several dealers, joined the Shafrazi Gallery in Soho. Haring, Basquiat and Quinones were invited to exhibit at Documenta 7, a prestigious international art show held in Kassel, West Germany, while other graffiti writers began appearing in various galleries on 57th Street, once a bastion for conservative, blue-chip art. It may have been started by a hodgepodge of impoverished art school dropouts and unschooled graffiti writers, but by 1982 they had turned it into one of the hottest art movements in America.

BREAKING OUT

In 1976, Tito and Macho were members of the RCA Rockmasters, a crew of Puerto Rican teenagers based in the Tremont section of the Bronx around 180th Street and Southern Boulevard. Like many crews during the period, RCA started as a group of fun-loving disco dancers. Unfortunately, as the group got larger, they began acting more and more like a streetgang. Tito and Macho were not comfortable being in a gang, so they convinced several friends to quit RCA and form their own crew. "One night we made a big pile of our RCA sweatshirts and burned them. Then we started thinking about a new name. I said, 'How about "Rockwell"?' Everybody liked that, so we became the Rockwell Association."

The group included Willie, Carlos, Victor, Hector, Pops, Rubberband, George and Shorty. They were a Puerto Rican crew during a time when communication between blacks and Puerto Ricans was somewhat limited. Both groups were into music and dance, both threw block parties, but the similarities stopped there. Puerto Ricans played disco music, while blacks played hard-core funk. Puerto Ricans dressed in flower-print shirts and pointy-toed shoes and danced the Hustle, while blacks wore bell-bottoms and sneakers while break dancing. However, around 1977, a Puerto Rican deejay named Charlie Chase helped bring about a merger of the two styles.

"From 1974 to 1977 I was in a band at Alfred E. Smith High School," said Chase. "But then I got interested in deejaying. There was a crew around my house called the Monterey Crew. They were the first I saw getting into the b-boy style. They didn't do any fancy cutting with their music, but they played 'Just Begun' and records like that. My deejay friends would only play disco music, which was all right, but it didn't really turn on the crowds like 'Just Begun.' So, I started doing a little deejaying. My friends would say, 'Okay Charlie, here's your turn to play your black music,' and I would get fifteen minutes to do my thing. When I was on the set, everybody would dance and my friends couldn't understand why."

Willie Will was 16 at the time and had just learned to break dance. "Pops taught me," he said, referring to a friend a year younger than himself. "He learned from the Zulus. They had one dancer named Chopper who was real good. Breaking was like a hobby. We'd go into a hallway and practice until three or four in the morning. Get drunk. Fight. There was nothing else to do. I don't know where the spinning came from, but it was out in 1976. The Zulus had footwork, headspins, backspins. We used to break on the concrete in Belmont Park. If you did a backspin, you'd only spin around once or twice. Everybody was in crews and the crews would break against each other. First the whole crew would dance and then the best one from each crew would go down."

After developing the dance for over five years, many blacks grew tired of breaking and had stopped by 1978. Some got into the Hustle or the Freak. Others did the Electric Boogie, a robotic mime-like dance popular in California and down South. However, the Puerto Ricans were just getting into breaking and had no intention of giving it up. Saint Martin's, a Catholic church located on 182nd Street and Crotona Avenue, began sponsoring breaking battles in their gymnasium with the local priests acting as judges. Well-known crews participating in the battles included The Disco Kids (TDK), the Apache Crew, Star Child La Rock and TBB. However, the Rockwells were widely considered the best.

"We beat everybody," said Macho calmly. "There was nobody else to challenge. The next year they picked the best guys from each crew to gang up on us. TBB had Bobby Lee, Spy, Track and Mongo. Spy and Willie were always going throat to throat."

"Believe it or not, I used to hang out with Spy," said Willie. "We used to practice together. One day I did a swipe and landed on my head. I was trying to work out a new routine. 'Do a headspin! Do a headspin!' said Spy. He helped me find a new move."

The final showdown of the Rockwells versus TBB and the rest of the Bronx was held at Saint Martin's during the summer of 1979. "The place was packed," said Macho. "They had chairs arranged in a circle. We had ten dancers. They had about twenty-five. Everything came down to Willie and George against Spy and Mongo. Then the priests said, Okay, one more move: Spy against Willie. Willie flipped the coin and Spy went first. He did a sweep, messed up and fell down. The crowd booed. Then it was Willie's turn."

"I did my new routine," said Willie. "I started with a split, into a tumble, into a swipe, into a headspin. I got him with the same move he told me to do! Hahahaha. I bet he regretted that one!"

"We won the trophy," said Macho, "but the other crew didn't want to admit we won. They said it was fixed. They said we bought the fathers! They wanted to fight. See, breaking is not only breaking. There's a lot of fighting too. You go to a party and burn this guy and he says, 'You want to battle, man? Let's battle with the hands. You're a punk,' and this and that. Then you go outside and find fifty dudes waiting for you. TDK was like that. They always looked at us wrong and would never speak to us."

After the Saint Martin's battle, many of the Rockwells felt they were too old to continue rolling around on concrete, getting skin cuts and tearing their clothes. Tito and Macho bought a sound system and became deejays. "A lot of young kids still wanted to get down with Rockwell," said Macho. "Richie Colon used to hang out. He wanted to get down, but we wouldn't let him because he was too young. His cousin Lennie was down. Then I heard Richie moved to Manhattan and we didn't see him for a while. He said he wanted to form a part of Rockwell in Manhattan."

Colon, a soft-spoken, polite 14-year-old, had spent two years practicing the dance and was just getting good enough to join Rockwell when everyone stopped breaking. He must have felt cheated. Then he moved to Manhattan and discovered that many of the kids around his new neighborhood didn't even know what breaking was. He tried to teach a few, but it wasn't like the old days. Breaking didn't make much sense if you didn't have a rival to battle against. Despite being isolated from his former friends in the Bronx, Colon remained a devoted b-boy. He had never met Kool Herc, Bambaataa or Flash, but he always spoke reverently of them and of all the original breaking crews. He dreamed of forming his own crew someday, one that would be just as famous as the Zulu Kings, the Rockwells or TBB. He changed his name to Crazy Legs, kept practicing and spent every weekend traveling around Manhattan looking for breakers. He finally found some on a playground at the corner of 98th Street and Amsterdam Avenue. "I met Ty Fly first," said Crazy Legs. "He introduced me to Ken Rock, Frosty Freeze, Doze, Mania and Take 1. I went against all of them. I'm not gonna even say what happened 'cause they later became my crew."

Meanwhile, Henry Chalfant was exploring the possibilities of publishing a book on graffiti with Martha Cooper, a former *New York Post* photographer. "After I met Fred [Brathwaite] I became aware of rap music," said Chalfant. "But my first indication of breaking came from Martha. We'd been comparing notes on graffiti for some time and one day she showed me a photo she'd taken in 1978 of a break dancer. She wanted to do a story on breaking but was having trouble finding kids still doing it. At the same time, I was approached about putting on a graffiti performance show at Common Ground. I agreed to do the show and asked Take 1, one of the graffiti writers, about breaking. He said, 'Sure, I break and I know the best crew.' The next day he walked in with Crazy Legs and Frosty Freeze from the Rock Steady Crew." Chalfant was stunned when he saw them dance. "It was amazing that this had been going on for years and nobody knew about it. In fact, it was about to die out when I found it."

The media found out about breaking on April 22, 1981, when the *Village Voice* published a cover story on the dance, written by Sally Banes with photos by Cooper. Although it was still nearly impossible to publish articles on graffiti or rap music, both of which seemed to be universally hated by magazine editors, breaking had immediate appeal for the national press, possibly because a quote in the *Voice* credited the dance with replacing fighting as an outlet for urban aggression. "In the summer of '78," said Tee, "when you got mad at someone, instead of saying, 'Hey man, you want to fight?' you'd say 'Hey man, you want to rock?'" The statement was not entirely accurate (break dancers were notorious for getting into fights, especially with each other), but it was just the sort of quote that makes good newspaper copy. When the article appeared there were only a handful of breakers left in the city, but within months television camera crews, reporters and independent filmmakers were scouring the city in search of more. The attention lavished on the dancers allowed graffiti writers and rappers to get media exposure as well. Graffiti and rapping were no longer thought of as bizarre, isolated phenomena but as integral parts of a complex subculture.

Until 1981, it was difficult for a white, downtown audience to experience live rap music or see a break-dance contest, because these activities took place well inside the ghetto, where few whites were willing to travel. However, as the popularity of break dancing spread, it became apparent that whites would flock to any club associated with hip hop, as long as the club was located below 96th Street in Manhattan. On Second Avenue around the corner from the original Fun Gallery was a small basement nightclub called Negril, which had been unsuccessfully trying to cultivate an audience for Jamaican music. Ruza Blue, a concert promoter from England, and Michael Holman, an independent film and video maker from California, began throwing hip hop parties at the club on Thursday nights. Herc, Bambaataa, the Treacherous Three, Cold Crush, the Rock Steady Crew and other hip hop celebrities began appearing at the club, which catered primarily to a white audience—although there were always plenty of Bronx b-boys on hand to give the place an authentic flavor. Negril's greatest moment probably came the night the Rock Steady Crew battled Floormasters, a crew from the Bronx later known as the New York City Breakers. For the first time the audience got a taste of the competitive nature of breaking. Rock star David Byrne and painter Francesco Clemente began frequenting Negril, which, because of its small, intimate dance floor, often seemed more like a private party than a nightclub. Much of the intimacy was lost when the operation moved to the Roxy, a cavernous roller rink on West 18th Street. However, by 1982 the downtown hip hop scene had gotten far too big for a tiny club like Negril.

Much of the credit for the growing acceptance of hip hop was undoubtedly due to Robert Christgau of the *Voice* and Robert Palmer of the *New York Times*, two of the most influential rock critics in New York at the time. Both were early supporters of rap music. For several years Christgau and Palmer were among the only mainstream rock critics regularly reviewing 12-inch rap singles put out by small, independent labels. On March 25, 1981, Christgau's "Consumer Guide" column in the *Voice*, once a bastion for progressive rock albums, contained reviews of no fewer than six rap records. These critics realized that hip hop was the first progressive movement to appear in black music in several years, and that it had the potential to cross over to a wider audience.

In 1981, Bambaataa had just established a relationship with a fledgling label called Tommy Boy Records when he began deejaying at clubs like Negril and the Mudd Club. He immediately went to work on a record designed to appeal to the new wave crowd as well as hip hoppers. Under the guidance of producer Arthur Baker, he raided musical fragments from sources appreciated by both groups: the pioneering German synthesizer band Kraftwerk, the film *The Good, the Bad, and the Ugly*, Captain Sky and Babe Ruth. A Roland TR 808 drum machine replaced a studio drummer, and the musical track was provided by a single keyboard player, John Robie. The result, titled "Planet Rock," unalterably changed the sound of dance music.

"Planet Rock" was released in May 1982 and, according to *Billboard*, was "an instant club and retail hit of formidable size, shipping near-gold upon release." Part of the success of the record was due to a new style of rap, which appeared on the record for the first time. Invented by G.L.O.B.E., a member of Soul Sonic Force, the rap was the result of years of experimentation. "The problem with a lot of rappers is they were stuck in the Bo Diddley syndrome," said G.L.O.B.E. "They just wanted to brag about themselves. I was working on something different and when I showed it to Bam, he really liked it." The lyrics were a dreamy, utopian throwback to the '60s, with lines like: "You're in a place where the nights are hot/where nature's children dance and say the chants/of this mother earth which is our rock/The time has come it was foretold, to show you really got soul."

G.L.O.B.E. also created a new style of rapping to augment the lyrics. "I call it MC Poppin'," he said. "It's a step above rapping and a little less than singing. It's an acrobatic way of saying words. The tongue moves faster and it has more melody to it. Today a lot of people imitate it but MC Poppin' is mine. I invented it in 1978."

Richard Grabel, New York correspondent for the British newspaper *New Musical Express*, began writing extensively about rap music, which found a devoted following in England, where rock groups imitated the "Planet Rock sound" using Roland drum machines and synthesizer effects. The Clash hired Futura 2000 to paint backdrops during their performances, shows that often ended with Futura climbing down from his ladder, throwing aside his can of spray paint and rapping his own song, "The Escapades of Futura 2000."

In 1981, Chris Frantz and Tina Weymouth, both members of the rock band Talking Heads, formed the Tom Tom Club, a group that specialized in a pop-oriented, electro-funk sound. They recorded an intellectual rap single titled "Wordy Rappinghood," followed by the more successful "Genius of Love," which became an extremely influential record in the world of hip hop. Ed Fletcher, resident percussionist for Sugar Hill Records, would soon design a musical track inspired in large part by "Genius of Love" and offer it to Grandmaster Flash and the Furious Five.

"At first, nobody wanted to do the song 'cause it was too low down," said Melle Mel. "The basic structure of rap is to get people to participate in a party, and all the rappers, including us, were scared to try something more serious. Why take your problems into a disco? I think Sylvia Robinson was the only one who really believed in the song. Ed Fletcher had the concept for two years and never did anything with it, but Miss Robinson knew it would be a big record and convinced us to do it."

Actually, the merger of rap with a serious message had first successfully taken place in 1980 with the release of "How We Gonna Make the Black Nation Rise?" by Brother D and the Collective Effort. Brother D (whose real name was Daryl Aamaa Nubyahn) was a member of the New York Family of National Black Science, a revolutionary organization "dedicated to the uplifting of black people and to the acquiring of knowledge and skills."

"I noticed kids around my block in the Bronx doing rap, but there was no message," said Nubyahn. "I was teaching math in a vocational training program and I started running some raps for the kids in my class. I made deals with them like, you do a certain amount of work and I'll rap for you at the end of the period. And they loved that. There was a strong desire in rap records for people to soup themselves up. Big fantasies—folks in their teens talking about my big car, I'm a movie star, I've got all the women in the world. People are very materially centered. Something flashes on TV and they have to go out and get it. With the idea of hooking rap up with political information and the practice I got rapping for my students, I began to write."

Set to a musical track taken from Cheryl Lynn's disco hit "Got to Be Real," Nubyahn repeated an angry refrain: "We're rising up, we won't take no more! We're rising up, we won't take no more!" Although it was an explosively effective record, it was far too political to ever attain wide popularity in hip hop circles. By 1982, when Grandmaster Flash and the Furious Five went into the studio to record their own version of a "serious" rap record, they hadn't even heard of Brother D and the Collective Effort.

Fletcher became the principal architect of "The Message," a song that would soon become rap's greatest single. Although his lyrics carried an emotional intensity equal to "How We Gonna Make the Black Nation Rise?" Fletcher left out the political ideology. The persona portrayed in the song was that of a typical South Bronx resident pressured to the point of desperation by his environment. "Don't push me, I'm close to the edge," warns the voice. "I'm trying not to lose my head. It's like a jungle sometimes, it makes me wonder, how I keep from going under." The cause for this tension was graphically illustrated: "Broken glass everywhere, people pissing on the stairs, you know they just don't care. I can't take the smell, I can't take the noise. Got no money to move out, I guess I got no choice. Rats in the front room, roaches in the back. Junkies in the alley with the baseball bat. I tried to get away but I couldn't get far, because the man from Prudential repossessed my car."

Fletcher and Mel took turns reciting the lyrics on the record, carefully juxtaposing their voices for a unique effect. Fletcher provided a more low-key, disco-style rap, which served to heighten the angry aggressiveness of Mel's delivery. In fact, by varying his tones, inserting slight, dramatic pauses and occasionally speeding up his tempo to create a sense of urgency, Mel gave a performance as meticulously planned and executed as any aria, completing the song with a rap he wrote in 1980 describing the birth, decline and eventual death in prison of a South Bronx hoodlum, a story told in sharp, cinematic imagery. A rapping tour de force, "The Message" stands as one of the most powerful poetic performances ever captured on vinyl.

"The Message" received the maximum rating of five stars from *Rolling Stone*, where Kurt Loder called it "the most detailed and devastating report from underclass America since Bob Dylan decried the lonesome death of Hattie Carroll—or, perhaps more to the point, since Marvin Gaye took a long look around and wondered what was going on." Several months later it topped nearly every critic's list as best single of the year. "Planet Rock" may have provided the musical inspiration for the further development of hip hop, but "The Message" created the impetus for greater lyrical complexity. Appropriately, the song that represented one of hip hop's finest moments described the South Bronx, the territory where hip hop began.

THE SAUK CITY SHOOTING

"For the sake of our children, I implore you to be unyielding and inflexible in your opposition to drugs."

—President Ronald Reagan
September 14, 1986

On September 16, 1986, a self-employed building contractor was traveling east on Highway B—a two-lane road linking Plain and Sauk City, Wisconsin—when he accelerated to pass a pickup truck. Normally, he would have paid little attention to the pile of green plants in the back of the pickup, but this was two days after President Reagan's nationally televised address on the war on drugs, and the plants looked suspiciously like marijuana. Even more damning, the truck had out-of-state plates. So the civic-minded contractor followed the pickup five miles into Sauk City. He intended to follow the suspected dope dealer home and report his address to the police.

Halfway through town, however, the driver of the pickup realized he was being followed because he turned onto a dead-end street leading to August Derleth Park and drove to an isolated parking lot near the banks of the Wisconsin River (a site where police would later find 34 marijuana plants stashed in the bushes.)

Rather than follow the pickup truck into the park, the contractor spun his car around and drove two blocks to the Sauk City Police Department. He raced downstairs and confronted Betty Neumeyer, the dispatcher.

"I just followed a truck carrying marijuana into town!" he said excitedly. "He drove into Derleth Park. It's a white Ford pickup with Texas plates. The driver is wearing a cowboy hat."

Neumeyer picked up her microphone and called Officer 63, the only policeman on duty. She tried three times to reach the officer, but received no reply.

Conservation Warden John Buss happened to be standing at the Xerox machine, overheard the conversation and realized Neumeyer was having trouble locating a squad car.

"Betty," said Buss. "I don't have a firearm and I don't have my credentials, but I can drive down to the park and maintain radio contact. I won't stop the guy, but I'll watch him for you."

"I'd appreciate that," said Neumeyer.

Buss ran upstairs, hopped into his truck and drove to the park entrance. As he turned the corner, Buss spotted a white Ford pickup with Texas plates traveling toward him in the opposite direction. The pickup swerved around Buss and made a left turn on Water Street. The driver looked to be in his late forties, a typical good ole boy in a cowboy hat.

Buss radioed Neumeyer. "I'm following a vehicle matching the description," he said. "The tailgate is down and there appears to be a green leafy substance in the back... suspect is turning right on Washington Street...."

A few minutes later, Officer 63, John Mueller, returned to his squad car and was notified that a white Ford pickup believed to be containing controlled substances was parked in a driveway at the corner of Oak and Ash streets.

Mueller started his engine and headed across town. His day usually consisted of issuing warnings for minor traffic violations or refereeing family squabbles. Drugs were a different, more dangerous matter. He popped another piece of gum and began chewing furiously.

Mueller, 40, was considered a model officer: professional, polite and well groomed. Jeff Lawson, a local tavern owner, affectionately dubbed him "John Boy" because of his youthful appearance. On September 16, however, Mueller was short-tempered and haggard. His hair—normally greased and combed—was unkempt. His uniform—normally starched and spotless—was dirty and wrinkled. Mueller was planning on getting married in a few months and the change in his appearance could be explained by the proximity of the event—at least that's what some people thought.

The truth, however, was much more bizarre: In his own mind, Mueller was engaged in a top-secret mission for the federal government, a mission so sensitive not even the federal government knew of its existence. Mueller's directives, in fact, came direct from the White House. Mueller was admittedly a bit foggy on the exact nature of the assignment, but then messages were delivered in code, sometimes in newspaper head-lines, sometimes during incidental meetings on the street. These mes-sages were very difficult to decipher and their intensity had been mount-ing wildly since Sunday night... the night Mueller watched President Reagan's speech... the night Mueller stopped taking his Thorazine pre-scription... stopped taking his Thorazine because the President told him drugs were evil.

Hopefully, it would not be long before Mueller learned more details concerning his mission. Meanwhile, his snub-nosed .357-caliber magnum revolver was loaded and close by his side.

After following the pickup to the driveway, Warden Buss had execut-ed a U-turn and parked nearby. Obviously, the individual wearing the cowboy hat knew he was being watched: rather than get out of the truck, he stayed scrunched down in the front seat, occasionally peering over his shoulder at Buss.

Buss, 26, was a relative newcomer to town. In 1982, after graduating from the University of Wisconsin with degrees in both biology and envi-ronmental law enforcement, he'd become a state conservation warden. He'd been assigned to the Sauk City area in October 1985. Buss was a devoted outdoorsman with a wife, kids and a pair of pedigreed hunting dogs. His number-one concern at the moment was the apprehension of midnight dumpers who were polluting nearby lakes and rivers. He had never been involved in a drug bust before.

In a statement given at the Sauk City Police Department later that day, Buss described the arrival of Officer Mueller at the scene of the crime:

When John arrived, I advised him to look over his right shoulder at the pick-up truck. I advised him I was unarmed, did not have my credentials, but I'd stay and backup. John turned on his squad lights and parked behind the pickup. I got out, walked over to him and explained the whole scenario. John got out and approached the truck. I stood to the left behind him. John opened the door and asked for identification.

"What for?" said the individual.

"Get out of the truck," said John.

The individual swung his body around, placed his feet on the running board and said, "This is as far as I go."

John grabbed his arm and started wrestling him out of the truck, I came over and grabbed the guy's left arm. John slammed the guy to the cement, and I was pulled down with him—like hanging onto a rope. I mean, BOOM!, we went down. There was really no need for that because the guy wasn't really resisting to the point of fighting. John pulled out his handcuffs and put them on one wrist. I put them on the other.

"Relax," I told the guy. "I'm a state conservation warden."

I searched him for weapons, pulled out a pocketknife and wallet, and tossed them back at John. John was saying a bunch of stuff. I don't remember what, but it was like he was talking to someone else. Then John walked to the back of his car. The guy started to roll over on one side.

"Just lay there and hang tight," I told him.

I walked behind the truck and found some green leafy substance in the back. I was looking at some seeds when John came up.

"John," I said, "Do you have any evidence bags to put this in?"

"Don't worry about it," said John. "This is resisting a federal agent."

He was talking slowly, chewing his gum overly hard, and staring at the truck as if he could eat a hole right through to the pavement. It went through my mind that maybe John was working with the Feds somehow. I just kept picking up leaves and seeds. John walked over to where the individual was lying on his belly in handcuffs.

I heard a shot, looked up and saw John shoot the guy in the back of the head a second time. I saw an orangish muzzle flash coming from his gun. John was standing upright, holding his gun with both hands.

John turned around, looked at me with real starry eyes, and started marching toward me, as if he was in front of a drill instructor. He was holding the gun at a 45-degree angle. He stopped about three feet away, with the gun pointed at my belt.

"John," I said. "You're not going to shoot me, are ya?"

I was going to take off running because the guy was lying down on his back and John shot the fucker... I'm sorry... the individual... in the back of the head. But there was no place to run.

John was looking right through me. "Don't... worry," he said. "This... is... resisting... a... federal... agent..." I mean I was scared. I wanted to disappear—just disappear. John holstered his gun, walked back to his squad car and got inside.

I looked at the guy on the ground and saw a lot of blood. The body was quiv-

ering. I knew he was dead or mortally wounded. I don't know if I ran, walked, flew or what, but I went back to my truck, got in and backed down the road. When I felt I was far enough away, I stopped and opened the door. This might sound crazy, but I had a shotgun loaded with buckshot in the truck and I thought, "If John comes down the road I'm going to have to kill him."

I tried to call in, but John got on the radio before me, so Betty told me to stand by. Basically, John said he had a 10-42, which means end of duty, although we sometimes use it to mean a traffic fatality, instead of saying over the radio that someone is dead. He requested an ambulance.

Finally I got on the radio and said, "We got a 10-33, we need officers. Get one and two down here," meaning the sheriff and chief deputy. At the same time I made a few notes.

John got out of his car, walked up to the body and took off the handcuffs. I think he felt I'd left. He was looking around, but he never made eye contact with me. Then he marched into the middle of the road. People were coming out of their houses, gathering around. John stopped in the middle of the street and started directing traffic like a Milwaukee police officer — real rigid. But there wasn't any traffic.

The twin cities of Sauk City and Prairie du Sac are nestled around the bend of the Wisconsin River about 150 miles northwest of Chicago. The towns have a combined population of 54,000, and share a school district, sewer system, weekly newspaper and police force. Despite their closeness, they maintain separate identities: Sauk City was settled primarily by Germans, while Prairie du Sac was settled by the English. The nearest major city, Madison, is 25 miles to the southeast.

Sauk City has a rich past: on July 21, 1832, Black Hawk and 50 braves fought a holding action against 1,000 government troops in a forest south of town. The lopsided battle succeeded in giving the Indian women and children time to cross the Wisconsin River to safety. Unfortunately, the tribe was massacred 12 days later at the Battle of Bad Axe.

After the Indians were disposed of, white settlers moved in, led by Count Augustin Hrzstzy, who founded a vineyard nearby. His vines continue to produce grapes today, even though the Count left abruptly (moving to Napa Valley, where he founded the California wine industry). "Many Germans who came here were members of the Frei Gemeinde," says Tracy Madison, editor of the weekly *Sauk Prairie Star*. "They were the local intellectuals, very cultured and well read."

A larger, less progressive contingent of German settlers moved into the state and formed the Wisconsin Synod, an ultra-conservative wing of the Lutheran Church. It was in this tradition that John Mueller was raised, the second of seven children.

Mueller was born in Jefferson, a town similar to Sauk City but located halfway between Madison and Milwaukee. His father changed careers several times, working as a security guard, mortician, postal clerk and finally food store manager. In 1964, Mueller graduated in the middle of his class at Lakeside Lutheran High School, where he was a member of the school band. On the surface, Mueller seemed like a typical teenager: He worked a paper route, collected stamps and restored old cars. There was, however, something odd about the boy. "John was a good kid, but always just a little bit different," says Harry Minshall, owner of the funeral home where Mueller's father was employed.

Upon graduation, Mueller enlisted in the Air Force. He was granted high-security clearance, became a communications officer, and was posted in both Japan and Thailand. Mueller refuses to discuss his work for the Air Force—except to say that he was a radio technician involved in top-secret matters. Immediately after leaving the service, he was hired by the National Security Agency (NSA).

Don't bother looking for mention of the NSA in government press releases: Even though it's the most powerful intelligence agency in America, larger and more influential than even the dreaded CIA, its very existence is considered classified. The NSA headquarters is located inside Fort Meade, halfway between Washington, D.C. and Baltimore. According to James Bamford, author of *The Puzzle Palace*: "The NSA's joint Headquarters-Operations Building is the Taj Mahal of eavesdropping, almost the size of the CIA building with the United States Capitol sitting on top... In 1978, the agency controlled 68,203 people—more than all the employees of the rest of the intelligence community put together... No law has ever been enacted prohibiting the NSA from engaging in any activity."

Since its inception on November 4, 1952, the NSA has tapped phones, intercepted private cables and compiled endless computer printouts with names of individuals considered to be a threat to national security. The agency's capacity for electronic surveillance is staggering. In the late '60s,

President Richard Nixon asked the NSA to help him dismantle the anti-war movement. The plan failed, but Nixon turned to the agency again in 1971 when he launched the first war on drugs, during which period the NSA instituted a watch list for suspected drug offenders. Fortunately, this project was shut down in 1973. Despite its power, size and influence, not one American in 10 has ever heard of the NSA.

In 1969, at the close of his second tour of duty, Mueller called his parents and informed them he was going to England for a three-year tour. They assumed he was still in the service. But he wasn't. Mueller's work in England was sensitive and he couldn't tell his parents the truth. He relocated to Cheltenham, Gloucestershire, a peaceful community 80 miles west of London, and purchased a red MGB sports car.

Like many servicemen during the waning years of the Vietnam War, Mueller had difficulty adjusting to civilian life. Within a matter of months, he was displaying signs of serious psychological problems. His first nervous breakdown seems to have been precipitated by an unhappy love affair. A nurse who interviewed him later wrote: "John talked about the girl with whom he was serious. He appeared to have many feelings, some of resentment, but could not express them. It was shortly after John wrote her a letter and got no reply that he smashed up his car while drinking." After wrecking the car, Mueller returned to his apartment, went into a frenzy and smashed everything in sight. He was hospitalized and lost his job. Three weeks later he was discharged with a prescription for Stelazine, an antipsychotic medication.

In September, 1970, Mueller boarded a plane and returned to his parents' house in Jefferson, where his mental health continued to deteriorate. Despite his emotional problems, Mueller made an unexpected move one week after coming home: He married a woman five years his junior. At the time, the family knew something was wrong, but everyone kept silent. Mueller found a job working for the Jefferson Well Drilling Company and seemed determined to lead a normal, domestic life. The plan failed.

On the night of June 30, after much encouragement from his family and his wife, Mueller admitted himself into the Madison Veteran's Administration Hospital. According to a psychiatrist's report: "Several family sessions were held and it came out that John thought he had murdered a prostitute while in England. The accuracy of this statement was not confirmed, but John continued to believe that he had committed such an act. He told his minister that he knew he would never be forgiven for anything he had done, and would never accept the minister's reassurances that he would be forgiven." The diagnosis? Acute paranoid schizophrenia.

On August 5, Mueller was discharged on a daily dose of 800 mg. of Thioridazine (the maximum allowable dosage), combined with 200 mg. of Thorazine. (In other words, enough tranquilizer to turn the average human into a lead-footed zombie.)

Six months later, Mueller was hired as a law enforcement officer, working for the Jefferson County Sheriff's Department. The following year his wife gave birth to a boy. Mueller was not present at the birth, however, having been recently admitted to the veteran's hospital, where he remained for four months. Hospital records made public during his trial contain the following summary:

"After exhibiting several days of agitated schizophrenic behavior including gouging his eyes superficially with a pencil, (Mueller) tended to gradually improve his behavior... Although we had some hesitation about his return to police work, and are hopeful that he will begin to consider other less threatening work options, we discharged him to outpatient treatment, to be followed weekly by psychology and social work service. He was to continue his medications, Thorazine 50 mg. four times daily."

The sheriff of Jefferson County wanted to keep Mueller on the force, but on a part-time basis, working jail duty. However, Mueller grew dissatisfied with this arrangement and eventually quit.

Hopes that Mueller might regain his mental health received a severe setback in 1974, when he discovered his three-year-old son Danny was suffering from reticuloendotheliosis, a rare blood disease. Mueller had difficulty accepting his son's illness, eventually concluding it was God's punishment for his own sins. In March, Mueller suffered another breakdown and was taken to the hospital, where he exhibited inappropriate behavior (smiling while discussing his son's illness and boasting of earning $100,000 a year as a salesman).

Strangely enough, after being discharged Mueller was hired as police chief of Mazonanie, a small town south of Sauk City with a reputation as the local "Dodge City." He held that position for four years and remained emotionally stable, despite his son's death in 1975. In 1978, a daughter, Paula, was born. Mueller and his wife met with their pediatrician, Dr. Dvorak, and discussed Danny's death in detail for the first time. Although Dvorak wasn't sure of the cause of death, he admitted that cortisone and cobalt treatments may have been a contributing factor. According to Mueller's wife, the statement had a lasting effect on Mueller, leading him to believe his son had been killed by drug treatments. Later that year, after a dispute with the town board (a board Mueller would later accuse of being involved with drugs), he was fired. Mueller went to junior college for a period and attended a training session in Texas in hopes of buying into a job-motivational teaching franchise. The night he returned, his wife jokingly spoke of getting a divorce. Mueller was unable to sleep and had a number of crying spells. His wife called the hospital and Mueller's doctor recommended an additional 25 mg. of chlorpromazine, which allowed Mueller to sleep. The following night, however, Mueller was unable to sleep even with the additional medication. Several times during the night he hallucinated blood on his wife's arm and leg and was unable to stop thinking about his son's death. On July 9, he was driven to the hospital and remained under observation for six days.

"We felt John's calm appearance and behavior represented his attempt to control with rigidity his fragmented thinking," wrote the attending doctor. "With his observing ego, he was probably acutely aware of this fragmentation and wanted to appear normal. As he had been maintained on chlorpromazine as an outpatient, we attempted to control him by increasing doses. However, on the second hospital day he acutely decompensated, became acutely agitated, disorganized, and paranoid, with blocking and required tranquilization with I.M. and seclusion."

After his release, Mueller went through a succession of menial, dead-end jobs. His wife insisted that they separate; they remained apart until their divorce became final in 1983. (At the divorce proceeding Mueller's wife suggested a program of "mental health consultation" be established for her husband, a suggestion that went ignored.)

Mueller's violent tendencies surfaced several times during his visits to the hospital. On January 1, 1982, he escaped while undergoing treatment and wound up in a "scuffle" with a stranger in a city building. The stranger later dropped charges against Mueller after discovering he was a mental patient. However, the following morning, Mueller refused medication and again attempted to leave his ward without permission. He was stopped by a nurse smoking a cigarette.

"What's that smell?" he said. "That's cyanide. Put it out."

Mueller grabbed the cigarette and tried to put it out on the nurse's arm. After "Code Orange" was called, he was removed to the quiet room.

"Is it God's will that I go in there?" he asked repeatedly. "I want to see God's will. I'll go into the quiet room but it's against my will."

Mueller continued to refuse medication, stalked around the room and constantly looked over his shoulder as if someone was sneaking up on him.

The next day, Dr. John H. Greist, the psychiatrist who has written the most probing and detailed analysis of Mueller, visited the quiet room. According to his notes (which became available at the trial):

"Entered seclusion room at 11:41 A.M. with Mrs. Keepman while Mr. Mueller was asleep. He appeared to be asleep. When awakened, he attempted to sit up, then lay down again. I asked to feel his pulse and he quickly rose and moved back against the window, pointed at me and said something about 'Satan.' He appeared frightened, was staggering, and moved toward the door, grasping, but not hurting, Mrs. Keepman. We gradually moved outside the room and Mrs. Keepman was able to get him to return to his mattress after considerable persuasion."

In the spring of 1983, Mueller's brother, Wayne, was working for a car dealership in Sauk City, and noticed an announcement in the *Sauk City Star* for a police officer. He sent the paper to his brother and suggested he apply for the job. Mueller passed the oral exam with flying colors and was sent to the Madison Area Technical College Police Academy, where he also excelled. He was chosen to give the class valedictory speech, which was later described as being "carefree."

Thanksgiving was frequently an upsetting holiday for Mueller, and shortly after assuming his duties with the Sauk City police force (the weekend before Thanksgiving), Wayne noticed his brother was having problems sleeping again. A restraining order had just been placed on Mueller limiting his visits with his daughter.

"John talked slow, in left field, cooked supper, which was cold, was drinking more beer than usual and wanted me to leave the apartment to see a friend even though my family was there," recalls Wayne. Later that night Mueller's landlord informed Wayne that his brother had been up the past two nights pacing the floor. Wayne visited his brother, who claimed to be upset over his recent divorce. John also objected to his daughter being allowed to dance to rock music, which he described as being "really evil." Wayne went home, but had to return after a late-night phone call. This sequence was repeated a second time, and Wayne drove his brother to the hospital. He returned home at 5:30 A.M., and received yet another phone call. "I should watch out if I were you," said John, "because they are out to get me." Wayne asked who "they" were, but received no reply.

Later that week, when Wayne visited his brother in the hospital, John informed him that he had "to go to Washington, D.C. to meet the generals in the Pentagon to solve the world's problems." Wayne told a psychologist his brother "went into a trancelike state, babbling words that were recognizable but didn't fit together to make any sense, and then said, 'the Holy Ghost has just spoken, believe it.'"

Although Mueller managed to hide his mental illness from most people, he had a harder time fooling women than men. At his favorite hangout, the Eagle Inn, where he ate most of his meals, the younger waitresses were certainly wary of him. Mueller asked a few for their phone numbers, but they refused. Mueller followed one of them home in his squad car, and she got so flustered that she fell and twisted her ankle.

However, there was one woman who was not afraid of Mueller: Patsy Murphy. An attractive divorcee with two children aged 8 and 11, Murphy had already been through one bad marriage plagued by alcohol and violence. As far as she was concerned, Mueller was a dream date who showered her with attention, sent her romantic letters and behaved with impeccable manners. Even more important, he was a quiet man willing to listen thoughtfully to her many problems.

In August 1986, Mueller and Murphy visited the Wisconsin Dells. Within a month, they were engaged to be married. Mueller found a house in Prairie du Sac he wanted to buy. He needed money and became interested in starting a photography business to supplement his income.

On September 10, Mueller visited a local attorney to seek advice on filing suit against a woman who had accused him of molesting young girls while on duty. The following day, he called his brother Lynn and asked him to come over and look at the house he wanted to buy. Lynn felt his brother was having trouble focusing his thoughts and asked what was wrong. Mueller replied, "There's lots of pressure, a lot going on."

On September 14, Mueller got off work at 7 P.M. and drove straight to Murphy's house. For several days, he'd been looking forward to seeing the President's speech concerning the "War on Drugs." Still dressed in his uniform, Mueller sat rigidly in front of the television, staring intently at the screen, saying nothing until the speech was over. After dinner, he drove home and threw all the alcohol in his apartment away. The President had told him drinking was evil, and Mueller always obeyed his President. He also decided not to take his medication. Without a tranquilizer, however, Mueller was unable to sleep. He spent the night pacing the floor, listening to a cassette tape titled "How to Relax" by Norman Vincent Peale.

The following day, Mueller and his fiancee had a meeting with Mueller's pastor concerning their upcoming wedding. Murphy, a Catholic, was planning to convert to the Lutheran faith. Mueller arrived at Murphy's house looking unkempt and frazzled. He explained his unusual appearance by saying he'd "been up all night with diarrhea." Murphy offered him coffee, but he requested water. "Well, you know where the water is," said Murphy. Mueller then changed his mind and asked for coffee.

While driving to the church, Murphy admitted she was nervous. Mueller uncharacteristically walked ahead of her into the church.

During the meeting, Mueller seemed preoccupied with minor matters, while Murphy tried to plan the details of the ceremony. The pastor asked if Murphy was aware of Mueller's background. Murphy confessed she knew very little about her prospective husband. At this point, Mueller became agitated and asked to leave the room. While he was gone, the pastor told Murphy about Mueller's mental problems. Mueller abruptly entered the room and stated it was time to leave.

The couple drove to Mueller's apartment, which was, atypically, in a state of disarray. A bottle of pills from the Veteran's Administration hospital was on the table.

"What are these for?" asked Murphy, picking up the bottle.

"You know, for a chemical imbalance caused by my drinking problem," said Mueller evasively, while leading her into the living room.

"What do you want to tell me?" asked Mueller.

"I don't think much of your pastor," said Murphy.

Mueller began to cry. "If he's going to get personal, I don't ever want to go back to that church."

Later that night, Mueller arrived at the Eagle Inn for dinner and discovered the booths were full. He took a seat at the counter and ordered the daily special. Les Tesch, the owner of a local gardening store, sat behind him.

"I always had a lot of respect for John," says Tesch. "I felt he was the most sensible, down-to-earth officer on the force. We got into a discussion while he was waiting for his food. I told him I was one-hundred percent behind Reagan. I don't think we have room in our society for people who take drugs. I told him they should get capital punishment—they should be blown away. John didn't say anything. He just nodded his head."

That night, Mueller was unable to sleep and paced the floor continuously. At 8:30 A.M. he arrived at Murphy's house for breakfast looking wild and glassy-eyed. His hair was uncombed, he couldn't sit still and he swore repeatedly. "He's been caught with his pants down in the squad car," he said of one of his fellow officers. Mueller's hands were shaking. He ate a slice of toast with peanut butter, got up to leave, kissed Murphy, and left a smear of peanut butter on her face.

Later that day, he called Murphy at work and spoke in a slow, robotic voice. "Is this Patricia or Peaches?" he asked. "What are you doing? Don't ask me any questions. I'll do the asking. You tell me the whole story. Tell me what you did. I know it's been bothering you for a long time."

"What's the matter?" asked Murphy. "Give me a hint."

"You know," replied Mueller.

"Stop it," said Murphy, breaking into tears. "You're scaring me."

"Keep it warm, keep it real warm just for me," said Mueller. "I'm hanging up now. I'll be here until two. You can tell me the whole story. Bye-bye."

Murphy knew something was seriously wrong and called Mueller's pastor. The pastor called Mueller, but Mueller refused to discuss anything, saying he had to leave for work. Murphy then called Neumeyer at the police station and asked to speak with Chief Rentmeester.

"John sounds really strange," said Murphy. "I'm afraid something is wrong."

Neumeyer relayed the message to Rentmeester, who responded by saying that Mueller had been quiet lately, but that he was always quiet.

A few hours later, Mueller unholstered his .357 and pumped two bullets into John Graham.

Fired at point-blank range, one of the bullets entered on the left side of Graham's neck, creating fractures in and around the second and third cervical vertebrae and damaging the spinal chord before exiting on the right side of the neck. The second bullet entered behind the left eyebrow, causing extensive brain damage, and exited through the right ear. Either shot would have been sufficient to kill.

Det. Sgt. Manny Bolz was the first member of the Sauk County Sheriff's Department to arrive at the scene of the shooting. After hearing details of the murder, he arrested Mueller and delivered him to the county jail. Bolz searched the August Derleth parking lot and found 34 marijuana plants in the bushes. He also searched Graham's toolbox in the truck and found a baggie containing a groomed marijuana bud. Bolz's case was not against Graham, however, who was dead, but against Mueller, and a search of his home proved even more revealing.

Mueller's small, second-story apartment was filled with religious books and Republican Party propaganda. Bolz discovered framed photographs of George Bush, Sr. and Reagan, a flag folded military-style on a chair, a notebook filled with letters addressed to Reagan and several self-improvement books, including *How to Sell Yourself*; *Write Better, Speak Better*; *The Miracle of Speech Power*; and *Professionals at Their Best*.

While Mueller's strange life was gradually uncovered during the trial, the unfortunate victim remained something of a mystery. "I didn't even know John Graham existed," Chief Rentmeester told James Romenesko of *Milwaukee* magazine. "Nobody in our department ever had contact with the man, even as much as given him a warning ticket."

Unfortunately, Crystal Graham couldn't provide much insight into why her husband might have been driving a load of marijuana, and continued to insist he did not smoke or cultivate the plant. Mrs. Graham portrayed her husband as a genial, laid-back country boy whose only interests were hunting, fishing and listening to the Statler Brothers. This does not seem strange, however, when one considers that Mrs. Graham is a former undercover narcotics officer herself.

"(My husband) would talk to most anyone," Mrs. Graham told Romenesko. "he couldn't sit still. Four walls would get to him. He was a collector of anything and everything, and especially if it had something to do with hunting. He loved knives and guns."

Born in Winter Garden, Florida, John Graham was the son of migrant workers, and he spent most of his youth traveling the country working on farms. He joined the Air Force and was stationed in San Antonio, where he married Crystal Olson. That same year he obtained a job with the phone company in Orlando, Florida. Crystal, meanwhile, joined the Orlando Police Department.

Mrs. Graham refused to talk to this author, but according to *Milwaukee* magazine: "In 1971, she was given the plum assignment of infiltrating the office of a local chiropractor who was suspected of dealing drugs. Crystal, who enjoyed this kind of clandestine work, got into the office by answering a help-wanted ad placed by the chiropractor. She got the job. For several weeks, she witnessed drug transactions and later became the state's chief witness at the suspect's trial."

As a result of her undercover work, Mrs. Graham became the first female officer to win the National Police Officer of the Year award— which is why she bristles at any suggestion that her husband was a drug user. According to her somewhat far-fetched scenario, her unemployed husband was coming home with the marijuana just to show it to her so he could say something like: "Honey, you ain't going to believe this, but this is growing wild out here. Now just look. I can go down there and cut it, and here it is…" as she told *Milwaukee* magazine.

Four days after the shooting, at the suggestion of his attorneys, Mueller was interviewed by Dr. Greist, who attempted to find out if Mueller was mentally ill during the murder. He asked Mueller to describe what happened on September 16, 1986, beginning at any previous point in time that made sense to him. Mueller chose January, 1983. What follows are his verbatim statements, which were easily written down since he spoke at the incredibly slow rate of 10 words per minute.

"I was laid off and initiated looking for work in various aspects of the employment market, and during the months of employment search learned of the Sauk-Prairie Police Department opening… On April 11, 1984, Deputy Ward, Officer and Mrs. Chileen and I attended a meeting in Milwaukee. Vice President Bush presented an address at this meeting… Christmas, 1984, is a memorable event. The White House received Christmas cards from me. The President and Mrs. Reagan sent me a Christmas card. The Christmas card arrived on or about January 12, 1985. The return address on the Christmas card was the White House. The President and Mrs. Reagan's congratulations for my support are contained in the Christmas card. Continuing correspondence made many changes... In September, 1985, I traveled to Washington, D.C. for the purpose of sightseeing. The Capitol tour is a highlight of my trip... When I returned to work, I was blessed with much work. Since then, my interest continues with the programs of the President... My familiarity with all programs is limited... On Tuesday, September 16, Lieutenant Harmon reported to my residence at his convenience. At approximately 1410, Lieutenant Harmon and I proceeded to Lieutenant Harmon's residence. Lieutenant Harmon stated a phrase that was not familiar to me. However, I interpreted his phrase in connection with government action. The phrase was 'The wild geese are flying.' The meaning has been defined to me as specific commando action. I never heard that phrase prior to Tuesday, September 16. Continuing our travels to Lieutenant Harmon's residence, we met no opposition—that is, we did not receive any calls. When I changed shift, I then proceeded on patrol and was requested to ask the police chief to call the police department. I delivered that message to the police chief and then was requested to assist another officer. Conservation Warden John Buss requested assistance with a vehicle containing controlled substances... My thoughts were to administer action to prevent illicit controlled substances. At the time, I believed to be serving in my official capacity as a government servant. I believed that a continuing obligation existed and continue to believe this obligation exists. The obligation I believe exists with the specific nature of my duties with the National Security Agency. In 1969 and 1970, I believe a formal obligation existed. The shooting cannot be considered a part of my informal obligation. The actions taken at the scene of the controlled substances on Tuesday, September 16, are not a part of the written informal obligations that exist. The reasoning I use with that is at the present time our nation is plagued with illicit drugs. Everyone concerned about this devastating enemy is doing what they can do in their own way to eliminate the existence of illicit controlled substances. I believed and still believe that the action I took is a service to our country... I believe that in defense of our country, state and cities, an action that is threatening to harm the people of our nation, a strengthening move must be taken."

"Blessed are those persecuted on account of righteousness, or theirs is the kingdom of heaven."

Lt. Col. Oliver North
February 26, 1987

Three days before Oliver North claimed innocence in the Iran-Contra affair on account of righteousness, John Mueller appeared in Circuit Court in Baraboo, Wisconsin. The proceedings did not take long. The prosecuting attorney, defense attorney and four psychiatrists all agreed Mueller was suffering from chronic paranoid schizophrenia. Judge James Evenson ordered Mueller taken to the Mendota Mental Health Center in Madison. During the sentencing, Mueller looked passively around the room, an eerie smile fixed on his face. He continued to maintain his innocence, and was quite upset to learn he'd been fired from the Sauk City police force.

Mueller is an unfortunate man suffering from a serious illness. For many years, his grasp on reality has been tenuous, his mind clouded by psychoactive chemicals. Mueller realized his illness and reached for the firmest anchors he could find: God and country. Both let him down. He could never completely accept the Christian doctrine of forgiveness and spoke with ministers frequently throughout his life. None were insightful or caring enough to insist he give up police work or stop carrying a revolver. As Mueller shifted away from his Lutheran upbringing, he came to depend more heavily on President Ronald Reagan.

Strangely enough, Mueller was eager to talk. "I would like to allow you to make some interviews," said Mueller, calling me from his private cell in Mendota. He sounded confident, clearheaded, and was effusively polite and gracious. "The condition would be some monetary amount," he continued. "The amount would be $10,000. Until you meet this condition, I would ask you not to speak to my fiancée or my family."

When asked if he was following the unfolding scandal in Washington, Mueller replied: "Oliver North was a man who ordered generals around. It's strange that my life would be connected with his."

PARADISE NOW!

"We are opening up in sweet surrender to the luminous love light of us all."
—Traditional Rainbow Circle Song

The Canadian shield of North America is one of the oldest land masses on Earth—somewhere between three and five billion years old. I get my first sight of this ancient land as my rental car climbs the crest overlooking Duluth, Minnesota at 1:35 P.M. on June 30, 1990. I'm traveling to my first national Rainbow Gathering, a mysterious, little-known event which draws between 10,000 and 20,000 people, and has been held in a different National Forest each year since 1972.

Who are the Rainbows? And how have they managed to survive the yuppification of America? The media usually portrays them as either an embarrassing anachronism—the last of the hippies—or as a potential environmental disaster. For example, in 1988, *Newsweek* reported that "Texas Gov. Bill Clements was prepared to call out the National Guard to control a 'hazard to the forest.'" Later on in the same article U.S. Forest Service Special Agent Billy Ball explained, "… their brains are baked anyway."

Although *Newsweek* took great pains to interview local residents and the police, they neglected to interview any members of the Rainbow Family. They also forgot to mention the primary function of the event: group prayer for world peace.

Yet, despite over 30 years of media misrepresentation and government oppression, the Rainbows have survived. In 1972, over 35,000 gathered near Granby, Colorado. Two years later, less than 1,000 came to the Virgin River in Utah. That was the low point of Rainbow. During the '80s, attendance grew steadily. In 1989, over 10,000 gathered in Robinson's Hole, Nevada, and at least that many have shown up every year since.

Unfortunately, Rainbow has also attracted the attention of the narco police. In 1988, over $500,000 of our tax money was spent harassing the national Gathering in Texas, while the government spent thousands more bringing suit against Rainbow in an attempt to block the Gathering in court. The Rainbows have always maintained that the right to peaceably assemble on public land is protected by the Constitution. Apparently, our federal judges agree—almost every time Rainbow goes to court, they win.

I've never camped in a National Forest, never been backpacking, but something pulls me toward Minnesota. Maybe it's the lack of spiritual input in my own life, or just that I've spent the last 10 years living in New York City. Our all-American fast-food TV-consumer culture has never had much appeal for me, but lately I've grown increasingly irritated by it. I've watched my nation turn into a police state with a higher percentage of its population in jail than any other country in the world. Meanwhile, the average American complacently exists in TV-world reality, stretching paychecks from week to week, and understanding little of what's really going on. In 1988, I stopped eating meat—an indication I must be on some sort of spiritual quest. There has to be an alternative reality somewhere. I want to find it.

Two hours later, I arrive at the entrance to a gravel pit high in the Sawtooth Mountains.

"Welcome home, brother," says a girl by the side of the road. "Park in the gravel pit, not by the side of the road."

After parking, I shoulder my pack and hike over to a small crowd gathered at the entrance of the pit. Even though the people here are strangers, they call each other "brother" and "sister" and hug each other. The vibe in the air is so positive it envelops me immediately.

"Wait here for the shuttle," announces a longhaired teenager who seems to be supervising the area.

Within a few minutes, a truck arrives and we all squeeze in. The dusty ride to the Gathering takes 20 minutes and we pass through several makeshift checkpoints along the way. Finally, we are deposited at the "Info Center." A few of us who have never been to a Gathering approach the center, hoping to get some advice on how to proceed.

"Go to work. Get a job," says a man behind the counter.

A mountain man clad in leather approaches us. He carries a homemade two-string guitar. "Got your bowl? Got your spoon?" he asks in a booming voice. He quickly draws a crowd and delivers a speech on how to survive at the Gathering, carefully explaining the importance of sanitation.

"Don't drink the spring water unless you boil it for fifteen minutes, and don't shit in the woods—use the shitters," he says. After the speech, the crowd disperses. I stay behind to interview this mountain man.

Barry Adams

They call me "Plunker" because of the instrument I carry. I'm from western Montana and I'm 45 years old.

Some of the family that runs with me has been around since the Haight days. I lived in a crash pad called The British Embassy with Cheshire Cat, Gandalf and Lady Jane. I wrote a book called *Where Have All the Flower Children Gone?*

To me, the sixties meant sleeping in a crash pad with 40 others with no room to lay down. The door would bust down, maybe the cops would haul a few people off to jail. Everybody would jump up, raise money in the street, pass the hat, go down and get them out. There was a sense we were "The People." We called ourselves the tribe back then. We tried for that vibration. Now, we are that tribe.

I first went to a Gathering one spring when I was a young 'un in Montana. Next one I went to was called Vortex 1, outside of Portland. At that time we had these tipis we called the Rainbow Tipis. The people who stayed around for the clean-up at Vortex, they became the Rainbow Family.

In 1972, 35,000 of us gathered near Granby, Colorado, 150 miles from Aspen. We did a little dance with the government that was unreal. We ran blockades. The lieutenant governor called us "sons of bitches." On July 4, we walked to Table Mountain and did a silence to show respect for all the people who were doing their best for planet Earth. And while we prayed, airplanes buzzed around us. I was interviewed by *Rolling Stone* back then. They called me the Elmer Gantry of the hip.

The next day, I looked down at the parking lot and saw people were leaving. I couldn't believe it! We were alive in New Jerusalem and they were leaving! But people said, "Well I gotta get back to work in Michigan." I didn't think there'd be another Gathering.

In the early days, we would nudge each other. We had a good vibration even then. Now, we hug. We're really close.

To this day, I don't know how Rainbow happens. I know when the shuttle bus hits, I can walk out there, raise my voice, and the bus will park.

Then I have to think, holy mackerel, how did this thing get here?! Somebody volunteered their bus, and somebody else volunteered to drive it, and another somebody volunteered to stand by the gate and say, "Yeah, this one goes through." What holds these people together? Even when you've been coming for a long time, you get startled by the miracle.

Rumors are big at Rainbow. In 1976, when we gathered in Montana, I went to visit the governor. We had a good relationship. He held my two-string plunker. Shook it, admired it. Six hours later, when we got back to the Gathering, word had gotten back that I'd been thrown out of the governor's mansion.

There are road dogs and winos that come here. They build shitters and help gather firewood for folks from the suburbs. They all learn the masterful art of environmental living. You get future shock at the gate. You go from a 90-mile-an-hour world to walk at your own pace. It's almost like hippie Disneyland.

In West Virginia, in 1980, they executed two of our sisters. It was like a warning trip. Vickie and Nancy were hitchhiking in and they were executed. We got very little response from law enforcement. All the different forces got together and said, "Hey, let's not really investigate this."

Then the Forest Service spent a lot of money hiring a bunch of badasses, people who told us, "You are Satanists. You use black magic. You use crystals. You are evil." In Wyoming a federal officer told one of the brothers: "I'd shoot you like a dog if I had the chance."

Billy Ball was the toughest redneck of them all. FBI-trained. Used to be on the Dallas DEA narc squad. Very strong, very strict, very heavy. Billy Ball has strong beliefs, but so do we.

In 1987, they spent a million dollars harassing us in North Carolina. One day, a mysterious plane flew overhead and sprayed something. The next day a heavy fever spread through the camp. Swept through Kid Village first. They blockaded the gate and wouldn't let a water truck come through. That was Billy Ball. In Texas, in 1988, it got worse. They wouldn't let us close the gate. It became a parking lot gathering. They had patrols every 22 minutes with squad cars parked at Main Circle—radios blasting. They waved guns openly, deliberately, intimidatingly. We are like a church trying to live in peace. We have brothers and sisters here who have been through wars. Please, out of respect—out of sight. We don't flash marijuana on the police, we ask them not to flash guns on us.

That's respect.

That year they tried to sue me and the other organizers. But for the first time in 200 years a federal judge actually ruled that the common people had a constitutional right to gather on public land. That was William Wayne Justice, better known as Justice Justice. We won. At the trial, the Feds asked: "How is everything done at a Gathering?" I said, "If there's a big need out, I just go out and tell everybody I meet."

In Texas, Billy Ball jumped Neosho, a traditional Native American tribal person who had eagle feathers on his staff. They beat on him. We surrounded them. They expected a riot. But everyone just said, "Easy, easy, peace, brother." Billy Ball got real shook up. He took me aside. He said, "I'm gonna release this guy into Rainbow custody." Neosho had papers for the feathers in camp.

Next year in Nevada, they used tactics like Vietnam. They'd go in, make lightning raids. Then they'd send in people to check out the psychological effect.

Right here in Minnesota, there's no buildup of cops internally. They're letting the district rangers handle everything. The district rangers are good people. They come in and say, "This is fantastic." They're blown away.

According to Forest Service figures, we've had over 400,000 people at all the Gatherings. We've had two rape cases, two or three sexual assaults on children. Right now, our council process is a little weak. But consensus is growing all around the planet; look at China, Romania, Poland. You know, I did get Billy Ball to shake my hand. He got righteous with us. But that's another story....

I thank Plunker for the interview and he responds by giving me a bear hug.

Across the trail from the Info Center is a huge map of the site. On my left is a trail marked "Yellow Brick Road" which leads to the Brewhaha Tea Kitchen, Krishna Kitchen, N.E.R.F. Kitchen, S.P.O.T. Theater, and finally, at the end of the trail, Main Circle. The other trail passes C.A.L.M. (the Center for Alternative Living Medicine), Popcorn Palace, Kid Village, Lovin' Oven, Sunrise Camp and Taco Hilton. It also leads to Barker Lake. Since the temperature is in the high 80s, I opt to camp by the lake.

It takes me several hours to find a campsite and set up my tent. As soon as that's out of the way, I wander over to Kid Village, the Rainbow day-care center. The kitchen is being run by a barrel-chested Native American. I approach him for an interview. At first, he seems reluctant, but soon changes his mind. We wander down to the lake and the sun sets while he tells me his story.

Felipe

I'm 51 years old. I was raised on the West Coast by grandparents, who were connected to the old ways, the traditional ways. Chavez, that's my grandparents' name. I started drinking at 14. My family was into alcohol. It affected our whole lives.

In 1955, I joined the Marines and then the 82nd Airborne. I went to Europe. Came back and worked in aircraft plants. By this time I was an alcoholic.

What really changed my life—gave me a whole different perspective—was coming to a Rainbow Gathering 15 years ago in New Mexico. I'd been drinking. Found myself on the way to New Mexico in a car, passed out drunk. When I woke up, I was on the top of this mountain. I looked down and saw all these tipis and children playing. I broke into tears. People came and sat around me. Pretty soon, the tears were tears of joy. It was a purification.

I went down that mountain into a sweat lodge that was run by a brother from Massachusetts named Medicine Story. He really touched my heart, got to my spirit. I couldn't go back and live the same way. It changed my whole life. I started getting more connected with my people through the American Indian Movement, going on walks, meeting medicine men. I've been participating in the Sun Dance in South Dakota, which is directed by Leonard Crow Dog.

I feel honored to be serving my family, especially the kids. You know, I used to do the main kitchen, but I got to the point I didn't want to deal with the stress. So I said, I'm gonna do Kid Village. Children give me energy. Every year we come together, a big family reunion. We come through life as a child, and—in a sense—we go back to that stage.

We've had people come in here and try to violate our children. So we take precautions. There are predators out there. They're sick and need help. We have security around our children. It's unfortunate, but we have to.

Past couple of years, Rainbow has had to struggle with the Forest Service. Every year we go to court. This year we avoided court because so many people wrote letters. I believe a lot of people in Washington are pressuring the Forest Service to harass us because they feel threatened by our coming together. They don't want people to go back to the old ways and live with nature.

Right now, my life is committed to serving the homeless. I go to reservations and ghettos, do soup kitchens and try to educate them by showing them videos of the Nevada Test Site. I'm pretty involved with the Shoshones now. I put my tipi up there last September near the test site.

I hope that when my time comes, and I graduate from this life to go to the spirit world, I do it right here with my family. I'd be real happy. I'd want them to party afterwards. Play drums and have a big feast. Live together in harmony and really create this peace on Earth that we talk about...

After I leave Kid Village, I walk over a mile to the Northeast Rainbow Family Kitchen (N.E.R.F.), hoping to find my photographer, Gabe Kirchheimer. Gabe is nowhere to be found, but the kitchen is serving dinner, so I help myself to some vegetarian stew. After dinner, I'm too exhausted to do anything except go back to my tent and fall asleep.

Next morning, I discover a young girl camped next to me. I'm surprised because the girl arrived at the Gathering with only a sleeping bag and space blanket. I fire up my camp stove, offer her some tea and turn on my tape recorder.

Soma
I'm 15 years old and I'm from Santa Barbara, California. I'm in college studying psychology, philosophy, math and English. My parents named me Soma after [the sacrament of the *Rig Veda*]. Soma means different things in different languages. It's also in the book *Brave New World* by Aldous Huxley.

My parents started bringing me to Kid Village when I was three years old. They've been coming here since it began. I always loved it. There are a lot of people like me who have grown up with Rainbow. It's a very lasting influence. I met my first boyfriend here. We roamed around and played in the woods. It was a really open experience. I've never taken any drugs. They're freely available but there's never any pressure to take them. I choose not to. I used to come to the Gathering with loads of stuff. Now I just come with my sleeping bag.

A few years ago, I saw some fairies—that's what gay people call themselves here—kissing each other, and I was a little shocked. But then I realized it was wrong to act like that. This is a place people can be happy and free and not have to worry about other people making judgments. This is the only place where I've felt like that.

After breakfast, I decide to visit Main Circle, which is a good hour's hike away. Along the trail I run into some rangers from the Forest Service who are on their way to the Rainbow Family Council. The rangers are very friendly.

"This is my fifth Gathering," says Butch Marita. "I think they're a good thing."

The rangers tell me over 5,000 people are already on-site, with many more cars arriving every hour. They're not concerned with the number of people because they know that Rainbow will leave this site in better condition than they found it. They always do. The rangers are surprised, however, by the total lack of blackflies and mosquitoes in the area. "Go five miles from here and you'll be eaten alive," they tell me. For some reason, Barker Lake is infested with mosquito-eating dragonflies.

When we arrive at council, the water crisis is being discussed. Everything at council is done by consensus, which means it takes only one negative vote to veto any action. Garrick Beck asks for permission to collect Magic Hat funds to pay for a water truck. After a half hour, all 50 people at council say "Ho!"—signifying their agreement with Garrick's plan. Garrick tells me it's the quickest council decision he's ever seen. (I learn later that some councils have gone on for three days before reaching consensus.)

Since fresh water is becoming a problem, I decide to return to my car and pick up the two gallons I left in the trunk. Unfortunately, when I get back to the Info Center, I learn the shuttle bus is no longer running, but is being stopped at Bus Village, a mile down the road. When I get to Bus Village, I pass the checkpoint that is preventing vehicles from coming into the Gathering. It's being run by a large, bearded man in a rocking chair. Someone tells me this man is responsible for the lack of mosquitoes in the area, so I interview him.

Frenchie

I was born in 1930 in east Texas. My mom was full-blood Cherokee and my father was a German Jew. I grew up on a cotton farm in the east Texas woods. We grew pot, too. It was still legal when I was born and didn't become illegal until way after I started smoking it. My dad gave me a reefer when I was six years old and I've been smoking it ever since. I intend to continue.

My ma was a traditional east Texas Cherokee. She was descended from folks who came to Texas from eastern Tennessee right after the Texas War of Independence with Sam Houston. The government gave them land and they settled down in houses. But my mom used some of the old traditional herbal medicines and stuff.

In the sixties, I was a typical revolutionary hippie, living on the street in San Fran, Berkeley, Oakland. I went to the Vortex Gathering in '72. In a way, Vortex was the beginning of Rainbow, but all gatherings are Rainbow Gatherings. When one of Noah's kids stepped out of the boat and said, "Hey, come look here at the birdie," that was the first Gathering. To my notion, the Rainbow Family has always been around. It just hadn't been defined as the Rainbow Family until the late sixties. We're no different than we were 1,000 years ago. The same people with the same peace in our hearts.

I got here June 13. On June 12, we stopped for a night at the site we were at in Michigan in '83. In the morning we walked over the old meadows and I talked to the dragonflies. I said, "Hey, remember all those hippies you saved from the mosquitoes a few years ago? Well, we're gonna be across the lake. Come visit." So we drove on here, and, sure enough, there were no dragonflies. Spent the night. In the morning dragonflies were all over the camp.

The scout camps arrived here first. That's when the seeding of the camp begins, before the lotus opens. We don't want too many vehicles inside. We don't need 'em. Anybody who was at Nevada shouldn't mind this walk in. The biggest problem working the gate is our own people claiming: "But we're different! We have to drive in!"

Solid prayer for peace is the focus of the whole Gathering. One day we'll get everybody tuned up just right and it's gonna happen...

It takes me the rest of the day to return to my car, parked in the gravel pit, and hike back to my campsite. I eat dinner at the Krishna kitchen, watch a performance at S.P.O.T. Theater and visit several late-night kitchens, where people have gathered to sing Rainbow songs around campfires. Apparently, the songs belong to no one, but have been handed down from one Gathering to the next. Like every other aspect of Rainbow, the words to these songs are easily learned in a few minutes and before long I find myself sitting around the fire singing with strangers. It's a great feeling.

The next day I go looking for Shanti Sena, the Rainbow police force. Technically, everyone at Rainbow is Shanti Sena, which means if you see something negative happening, you're supposed to alert the rest of the camp. There are few rules at Rainbow, but the Family does strongly discourage guns and alcohol.

Suppose, for example, a hunter wandered into the Gathering. Before he got far, he'd be stopped and told: "Hey, brother, no guns in the church." If that didn't work, the shout "Shanti Sena" would probably go up, drawing several hundred Rainbow brothers and sisters to the area. Although Shanti Sena practices nonviolence, they will resort to force if necessary. After asking around the camp, I'm introduced to Amazin' Dave, a martial arts expert who serves on the Shanti Sena Council.

Amazin' Dave

I grew up in Fort Worth, Texas. My old man was a civil judge and I was supposed to become a lawyer when I grew up. I got drafted in the sixties and survived by going to Korea instead of Vietnam. The Army gave me time to read. I went to the library and read a book about the Kennedy assassination—*Heritage of Stone* by Jim Garrison—that changed my life.

I got out of the Army in '71 and went to graduate school. I did most of my graduate work while living in a log cabin in the woods. One day, I went to an alternative technology fair in Washington, D.C. I drove in early with my truck and tools, went down to the middle of the site, helped shuttle people in and set up tents. I set up the first tipi I ever saw. It was a wonderful introduction to what America could be.

You might call me a Jeffersonian. I visit his memorial every month. Unfortunately, this country no longer has any resemblance to what Mr.

Jefferson envisioned. His words are very explicit: We all have responsibility to try to better our government.

The problem is that capitalism has developed a stranglehold over our industrial development. The pretense that we have an energy crisis, the energy discoveries that have been suppressed—all lies. They have created a narrow-minded world for us to live in and pretend it's a reality. America needs to know that we are out here. That we're trying to create this New Jerusalem in just a few days of free sharing and caring. They need to step away from government influences. Step away from sexism, racism and all those bad feelings.

When you are in an environment where 85 to 95 percent of the people are loving and caring, and there is no money involved, people find themselves more civilized. They relax a bit. There will be problems. Some theft. It's tough. We're so open here. We go on faith. But there are very few predators here. Most people come to be healed.

Shanti Sena started a long time ago. Some brothers and sisters got together and wanted to make sure any negativity was handled appropriately. Our council process allows even the smallest voice to be heard. We want even the shy voices to speak. We give respect to all. Decisions are made in silence, after long, exhaustive hours of council. There is the big council, and there are many smaller councils.

The police are our only impediment. This drug issue is a red herring. The police here have been randomly stopping vehicles heading in this direction. People tell me this has never happened in their area before. There has been a recent Supreme Court decision that supports sobriety checks, but these checks have been safety checks with dogs and video cameras. It's a blight upon the Constitution and our legal right to assemble...

Today, Shanti Sena seems preoccupied with the roadblocks the police have set up near the Gathering. Dave takes me to meet a girl who was stopped and searched at one of these.

Kimmie
I'm 18, from Indiana, close to Indianapolis. This is my first Gathering. I met the family through the Grateful Dead tour and I came here to be close to them.

While me and my fiancé were coming into the Gathering, the police stopped us. They were doing random driver's license checks, basically on young people from out of state. If you were going to the Gathering, they made you step away from the car and got the dogs out. The dog made a hit on the back of our car, so they got us out and searched the car. About 20 state cops were all around the car. They were very rude and cold, and videotaped part of the search. I was wearing just a tank top and shorts, so I was really cold. I asked if I could get a shirt while they were throwing our clothes on the ground. They said no. After the dog made a second hit, they found four ounces of marijuana in the bumper. They grabbed my fiancé. I asked if I could talk to him but they told me to stay away from him, not to touch him or talk to him. They told me to leave. I said, "Where do you want me to go? You have my love, my home, my belongings." They said, "Little girl, why don't you go call your mommy?" So I took off without my things. I was seven or eight miles from the Gathering. Some sisters and brothers picked my up and brought me here. I could have been raped. They're holding my boyfriend at the Holiday Inn because the jail is full of people.

Hours later, when I get back to my tent, I find there are many new arrivals in my neighborhood and they are organizing a sundown jam session. The leaders of the party seem to be Fantuzzi and Herkimer. Although the party starts at sunset, it wails until late in the evening.

Next morning, I wake up and go for a canoe ride with Fantuzzi, who tells me his life story.

Fantuzzi

I'm from the Upper West Side of Manhattan, born September 17, 1951. My mother and father were from Puerto Rico. I started out dancing and then music took over my life. I just completed my third album—*One Earth, One People.*

In the sixties, I used to throw parties in New York that were famous. Barry Plunker came to one at a church on West Fourth Street. Barry said, "What is this, capitalism? Why are you asking for money?" But he stayed and helped clean up afterwards.

The last party I threw was to raise money for me to go to India. It was called Fantuzzi's Blowout, and the *Village Voice* wrote about it. I held it in

a ballroom on 43rd Street and 1,200 people showed up. There were business people, transvestites, yogis, Lower East Side LSD people. Actually, I
lost money, but I didn't care.

I went to Woodstock. I think that was the first real Gathering. We were
called the Butterfly Family then and we did pageants and shared our
heart songs. In 1971, I joined a group called the Rainbow Gypsies. We
traveled the world, singing, dancing. We ran into Rainbow people everywhere we went. We went to India and the group got into a guru. I didn't
want that, so I came back and discovered the Rainbow Family. Part of the
Living Theater was also connected with the Rainbow Gypsies. I lived
with Ira Cohen, who photographed the Living Theater and made a movie
about them.

Basically, I'm going around the world trying to help the evolution that
needs to take place. I just spent five years living on the Big Island in
Hawaii. Now I'm based in Los Angeles. From there I go to the Oregon
Country Fair, then the Jamaican Sunsplash, then I do an East Coast tour,
then I go to Japan for an ecology event…

Gabe finally shows up and we go to a wedding celebration for Felipe
that is taking place at the S.P.O.T. Theater. On the way, we run into a can-
didate for governor of Minnesota. I get out my tape recorder.

Heart Warrior
I come from the last Native Indian family that still lives in the Boundary
Waters Canoe Area. This is a four-million-acre wilderness preserve, con-
sisting of islands and spring-fed lakes, located in northern Minnesota. It
is the greatest fresh watershed of this continent. I live where my ancestors
had their villages. My great uncles were Ojibway chiefs. The waterways
were their highways. They net-fished here, and lived in small families
because the habitat is so delicate.

I was a charity Indian, raised in a school designed to de-culture Indians.
That is how I earned the name Heart Warrior. I wouldn't go for all their
bullshit. I was always traditional, born that way, and they couldn't corrupt
me. I could see through the whole thing, so I took a lot of beatings. I went
to college and got interested in the Hopis, the Keepers of the West Polar
Earth, and the Tibetans, Keepers of the East Polar Earth.

This great freshwater source is in very serious jeopardy right now, with only a short time left to avert the danger. Minnesota has leased out almost the entire area to 35 mining companies. Back in 1976 the state commissioned a study into the effects of copper-nickel mining north of Laurentian Divide. It was found that copper-nickel mining in this watershed would destroy all trees, aquatic life and fur-bearing animals, consequently destroying the tourism-based economy of the area. People downstream and the effects of downstream water quality—Hudson Bay, the Great Lakes and the Mississippi River—were not even considered in this study.

The state has opted for mining rather than the present paper mill industry. They know mining will destroy this land. Our children do not deserve this legacy. I am running for governor of Minnesota and trying to warn everybody before it's too late...

Next morning, Fantuzzi is walking up the trail outside my tent. I start to speak, but he quickly silences me. I realize it's July Fourth, the day of silent meditation.

Two hours later, around noon, Gabe and I arrive at Main Circle, which is filled with thousands of silent Rainbowers. Suddenly, a man wearing an owl headdress jumps up and breaks the silence. "Stop nuclear war!" he shouts. Before long, this man's speech is interrupted by the pounding of drums. The entire camp breaks into a wild, tribal celebration.

Although the man with the owl headdress meant well, it's obvious his speech disturbed many people. Garrick is so mad that he storms over and tears off the man's owl feathers.

"I just want you to know that you ruined the silence for 2,000 people who were still on the trail on their way here," says Garrick.

The man protests his innocence, but soon falls to the ground and prostrates himself. An "Om" circle forms around him. Although I've never been involved in an Om circle before, I find myself joining in. I'm amazed by how easy it is to participate. The owl feathers are taken away and buried. A black vulture circles overhead. For some reason, I am overcome by emotion at this sight and start to cry. So does the man in the center of the circle.

An hour later a woman dressed in white breaks out some garbage bags and starts cleaning up the site. She is quickly joined by many volunteers. After the cleanup, I approach the woman and ask to interview her.

No Guns

I was born in Mobile, Alabama, March 16, 1948. My father was in the printing business, but printing got phased out so he got retrained into missiles. I grew up all over the country.

My first Gathering was 1972. I was living in the backwoods of Minnesota when I heard that somewhere in Colorado there was going to be this incredible Gathering to pray for world peace. I only had a dollar bill, but I felt that if I was ever going to connect with people, it would be at this Gathering. So I hitchhiked out of Duluth.

I got to Nebraska and prayed for a long ride because hitchhiking is illegal in Colorado. This van stopped and the driver said he was going to Granby. When we were 20 miles from the Gathering, he said, "Well, if this Gathering is as big as you say, maybe we'll hear something on the radio." So he switched it on, and sure enough we heard a voice say they had just opened the barricades. The driver turned to me and said, "I'm going to the Gathering too." There were about 20,000 people there when we arrived.

I camped at Kid City. Six babies were born in a big army medical tent. I focused mostly on information.

I got the name No Guns after the Arkansas Gathering in 1975. We were in the Bible Belt and this sheriff had gathered a posse to rid the area of these devil worshippers. He knew we were devil worshippers because we looked strange and danced and hugged. The posse arrived and we had the very first women's circle to deal with guns in the church. I got my Rainbow name from that council.

In 1988, some friends saw on the news that Rainbow was in trouble, so I immediately made plans to go to the Gathering in Texas. When I arrived, fences were up and men with guns were everywhere. I started singing, "We've got the right of the people to freely assemble."

I didn't know how serious it was until I walked into the Shanti Sena camp and someone said, "Do you think they'll round us up?"

This was the first time the police controlled the gate. They had 60 guys with guns there. I followed them around singing. "Lay your weapons down, boys." They seemed nervous. Then I would rap about the Reagan administration, and the CIA crack-cocaine connection. About how the CIA had taken the heroin trade over from the Corsican Mafia through the French intelligence. The family said, "Why don't you do the gate?" So, on

July 3, I stood at the gate and sang for about six hours straight.

We formed Rainbow affinity groups to stop cars from coming into Main Circle. If the police were going to come into the Gathering, at least we wanted them to cover their guns with their shirts.

I was talking to my affinity group when I saw these two brothers running alongside this jeep. I ran up to them. The driver said, "We got cows in here."

I said, "Come on, brother, there ain't no cows in here. Park your car and join the Gathering."

In my head, the jeep stopped, but in fact this never happened. I stepped in front of the jeep just as the driver accelerated. I felt a crunch over my chest. I felt all of my energy leave. I knew I was in pieces. I saw a face looking at me. I said, "I'm dead," and I got no reaction, so I thought, "Wow, nobody is talking to me. I *am* dead."

Then I saw my son and he just walked away, so I knew I was dead. Then I saw Barry and he said, "No Guns, don't you dare die."

And I went, "Wow, I'll try." So I said, "Total forgiveness, press no charges and no vengeance." Barry said, "You got it."

A helicopter arrived just as a storm set in and they had to send it back. I had to ride the rocky road in an ambulance. But the guys in the ambulance were so fantastic. They held me and came to visit me later. My doctor turned out to be a right-wing Christian, all freaked out about the crystals I was wearing. We had numerous discussions. He said I had nine broken ribs, two punctures in my lung, a blood clot and a leg jammed in the socket.

My nurse came in and told me that Justice Justice was threatened by the KKK for allowing us to gather in Texas. The judge had risked his life for the Rainbow people.

Now I'm based in Santa Cruz, working for the homeless people. I believe our country has taken a very serious fascist turn. I do not believe there's a Constitution protecting us at all right now…

On the way back to my campsite, I have one more interview to conduct. Gabe insists I speak with Estar, one of the elders of the tribe. Elders are accorded great respect at Rainbow and Gabe says I mustn't leave without meeting one.

Estar

I was born in Wisconsin in 1923. My parents were ordinary people. My father had a small bakery and my ma was a housekeeper. In 1971, I decided to travel across the country to check out all the communes. I visited Garrick Beck's Rainbow Farm outside of Eugene three times. They were making flyers for the big Gathering in Colorado and I decided to go.

The first day I arrived in Colorado, I met a brother who said, "Welcome home." He had been living in a tipi in New York State on a farm outside of Woodstock. That farm was called Rainbow too.

A few days later, we were in a circle humming and this airplane kept diving over us. We hummed up to the airplane and it went away. We had to do this dance so that we could influence world peace without being clobbered.

I don't go to the council anymore. I used to, but every time I stood up, a brother would say, "Out of order." I had the feather taken out of my hand once. Few women are brave enough to combat that. The women elders control council in Hopi tribes, but not here.

Rainbow keeps growing. One of these years when we do the hum, it'll be a true hum and we'll be centered. We still have a long way to go.

I embarrass my mom by being as funky as they come. She's still alive, 93 years old. She smiles all the time, but she's bitter about her hard life. I'm going to give her some Rainbow love before she dies, even though she doesn't approve of my lifestyle...

After five days in paradise, I'm reluctant to leave. Unfortunately, I'm under deadline pressure to file this story and have to return to New York. There are many aspects of Rainbow that continue to impress me after I leave. I realize I went the entire time without a beer or any other drug, and didn't miss them at all. Because I was constantly being bombarded with love vibes, my consciousness was already altered. I was on a natural ecstacy and didn't have the urge to do drugs, even though they were offered free on several occasions. I'm impressed by how well I ate. Good organic vegetarian food, something almost impossible to find outside Rainbow, is plentiful at the Gathering. Most of all, I'm impressed by how open, friendly and helpful I was to everyone around me. Whenever possible, I took time to help anyone in need. It's a feeling that stayed with me long after I left.

When I was back in the city, the real work of Rainbow was just begin-ning. Campfires, latrines and compost pits were filled in and dismantled. Shelters were taken down and all litter picked up. Hardened ground was spaded and trails were covered with branches, leaves and pine needles. As the last humans left the area, seeds were spread to revitalize plant growth.

Rainbow is not a perfect world. There are problems, including plenty of "Drainbows" who take from the Gathering and give little back. This element, however, is small in comparison to the dedicated workers who make the event possible. While our mainstream culture feeds on violence, sex, youth worship and consumerism, Rainbow feeds on love, respect for elders and environmentalism. Given an educated choice between the two, I have to believe most Americans would choose the latter. I only hope someday our mainstream culture discovers Rainbow's potential, instead of persecuting these peaceful people.

After I returned from the Gathering, I went to the East Village home of Garrick Beck for my final Rainbow interview. Garrick was born into one of the foremost counterculture families in America. His father, Julian Beck, was a prominent artist and member of the original abstract-expressionist scene of the fifties. His mother, Judith Malina, is an actress and director. Together they founded the Living Theatre, one of the original avant-garde companies. Hounded by the authorities for their political activism, the Living Theatre fled the US in the sixties. Garrick stayed behind and became a political activist, organizer and well-known raconteur. In the '70s, he helped found the Rainbow Family and remains one of its most respected brothers. Today, Garrick splits his time between New Mexico, New York City and his organic farm in Oregon.

Garrick Beck
I was born right here on Manhattan Island in 1949. I grew up in Manhat-tan. Played in the streets with people of different race, language and cul-ture. So, by the time I was nine I had an understanding of racial prejudices. My parents were Beatniks trying to rethink society. In the fifties, the Upper West Side of Manhattan was an enlightened zone. There were artists and writers moving in. There were performances. It was a scene that later moved into civil rights. A number of literary and artistic characters passed

through our house, but a lot of them never got known. Like Lester Schwartz. Lester never got famous. But he was one of the early rebels. He died about two years ago. By day he was a dockworker, and by night he was an FM-listening hashish-smoking compadre of jazz musicians, painters of the New York School and poets of the Beat generation. Lester had the quintessential Beatnik look: sandals, blue jeans, sweatshirt, T-shirt. "Work is what you don't want to do," he told me. "Pleasure is what life is for. Don't let them fool you. Don't believe what they teach you in school. In school you learn what the government wants you to learn. On the streets you learn what is really going on." Lester never got famous, but to me he was right in there laughing and talking with Larry Rivers, Allen Ginsberg, Herbert Huncke, Diane DiPrima, John Cage, Cecil Taylor. But from the eyes of a little kid, these were all just people. Much later I realized how inspirational Lester's life was, compared to the millions of people trapped in ruts, grinding out meaningless work, coming home and being satisfied by television.

My parents had a theater company, the Living Theatre, and I grew up around it, starting at the Cherry Lane Theater, which is still a functional theater in West Greenwich Village. In 1954, they moved up to a loft on 100th Street and Broadway, one of the last wood frame buildings on Broadway. They were puzzling over who would play a certain child's role. Actually they had a child actor who'd played the part, but I guess he grew older or moved somewhere. I said, "I can take the role." I really wanted to act. I played in *Tonight We Improvise, Many Loves, The Idiot King*. I learned to be professional about staging. And that became useful in demonstrations, street performances and in councils. Judith, my director/mother, taught me there are two great things you can do onstage: "fall in love and die."

The Living Theatre progressed from a poetic-philosophical theater to a politically relevant one. The theater was in the middle of a swirl of the New York painters and poets, many of whom had been young wildcats kicking around five years earlier, and now were receiving international acclaim. So, the Beatniks of the world would cruise through—like visiting dignitaries—coming from San Francisco, Paris, London. The city was becoming very politically aware. The Committee for Non-Violent Action (CNVA) sponsored the Polaris submarine protest at the launching of the first nuclear submarine at Groton, Connecticut. By 1960, the Living Theatre was discussing overt social problems, and this aroused the wrath of the authorities, who still had one foot in the McCarthy era. But then the IRS moved in and seized the theater on the grounds we owed back taxes. We were in negotiations with them over whether they had illegally delayed our not-for-profit status. The court later ruled in our favor and awarded us one dollar in damages. But in the intervening years, the theater went through an incredible ordeal. When I was 14, the government seized the theater, arresting the 23 people inside. My parents argued their own case and were cited for contempt. They never got nailed on the eleven counts carrying three years each that the government wanted. I watched the government throw the book at my parents because they were anarchists and artists. It had very little to do with a struggling theater company trying to meet its tax burden. They were found guilty on a couple of charges, like opening a dressing room door that had been sealed by police. Well, that carried a three-year penalty, and the government argued for that! Everything I'd been taught in school about democracy and due process of law suddenly seemed like a lot of hokum. Julian served 60 days, Judith served 30, and the company moved to Europe.

The adults were smoking pot. In the mid-fifties, the whole arts galaxy began experimenting with mescaline, but it was mostly a pot and hashish scene, which had arrived through the jazz connection. When the company went to Europe, I stayed in New York, moved in with my grandmother and finished high school. I worked with the High School Students Against the War and the Student Peace Union, and I learned a bunch about political organizing. In '66 and '67, we sponsored a High School Students Against the War rally on Fourth Street, sound truck, permits and all.

You want to hear the story of the first hippie? In '54 or '55, a young actress named Nina cruised through our scene and began wearing Indian print dresses with mirrors. She burned incense and wore flowers. She threw out the furniture, spread out Hindu-style rugs and put big cushions down. She ate fresh fruit and went barefoot. She lived in a magical land. Eventually, she moved to Vermont and is still leading a natural life as far as I know. Nina was a comet ahead of her time.

Ten years later, the theater was in Europe experimenting with tribal collective living. Little money, big cabins on the freezing Belgian coast, natural foods. In the summer of '66, I went over and visited them in Italy. I left Grandma's home, was met at the airport in Rome, got driven up to this house in the hills of Velatri. I walked into a big, sprawling living room with a rock'n'roll band, Dutch guys with long hair, and these lights flashing red, green, purple. It was a totally different world from New York, but I could see Nina and her influences of tribal culture. It was new, it was fun. Instead of taking one more step in protest, they had declared peace, beauty and love as revolutionary action, a unique and powerful concept.

In 1967, after returning from a summer in Europe, I entered Reed College in Oregon, where I met a real peer group. Like many campuses, Reed was torn apart by the war in Vietnam. A group of us chained ourselves to the doors of the local draft board. We pasted up a sign: Conscription is Slavery. We were arrested and it was headlines for days. Classes seemed very removed from the real problem of people being shipped over to Vietnam and coming home dead. There were some very brilliant professors at Reed, most of whom left or didn't get tenure. I gave a little speech to one of the faculty-student senates about hypocrisy. They were making a big issue out of sex and drug use in public, while many of them were dropping their britches and smoking joints in private. I took out a joint, waved it in front of their faces, and said, "I'm going to go under that tree over there and smoke this."

The powers that be brought an honor case against me to throw me out of college. I was brought before the five-person judicial board—the "J" board. The president of the college made a speech about how I'd broken the honor principle and put them in danger of being arrested by being in the same room with a forbidden substance. These hearings were open and I'd invited anyone with an interest in the case to attend. A lot of people showed up. In my defense, I spoke of the history of the American colonies, and paralleled the refusal of the Virginia Burghers to support the Revolution and the refusal of the college faculty and senate to endorse a statement against the war. I spoke of the Lexington Green and of the Chicago Democratic convention police riot.

I called my witnesses. I said: "Anyone who felt I represented them when I smoked that joint under that tree, come forward now and testify by smoking a little grass with me right now." And 200 people reached for their stash. I took a lit number and went over to the president. I said: "Mr. President, this is a large part of your student body. What do you think of this?"

And he stood up and stammered: "I don't know what to think."

And somebody in the back hollered out: "And you probably don't know how to think!" It was an awful moment for him. But that moment taught me that if you follow due process, you can get things done. Even if it's very slow.

Later on, I got collared by one of the right-wing trustees. "It's our school," he said. "You can butt your head up against us all you want, but you students just pass through here. Don't mess with our kitchen. Make your own."

So we moved into communal houses in Portland. We created food co-ops. We sought a larger vision and there it was: Go back to the land! What a vision! The vast green Earth. People all over the world left the cities and attempted to live an ecological lifestyle. A group of us got together, located a piece of land and bought it. We were new to gardening, water pumps and chain saws. There was the question: Are we self-sufficient? But it seemed to me there was always an interchange of supplies and materials. We grew organic wheat, organic apples, organic carrots. We learned that by living close to the Earth, we could survive.

Some people were on heavy guru trips or political power trips. We were on a circuit filled with hipsters, tripsters, dipsters and every kind of lipster. Romances happened, babies happened. Lots of babies happened. People screamed at each other. We had the vegetarians versus the meat-eaters, the New Age Christians versus Born Again Christians. In the many attempts to find the beautiful alternative society, we tried a lot of things that didn't work. We tried group marriage. We tried living without property. We learned the first basic truth: People are basically very good to each other, thus dispelling the myth for the need of standing armies.

A great deal of the lost knowledge that we need in order to survive as a human species resides in the old tribal ways of all our ancestors. And like the old tribes, we decided to hold a gathering, a World Family Gathering. So we sent out invitations for a Gathering to be held in Colorado in 1972. While we were working toward this first Gathering, we pitched in and worked on a post-Woodstock rock concert called Vortex 1, a Biodegradable Festival of Life. It was a rock'n'roll festival coupled with a cooperative, community village. This took place in McIver State Park outside Portland. Vortex was amazing. It was a very powerful event because the food supply was done by the co-op people, the cooking was done by

the restaurant people, the childcare was done by the alternative education people, the parking and road crew was done by the mechanic co-op,
and so on.

We said at Vortex: "Whatever the twin powers of darkness and
destruction have done to stop this gathering, it has not been enough!"

At a late-night celebration, we were given our name. We were drum-
ming, celebrating at the central fire. Someone hollered out: "We are...!"
Someone else hollered out: "The Rainbow...!" A bunch hollered out:
"Family...!" And one old man hollered out: "... of Living Light!" And
people cheered and threw hats in the air. It seemed like one lovely
moment. Honestly, I didn't think it was going to stick. But low and
behold, two years later, by the time we got to Colorado, no one called it
The World Family Gathering anymore. Everyone called it the Rainbow
Gathering.

We were camped at Strawberry Lake, near Granby. For the Fourth of
July meditation, we hiked to Table Mountain, a lonely small mountain
surrounded by high plateaus, where the headwaters of the Colorado
River spring from a split in the Continental Divide. It's a stupendous
place. The authorities found out we were going to gather there, so they
barbed-wired Table Mountain. There were 20,000 people near Strawberry Lake, and on the night of July Third, we counciled. The next day we
hiked the eight miles over to Table Mountain. I remember looking down
the mountain and seeing multicolored dots of people moving up two big
trails, like two legs. There was a huge array of fruit at the intersection of
the two trails, the belly. I sat on some rocks up at the head of the mountain, and Colorado breezes rolled across us while we sat in silence for
hours. I prayed for the tanks to turn into tractors.

Frankly, I was surprised when I came down and found it wasn't so. I
learned that if you want to be free from the banks, the governments and
giant corporations, you have to learn how to provide food, water and
medical needs. Whoever is doing that is running the ship. We have to
learn to pilot the spaceship Earth in order to get out from under the banks
and corporations. After three or four Gatherings, we learned there was a
basic set of information that needed to be communicated. It had to do
with hygiene, food, water supply and sanitation. We had to tell people
about things like fire safety. We used to have this process along the trail.
We'd serve tea and give Rap 107. As it developed, it evolved into written

form. We try not to prohibit anyone's freedom. But we certainly discourage buying and selling. We discourage weapons.

The children that have grown up in Rainbow are fantastic: self-reliant, unprejudiced, with many skills and talents. Kid Village is a big part of the Gathering. Rainbow is a society that is not at war with itself. We are reestablishing old tribal knowledge, knowledge of mutual respect, understanding and cooperation. We need to reestablish tribal experience. Everyone has a tribal heritage, whether it's Celtic, Siberian, African or Native American. And all these tribes had councils in the center of the village, where you went if you had a problem. We don't want to throw away the electronic age. We want to incorporate solar technology and all the high-grade communications.

We've talked endlessly about creating a permanent Rainbow village. We've looked at a lot of sites. The concept is a P.E.A.C.E. village that produces arts, crafts, energy devices, agricultural products, alternative housing and transportation, all in the village environment. I think that is the design of the future. Look what a terrible state our old people are in! How sad their lives are. We need a village environment where the old people can be with the young people. It's a powerful approach. We've invested 20 years of time, effort and energy communicating the idea that the human family can live happily in peace.

APPOINTMENT WITH THE APOCALYPSE

Morale at the Bureau of Alcohol, Tobacco and Firearms (ATF) might have been reaching an all-time low early in 1993. The previous summer, the agency had initiated and botched a case against Randy Weaver in Idaho. (Weaver later collected $3.1 million in restitution after the FBI killed his wife and son.) Then came widespread accusations of sexual harassment inside the agency. *60 Minutes*, the most-watched news show in the country, jumped all over that one.

The ATF brass wanted something to turn around the bad publicity, and they wanted it fast. In March, they were scheduled to appear before Congress to defend their annual budget. The solution? They began planning the biggest, most elaborate raid in ATF history. On February 28, a mile-long, 80-vehicle caravan pulled out of Fort Hood, Texas and headed 50 miles northeast for an appointment with the Apocalypse near Waco.

"Raiding is the expertise of the ATF, and statistically, it's not as dangerous as one might think," writes Dick J. Reavis in *The Ashes of Waco.* "In 36 months, the agency had called out its SRT or SWAT teams 578 times, executed 603 search warrants, mostly against dope dealers, and had seized some 1,500 weapons. It had encountered gunfire on only two of its raids, and the only fatalities (three of them) had been among suspects."

The ATF videotaped the planning sessions, as well as the training maneuvers at Fort Hood. Many agents carried cameras along with their flash-bang grenades, nylon handcuffs and assault rifles. A video camera was mounted on one of the three helicopters that were scheduled to arrive with the raiding party.

Unfortunately, there were serious problems with the raid's planning and execution. The search warrant contained inflammatory and prejudicial comments. Legal citations were incorrect. It contained blatantly false information about a methamphetamine lab, info which had been fabricated to obtain free military assistance. Two-thirds of the warrant involved charges of child abuse, a crime for which the ATF had no jurisdiction. Many consultants had urged the ATF to conduct the raid before sunrise, but the designated time had been moved to 9:30 A.M. The plan involved multiple "dynamic entries," which meant forced entry from numerous sides and levels simultaneously.

The planning was shoddy because the ATF needed the raid to happen fast, and they expected a cakewalk. The target, a religious community called Mount Carmel, had been under observation for over a month. It housed about 130 people, of which two-thirds were women and children. The occupants ranged from very elderly to babies and included two pregnant women. An undercover agent who'd penetrated the community reported endless hours of Bible study, with two communion services daily. The last thing the ATF expected was armed resistance in the face of their overwhelming firepower. Had they a better understanding of the Students of the Seven Seals who lived at Mount Carmel, the ATF would have realized they were about to stick their nose into a hornet's nest.

The Search for a Living Prophet

The Romans threw John the Apostle into a pot of boiling oil as punishment for spreading Christianity; but he survived and eventually was banished to the Greek isle of Patmos, where, around 90 AD, he wrote the Book of Revelation, a violent prophecy in which the unbelievers (read: Romans) are subjected to horrible tortures while the true followers of Christ are lifted into a golden city in heaven. Think of it as the original vengeance drama. Written before much of the New Testament, Revelation was placed at the end of the Bible. Martin Luther warned excessive study of it could lead to insanity. It ends with a plea for the Apocalypse to come quickly.

In 1831, William Miller launched the Second Advent Awakening, the biggest American-born religious movement in history. According to Miller's calculations, the end of the world was due on Oct. 22, 1844. Miller attracted a huge following of doomsday advocates, the survivalists of their time. When Jesus and the Apocalypse failed to appear at the appointed hour, the devotees had to recover from what they dubbed the "great disappointment." Miller's followers eventually blossomed into 84 groups of churches with over 10 million members worldwide, the largest of which is the Seventh Day Adventist Church, with about 750,000 members in the United States. Adventists believe the Second Coming is imminent, and that the power of prophecy will flourish in the final days.

Despite this, only one person since Miller has ascended to official "living prophet" status.

In 1935, Bulgarian immigrant Victor Houteff declared himself a living prophet and was promptly banished from the church. He assembled a large band of devotees at Mount Carmel Center in Texas. Upon his death in 1955, his widow took over and announced the Second Coming was due April 22, 1959. But when the date came and passed without an Apocalypse, 10,000 members were left in disarray. Most stopped sending in contributions, leaving self-proclaimed prophet Ben Roden and about 50 "Branch Davidians," as they called themselves, in charge of the once-prosperous Mount Carmel.

Following Roden's death in 1978, his widow, Lois, took over the church. Lois not only proclaimed herself a prophetess, she attracted a lot of attention in Adventist circles by declaring the Holy Spirit was feminine.

Vernon Wayne Howell joined the congregation in 1981. Born in Texas to a 15-year-old single mother, Howell had been passed between family members and physically and sexually abused during childhood. Due to dyslexia, he was held back many times in school, earning the nickname "Mr. Retardo." At age nine, he became a devout Seventh Day Adventist. By age 12, he'd memorized large tracts of the King James Bible.

When Howell arrived at Mount Carmel, he was a stuttering, insecure boy given to fits of self-pity. More than anything, he wanted contact with a living prophet. He formed a secret sexual liaison with Lois Roden, then in her late sixties. With his encyclopedic command of the Bible, Howell became an inspirational figure whose "visions" were taken seriously, despite his ninth-grade education. This angered George Roden, Lois' son, who saw himself as the future leader of the group. George suffered from Tourette's syndrome and frequently exploded with uncontrollable rage and inappropriate behavior. When Howell took a 14-year-old member of the congregation as his wife, Lois acted the jilted lover and confessed her secret affair during Bible study class. George expelled Howell and his bride from Mount Carmel at the point of an Uzi. Most of the congregation followed Howell to East Texas, where they lived communally in wretched conditions. Thus began his conversion from inspirational figure to actual living prophet. In 1987, Marc Breault joined the East Texas enclave and became Howell's right-hand man, helping recruit dozens of new members to the community.

After his mother died, George Roden became completely unglued. Determined to wrest back his congregation, he dug up a corpse and challenged Howell to see who could raise the dead. Instead, Howell reported the corpse abuse to the local sheriff. The sheriff wanted evidence, so Howell and several armed followers crept back to Mount Carmel under cover of night with a camera. Before they embarked on the mission, however, Howell outfitted everyone with identical camouflage fatigues and armed them with AR-15 assault rifles.

A gun battle ensued and Roden was wounded. He would have likely been killed, except the neighbors called the police, who broke up the gunfight and arrested Howell and his men for attempted murder. During the trial, Roden wrote angry letters to the judge, threatening to reign down a pox of AIDS and herpes on him. The judge sentenced him to six months in jail for contempt. The trial ended in a hung jury. Two years later, Roden was convicted of an ax murder and locked in an insane asylum.

Meanwhile, Howell and his followers rebuilt Mount Carmel, which had fallen into disrepair. They maintained a 24-hour armed vigil against possible retribution from Roden, who'd briefly escaped from the mental institution and continued to assert his ownership of the property. By paying back taxes and occupying the site, Howell hoped to gain full legal ownership within five years. In 1990, he changed his name to David Koresh and announced the Apocalypse was commencing in five years.

His group called themselves "Students of the Seven Seals," not "Branch Davidians," as they would later be known by the news media. Koresh yearned for recognition as a living prophet from the Adventist Church. His group lived a happy and communal life. They were an eclectic group of races, cultures and nationalities, some with advanced degrees in theology. One was the first black graduate of Harvard Law School.

Koresh formed a rock band, and the elders viewed him as a possible MTV-style prophet who could breathe life into a dying religious movement. He drove a souped-up Camaro and enjoyed target practice with semiautomatic assault weapons. He believed guns would come in handy during the 1995 Apocalypse. "What are you going to do when the tanks are surrounding us?" he'd ask his congregation.

Adventists believe the Bible contains clues concerning the date and nature of Judgment Day. They also have a religious obligation to take claims of prophecy seriously. By creating down-home explanations for many confusing passages in Revelation, and by memorizing all 150 Psalms and treating them as prophecy, Koresh created a fresh take on doomsday Christianity that was irresistible to some Adventists. His congregation was not a collection of brainwashed zombies, but an educated and highly spiritual community. Koresh frequently came to Bible class straight from work, his hands soiled with axle grease, the tones of his voice always conversational, never bombastic like a typical Southern Baptist.

Life at Mount Carmel was spartan, but people stayed because it was spiritually charged. One never knew what outlandish prophecy Koresh might spout next. He had a knack for constantly topping himself, like Jackie Chan dreaming up new stunts. Serious problems began, however, soon after Breault left the community and moved back to Australia, a split which coincided with Koresh's celibacy prophecy, which he called "The New Light." "At the time of the end, those who have wives should live as they have none," said Koresh, quoting the Bible to support the new policy. It was time for male members at Mount Carmel to become celibate, except for Koresh, who was obligated to sire 24 children by 1995. He already had several wives at Mount Carmel, one of whom he'd seduced when she was 12. (Koresh later admitted it was difficult keeping former couples from getting it on once in a while, just as it was difficult keeping his harem satisfied.)

It wasn't your typical American family, but the children were Koresh's jewels. They were reportedly extremely well mannered, quiet, obedient and showered with love. They'd never seen a television, never eaten junk food, never been to a public school. Their welfare had been monitored by the Texas Department of Human Services. The children showed no signs of physical or emotional abuse.

The community sincerely believed Koresh's interpretations of the Bible, and accepted him as "The Lamb," the only person capable of opening the Seven Seals that would bring about the Apocalypse. His matings with teenagers were unlawful, but they were conducted with parental approval. It was considered a sacred honor to bear his child. "It's not like I really want to do this," Koresh would always explain. "The Lord is telling me I have to."

Instead of turning his newlywed wife over to "The House of David,"

Breault embarked on a vendetta to expose Koresh. He hired a private investigator to document Koresh's history of statutory rape. When he couldn't get the press or authorities interested in the story, he began mixing exaggerations with real facts to produce a tantalizing stew of tabloid sensationalism. Eventually, he gave the story to an Australian TV show and began working on a book deal. Meanwhile, based on his evidence, the ATF elevated Koresh to "ZBO."

Zee Big One

Zee Big One (ZBO) is "a press-drawing stunt that when shown to Congress at budget time justifies more funding," wrote investigative reporter Carol Vinzant in *Spy*. "The attack on the Branch Davidians' complex was, in the eyes of some of the agents, the ultimate ZBO." In the spring of 1992, a United Parcel Service driver opened a box of grenade hulls being shipped to Mount Carmel and reported it to the local sheriff, who alerted the ATF. A member of Koresh's community was developing a profitable and entirely legal business selling firearms and survivalist fashion wear at gun shows. The empty grenade hulls were sewn into ammo vests, part of the official David Koresh survival gear.

On July 30, 1992, gun dealer Henry McMahon called Koresh, saying ATF agents were at his home asking questions about him. "Tell them to come out here," replied Koresh. "If they want to see my guns, they are more than welcome." The agents responded by motioning silently, "no, no," and getting McMahon to hang up. In January 1993, three undercover ATF agents occupied the house across the street from Mount Carmel and began videotaping and gathering intelligence. Although it was obvious they were government agents, Koresh welcomed their arrival and spent considerable time discussing the Bible with agent Robert Rodriguez, trying to convince him the government represented a false Babylonian power. He urged Rodriguez to move into Mount Carmel so he could have a better understanding of the community. They engaged in target practice together and inspected each other's weapons. Koresh noted Rodriguez's gun had a hair trigger, standard issue for a police sniper, and had been converted for full automatic fire, normally an illegal modification unless one registered the gun and paid the proper taxes. "This is a dangerous weapon," noted Koresh.

The day before launching "Operation Trojan Horse," the ATF reserved rooms in local hotels for over a hundred agents and personnel. They also alerted the national and local media to be ready for a big story that was about to break. A highly inflammatory article attacking Koresh as a child abuser appeared in the *Waco Tribune-Herald* the morning of the raid. It wasn't difficult to see a massive operation was underway, aimed at Mount Carmel.

David Jones, a local postman and Mount Carmel resident, was tipped off to the upcoming raid when a news cameraman asked for directions to "Rodenville." While they spoke, an ATF sniper team drove past and National Guard helicopters flew overhead. Jones headed for Mount Carmel and found Koresh discussing theology with Rodriguez. After speaking privately with Jones, Koresh told Rodriguez, "We know they're coming." He shook Rodriguez's hand and said, "Do what you gotta do."

Upon exiting Mount Carmel, Rodriguez called ATF Special Agent Chuck Sarabyn in an effort to cancel the raid. Instead, Sarabyn told the troops, "Hurry up, they know we're coming!" He had just led the convoy from Ft. Hood to Bellmead Civic Center, about 10 miles from Mount Carmel. Seventy-six ATF raiders loaded into two unprotected cattle trailers pulled by pickup trucks. Even though the element of surprise was lost, and the raid was happening in broad daylight, Sarabyn could not cancel ZBO.

There are many versions of what happened next, but the most believable accounts come from the surviving residents of Mount Carmel. Their perspective has been best documented by David Thibodeau, the drummer in Koresh's band, in his book, *A Place Called Waco*. "David appeared in the cafeteria accompanied by four or five men armed with AR-15s," writes Thibodeau. Koresh told his congregation to keep cool: "I want to talk it out with these people," he said. "We want to work it out."

A few minutes later the cattle cars filled with agents pulled up broadside to the front door. The first shots were probably fired into the dog pen in front of the building, where an Alaskan malamute lived with her pups. All the dogs were killed. There is also evidence an agent accidentally discharged two rounds into the radiator and windshield of an ATF vehicle.

Koresh opened the front door. He was unarmed. "What's going on?" he shouted. "There are women and children in here!" When he failed to hit the ground upon command, the agents opened fire, fatally wounding 64-year-old Perry Jones, who was standing next to Koresh. The door slammed shut and residents began to return fire. Under Texas law, defending oneself against excessive police force is legal.

Within seconds, Harvard Law graduate Wayne Martin, a local attorney, called 911. "There's 75 men around our building shooting at us at Mount Carmel," said Martin. "Tell them there are children and women in here and to call it off!" Ten minutes passed before Lieutenant Lynch, a deputy sheriff known to Martin, picked up the line. "I have a right to defend myself!" shrieked Martin, "We want a cease-fire!"

Strangely, there was no line of communication between local law enforcement and the raiding party, even though Lynch had visited the ATF command center earlier in the day. The command center was filled with phones and fax machines, all ready to blanket the news media with press releases, but had no communications with the raiding team. Apparently, none of the raiders had a cell phone.

It would take two agonizing hours to arrange a cease-fire, and it happened only after ATF agents ran out of bullets. During that time, six residents were killed and four were wounded, while four ATF agents were killed and 16 wounded. Many of the wounded agents were lying helpless on the field of battle. Of all the residents, Koresh was the most seriously wounded—a bullet had blown through his side. News photos reveal ATF agents in panic and disarray, loading their wounded on the hoods of vehicles.

The ATF had arrived in overwhelming force—including air support—and assaulted a church, only to be driven back by less than a dozen armed men. Suddenly, instead of a "ZBO," it had one of the biggest public-relations disasters in American history on its hands. The ATF agents were soon replaced by the FBI, the media were drawn back a mile from the scene and all lines of communication to Mount Carmel were severed. "A crazy cult is holding their children hostage," went the standard press release.

The most damaging "evidence" of what really happened that day is the bizarre disappearance of the videotape shot by the ATF. The only explanation given was the multiple cameras malfunctioned simultaneously, producing no tapes whatsoever. It's far more likely the tapes disappeared because they supported the claim of Mount Carmel residents, all of whom insisted the ATF fired first.

Even worse, no written reports were filed by any agents on the field of battle, a startling reversal of ATF policy. Later, when agents were questioned about the skirmish, interviews had to be canceled because they were producing evidence favorable to the defendants inside Mount Carmel.

Today, the ATF tells a much different story: "We were ambushed by a hail of machine-gun fire the moment we got off the cattle cars." This explanation doesn't hold up. Koresh had no machine guns, and photos reveal Mount Carmel heavily peppered with bullet holes, while the vehicles used as cover by the ATF bear no signs of incoming fire.

Dr. Alan Stone, a Harvard psychiatrist and law expert hired by the government to write a report on Waco, concluded: "If they were militants determined to ambush and kill as many ATF agents as possible, it seemed to me that given their firepower, the devastation could have been even worse... the agents brought to the compound in cattle cars could have been cattle going to slaughter if the Branch Davidians had taken full advantage of their tactical superiority."

Tragically, the fact that four ATF agents died while attempting the initial "dynamic entry" calls into suspicion any statements made by agents at the scene. Why? Because "testi-lying" (fabricating evidence against suspected criminals in order to obtain convictions) has become a standard operating procedure for police agencies, and an unofficial wall of silence protects police engaged in vigilante retribution against cop-killers. Many law enforcement officers will always believe Koresh and his followers got what they deserved, and if it requires a few lies to make it stand up in court, who cares?

The Siege
The FBI brought in 10 Bradley fighting vehicles, two Abrams tanks and a multitude of other armored vehicles. Shortwave radio and cell phones were electronically jammed. The only contact out was the single phone line the FBI ran from Mount Carmel to FBI negotiators off-site.

Koresh requested that Robert Rodriquez be installed as a negotiator, a logical choice since they already had established a relationship. The request was denied. Instead, the FBI created a team of revolving negotiators, none of whom developed any sensitivity to Seventh Day Adventist doctrine. FBI negotiators dismissed all religious talk as "Bible babble," not realizing Bible quotations were perhaps the best tool for bringing the residents out.

Early on, Koresh agreed to voluntarily surrender if a one-hour tape explaining his theology was aired on national radio. However, the night before, the residents had dug out the medicinal whiskey supply and held a party in the chapel while he lay wounded upstairs. Koresh abruptly canceled the surrender by saying God had told him to wait. "Some of us blamed the previous night's binge, saying we'd sinned and acted wildly," writes Thibodeau.

The FBI responded angrily and began a psychological war, playing loud music and the sounds of animals being tortured. Searchlights beamed into the building during the night. "Every time we thought we were cooperating, people were coming out, or we were doing what they'd asked, we'd be punished, almost right after complying," says Clive Doyle, one of the survivors. "The electricity being cut off, the music being played, all that kind of stuff just gave us the attitude they certainly did not mean what they were promising, that we couldn't trust them. All the things that went on for the next fifty-odd days just confirmed in our minds they had no concern for our children at all."

During the siege, snipers routinely mooned women with their exposed buttocks. They also gave the finger to the men inside and loudly called them "cocksuckers" and "motherfuckers," behavior that contributed to the residents' impression that they were surrounded by an immoral force sent by Babylon. Meanwhile, the tanks and armored vehicles circled Mount Carmel, crushing cars, trampling graves, destroying property and contaminating the crime scene.

During the siege, 35 residents voluntarily left Mount Carmel, mostly children and the elderly. The elderly were immediately put in chains and treated like hardened criminals, while the children were fed candy and other junk food. Most of the people remaining inside became convinced surrender was not a viable option by watching how the FBI treated those exiting Mount Carmel.

On April 15, after the residents celebrated several days of Passover, Koresh informed the FBI that God had given him permission to write down his interpretation of the Seven Seals, a major breakthrough since he had never written down any of his philosophy. He feverishly went to work on the manuscript. As soon as it was done, he planned to surrender. His aides expected the work to be completed within a week.

But the mood of the FBI had turned permanently sour. Residents were no longer able to peacefully surrender after April 15. Instead, anyone who left the compound was immediately subjected to a barrage of deadly flash-bang grenades. Apparently, the cost of keeping so much law enforcement personnel and equipment at the site (estimated at $500,000 per day) had reached the limit. Deep inside the bowels of the federal government, a final solution was being hatched for the Students of the Seven Seals.

The Final Solution

In January, 1993, the United States and 130 other countries signed the Chemical Weapons Convention banning the use of CS gas in warfare. Use of this toxic chemical had been condemned by everyone from Amnesty International to the US Army.

On April 14, 1993, the Department of Justice secretly flew in two military officers, Brigadier General Paul J. Shoomaker and Colonel William "Jerry" Boykin, then Commander of Delta Force (B Squadron) Special Ops at Ft. Bragg, North Carolina. They were flown by FBI transport to Waco to "assess the situation," then flown to Washington to meet Attorney General Janet Reno, to discuss "contingency plans that may be used to bring the situation in Waco to an end," according to an Army Operations Command memo obtained by WorldNetDaily in August, 1999.

On Saturday, April 17, Reno suddenly agreed to the use of CS gas in ending the Waco siege. She would later offer several reasons for approving the gas attack: Intelligence had indicated Koresh was sexually abusing the children, armed militia from around the country were converging on Mount Carmel to free the residents, the perimeter had become unstable and, finally, the agents at the scene were suffering from fatigue.

At 6 A.M. on April 19, while it was still dark, the huge speakers began broadcasting a new message to the 83 people inside. "The siege is over. We're going to put tear gas into the building. The tear gas is harmless, but it will make your environment uninhabitable. You are under arrest. Come out now with your hands up. There will be no shooting. This is not an assault."

From several sides at once, M60A1 tanks modified for demolition began punching holes into the walls of Mount Carmel. According to the plan signed off on by Reno, this phase of the gas attack was supposed to continue for 48 hours if necessary. However, in the fine print of the plan, the part Reno may not have read, rapid escalation of the attack was approved if tanks drew fire from the residents. Within a few minutes, four BV tanks began firing ferret rounds into the building. Four hundred canisters had been stockpiled for the attack. Ninety minutes later, they had practically expended the supply. They put out an emergency request for more canisters.

"By noon the building is a tinderbox," writes Thibodeau. "A thick layer of methylene chloride dust deposited by the CS gas coats the walls, floors, and ceilings, mingling with kerosene and propane vapors from our spilled lanterns and crushed heaters. To make things worse, a brisk, thirty-knot Texas wind whips through the holes ripped in the building like a potbellied stove with its damper flung open."

Shortly after two pyrotechnic ferret rounds were fired into the house, one in the rear and one in the front, two fireballs raced through the building. Within seconds, the entire structure was in flames. According to the survivors, the only logical exit for most people was through the cafeteria. Most of the women and children were huddled in a concrete vault nearby. The children had no gas masks, so they sought shelter under wet blankets. When people tried to exit, they were driven back into the building by sniper fire. With their escape route cut off, they roasted alive.

Nine residents survived, all of whom emerged from locations visible to the telephoto lenses of the network TV cameras. The presence of those cameras may explain why they survived, unlike the unfortunate ones who attempted to exit through the rear.

Fire trucks were available to put out the blaze, but were held back and not allowed near the scene until nothing but ashes were left. Meanwhile, the tanks ran over bodies and pushed debris into the fire to make sure nothing remained standing. Texas Rangers, who were not allowed near the scene until much later in the day, believed the FBI was salting phony evidence while destroying the crime scene to make an investigation impossible. What little evidence did remain disappeared quickly.

In the midst of the smoke and dust, the ATF flag was run up the Mount Carmel flagpole, signaling victory. Meanwhile, the official press release went out: "The cult set fire to the building and committed mass suicide rather than surrender."

Dr. Nizam Peerwani, medical examiner for Tarrant County, was in charge of the autopsies. Although 21 people appeared to have died from gunshot wounds, all bullet fragments were immediately confiscated by the FBI and never subjected to independent analysis. Many of the bodies were decapitated or mutilated beyond recognition. According to the official report, "There was a particular instance where all that remained was the arm and hand of a mother clasping a small child's hand and remains of an arm. You could see how tightly the child's hand was being squeezed by the mother." The body of one charred six-year-old was bent backward until the head almost touched the feet, the result of CS gas suffocation. Two fetuses died instantly, expelled after their mothers' death. The major question unanswered: How many residents killed themselves to avoid being roasted alive, and how many were massacred by snipers as they tried to flee the building?

The Cover-Up

The government engineered a slam-dunk cover-up almost immediately. A blatantly biased judge was selected for the criminal trial, held in San Antonio in 1993. "The government is not on trial here," he would say repeatedly. Eleven members of the community were charged with the murder of the ATF agents, but the evidence against them was weak. The judge gave the jury 67 pages of instructions on how to render a verdict. After four days of deliberations, the jury found all 11 not guilty of murder or conspiracy to commit murder. Four were found guilty of manslaughter, with four others convicted on weapons charges. The jury felt none of the defendants deserved long prison terms, and they expected another trial to take place, one for the architects of the original assault plan.

The judge ignored the jury. He accused the defendants of firing the first shots and setting the fire and proceeded to sentence four defendants to 40 years, one to 20 years, one to 15, one to 10 and one to five. The jury was outraged. During appeals, all sentences were greatly reduced.

Thanks to the work of independent investigators, the cover-up began unraveling as numerous assertions by ATF, FBI and Janet Reno kept turning up false. They claimed no pyrotechnic rounds were fired by the FBI during the siege or gas attack. They claimed no Delta Force assassins were on site. None of these assertions would hold up under scrutiny.

Journalists like Dick Reavis were paraded in front of Congress and lambasted for showing sympathy for Koresh and his community. The sickening bias of Congress is clear in the award-winning documentary,

Waco: The Rules of Engagement. The most damaging evidence uncovered by the filmmakers was an infrared videotape shot from a helicopter during the CS gas attack, which revealed two snipers firing into the cafeteria.

After the initial cover-up failed to hold, Reno appointed former Senator John Danforth (R-MO) to conduct an "independent investigation," which lasted 14 months, employed 74 people and cost $17 million. The investigation sifted through 2.3 million documents, interviewed 1,001 witnesses and examined thousands of pounds of physical evidence. Danforth stated emphatically that "the government did not start or spread the fire... did not direct gunfire at the Davidians, and did not unlawfully employ the Armed Forces of the United States." The report is a morass of obfuscation, utilizing Orwellian doublespeak at every turn.

In the preface, Danforth stated he investigated whether the government engaged in "bad acts, not bad judgment." He noted 61% of the country, according to a *Time* magazine poll, believes the government started the fire, a matter of grave concern. Instead of seeking truth, he set out to calm the citizenry. "When 61% of the people believe that the government not only fails to ensure life, liberty and the pursuit of happiness, but also intentionally murders people by fire, the existence of public consent, the very basis of government, is imperiled."

Only one man was criminally charged by Danforth: William Johnston, a former assistant US attorney in Waco who helped draw up the original warrant and was one of the three lead prosecutors in the San Antonio trial. He was indicted on five felony counts and threatened with 21 months in jail.

Apparently, Johnston's real "crime" had been to allow filmmakers into an evidence locker, where they discovered pyrotechnic rounds mislabeled as "silencers." Later, he came forward and admitted he'd lied by saying no pyrotechnic rounds had been fired into Mount Carmel. Johnston quietly worked out a plea-bargain agreement that resulted in no jail time.

The ATF fired Charles Sarabyn and Phillip Chojnacki, two of the raid's commanders. But when the agents threatened to sue, they were reinstated with back pay. ATF director Stephen Higgins was eventually forced to resign, and Deputy Director Daniel Hartnett and two other ranking ATF officials were temporarily suspended. However, one of them, ATF intelligence chief David Troy, was later promoted.

Today, the Internet is filled with contradictory statements about the massacre, and the survivors have split into several camps. The cover-up continues, and some Websites are undoubtedly counterintelligence operations designed to confuse the American people.

The most frightening development, the militarization of our police force, continues unabated. Today, every major police department in America has hired and outfitted a squad of professional snipers like those brought in for the final solution at Waco.

ART AFTER MIDNIGHT

When life gets unacceptably grim, people make fun of it. At least that's what happened in France during the Reign of Terror when a bizarre sub-culture known as *Les Incroyables* ("The Incredibles") appeared. Although barely remembered today, *Les Incroyables* were famous for an eccentric style of dress (which parodied the excesses of the deposed aristocracy), short, unkempt hairstyles ("Hair á la Victime") and a fondness for wrapping scarfs and bandages around their necks.

In the late '70s, life was almost equally distressing. The first generation to grow up under the specter of nuclear annihilation angrily came of age in an era of diminishing expectations. It was in this atmosphere that a rock club called CBGB opened in New York's East Village. The local music scene began undergoing a renaissance and a group of unknown artists moved into the neighborhood. Although they sprang from varied backgrounds, the artists shared a collective media-drenched conscious-ness, the heritage of the suburban teenager. In the '60s, this pampered upbringing was frequently a source of guilt, but in the '70s, it was dis-sected and rearranged, and eventually regurgitated into new forms.

CBGB launched the punk movement, and it's no coincidence that many of the early punks looked like survivors from a nuclear holocaust. Although routinely scorned by the press, the punks gave vivid reality to anxieties that had become submerged in the national psyche. Then Ronald Reagan was elected President on a hard-line, anti-Communist campaign. The election provoked an outbreak of doomsday fever across the country. For those who felt the world situation was getting increas-ingly hopeless, throwing a party seemed like an appropriate response. It was so appropriate, in fact, that it turned into a four-year-long binge that a lot of people attended: punk rockers, hip hoppers, new wavers, per-formance artists, fashion designers and drag queens. When it was over, the East Village had changed forever. Underground ideas became mar-ketable commodities, blatant careerism was in fashion, and young painters began to be treated like emerging rock stars.

CBGB & OMFUG

"Punks started as an attitude that celebrated American culture and the teenager as the Master Race. Punks were not asexual, faggot, hippie, bloodsucking ignorant scum as the media would have you believe."

—Legs McNeil, *The Punk Manifesto*

Tom Miller and Richard Lloyd, two aspiring, unemployed rock guitarists, were walking home through the East Village one afternoon in 1975 when they passed an anonymous bar on the corner of Bleecker and Bowery and decided to stop in for a drink. They entered a long, windowless room with a bar on one side, a stage on the other and a pool table in the back. The walls were peeling; the floor was littered with broken glass. The bar stools were filled with winos.

Miller and Lloyd took an immediate interest in the stage, which didn't seem to be in current use, even though it had a PA system. At the time it was difficult for struggling rock bands to find a place to perform. The Mercer Arts Center, a conglomerate of theaters and performance spaces that launched the New York Dolls and several other recent bands, had been condemned after a neighboring hotel collapsed. That left only Club 82, a hangout for transvestites and glitter bands at Second Avenue and East Fourth Street, and Max's Kansas City, the original home of the Velvet Underground. The rock scene seemed to be dying and bands were getting desperate for new venues. Under the circumstances, even a seedy bar on Skid Row seemed appealing.

Miller approached the bartender. "We're in a band," he said, "and we'd like to play here."

"What kind of music do you play?" asked the bartender.

"Well," said Miller, "whatta ya like?"

"Irish folk music."

"Yeah, we play that," lied Miller.

On the basis of this conversation, the band Television got its second gig in New York and the owner of the bar, Hilly Kristal, decided to rename his establishment in the hope of attracting a more upscale clientele. A burly ex-farm boy from New Jersey, Kristal was unsure what sort of music he should feature, so he picked a name designed to cover a lot of territory: Country, Bluegrass, Blues and Other Music for Uplifting Gourmandizers. Later on, he mercifully shortened it to CBGB & OMFUG.

Not too many people were coming down to the East Village in those days. Overrun by heroin addicts and drug dealers in the mid-'60s, the neighborhood was scarred by endless rows of abandoned tenement buildings—many of which had been torched and gutted, and were now functioning as "shooting galleries." The European immigrants and bohemians who had previously lent the community an Old World aura had been displaced by impoverished blacks and Hispanics. It was a dangerous place for white kids from the suburbs to be hanging out, but it also had the cheapest apartments in the city—which made it a haven for starving rock musicians, many of whom began congregating at CBGB.

A year earlier, Miller had formed a group called the Neon Boys with a friend from high school named Richard Meyers, who was now Television's bass player. Both had adopted stage names. Miller was calling himself "Verlaine," after a French symbolist poet, but Meyers wanted something a little more sinister and settled on the last name "Hell."

Television began playing CBGB on a weekly basis and was soon joined at the club by several other bands, including Patti Smith, Blondie and the Ramones. Although all four bands were distinctively different in sound and appearance, there were some connections between them. For example, Television opened each show with a rowdy rendition of "Fire Engine" by the Thirteenth Floor Elevators, a psychedelic garage band from Texas whose popularity peaked around 1967. Hundreds of garage bands had emerged across the country in the mid-'60s, and even though they experienced only a fleeting moment of success, their amateur enthusiasm was exerting a strong influence on the music of the '70s. In 1971, Lenny Kaye, Patti Smith's lead guitarist and a former rock journalist with a master's degree in American history, compiled an album for Elektra records that documented the emergence of this genre. Titled *Nuggets*, Kaye's record included songs by the Seeds, the Standells, the Shadows of Night and other seminal bands of the period.

"The garage bands were really naïve and innocent and just wanted to be a part of rock'n'roll so badly," says Kaye. "They were more at home practicing for a teen dance than going out on national tour."

By the time *Nuggets* appeared, bands had already begun self-consciously imitating the garage sound, which, in the true spirit of rock, rejected musical virtuosity in favor of raw teenage emotion and fuzzy guitar solos. (According to Kaye, the first of these revivalist groups was a California band called the Droogs. A few years later, another garage revivalist band called the Fleshtones formed in the East Village.) "A lot of interest in the garage bands grew out of the rock fanzine movement of the early seventies," says Kaye. "A whole cult developed around the groups." *Creem* magazine, a leading promoter of the music, named it "punk rock" and identified the MC5, Iggy Pop and the New York Dolls as true standard-bearers of the garage sensibility.

It was, however, only the beginning for punk rock, and the garage bands represented only one component of an emerging aesthetic that worshiped the sleazy underbelly of American consumer culture. '50s baby-boomers who had grown up on a diet of comic books, *Mad Magazine*, science fiction novels, illegal drugs, grade-B horror films and Saturday morning cartoon shows suddenly decided they much preferred *The Gong Show* to *Masterpiece Theater*, an attitude that had found early champions at *Creem*, especially in writer Lester Bangs. However, the sensibility didn't fully mature until 1975, when a new magazine centered around the CBGB scene appeared, a magazine appropriately titled *Punk*.

Punk magazine was founded by a 22-year-old graduate of the School of Visual Arts (SVA) named John Holmstrom, who was born and raised in a typical middle-class suburb in Cheshire, Connecticut. Among Holmstrom's early influences were Spiderman comics, *Creem* and the rock band Alice Cooper. While at SVA, he studied with Harvey Kurtzman, one of the principal architects behind *Mad Comics* (which later evolved into *Mad* magazine), and began drawing an autobiographical cartoon strip called "Joe."

"The East Village was really dead in those days," says Holmstrom. "The junkies had taken over. The talk on the street was that the city was going to tear down the whole neighborhood." After graduating, Holmstrom moved back to Cheshire, where he met Legs McNeil, an old friend from high school who convinced him to return to New York and start a magazine. They rented a storefront on 30th Street and 10th Avenue and went to work. McNeil invented the magazine's name and became its "resident punk." "We were going to CBGB all through the summer of 1975 and after I saw the Ramones, I was convinced something was happening," says Holmstrom.

Punk found its perfect incarnation in four guys from Queens, all in their early twenties, who dressed in black motorcycle jackets (a throwback to Marlon Brando's look in *The Wild One*), frayed jeans and long, shaggy haircuts. Outspokenly anti-hippie, the band reveled in American trash culture and parodied right-wing sensibilities so effectively many rock critics labeled them as fascists. Their music was short, fast and loud. Performances rarely lasted more than 20 minutes. Song lyrics discussed such matters as glue-sniffing and the band's favorite film (*The Texas Chainsaw Massacre*). Although dismissed by many as a one-joke band, the Ramones (along with Patti Smith and a few others) were consciously trying to resuscitate rock music, which had been virtually obliterated by the success of such laid-back groups as the Eagles and Linda Ronstadt. Naturally, they considered the mechanical, manufactured sound of disco (then the most popular music in New York) even more offensive.

The first issue of *Punk* appeared on January 1, 1976, with Lou Reed on the cover. Inside was an essay on Brando, who was acknowledged as the original punk. Page two contained a strident editorial: "Death to Disco Shit. Long live the Rock! Kill yourself. Jump off a fuckin' cliff. Drive nails into your head. Become a robot and join the staff at Disneyland. OD. Anything. Just don't listen to discoshit. I've seen the canned crap take real live people and turn them into dogs! And vice versa. The epitome of all that's wrong with Western Civilization is disco."

Although the first issue contained several standard interviews and essays, as well as a number of comic strips, the entire text, interviews and all, was lettered by hand, like a comic book. The Ramones were featured in the centerfold spread. "We love bubble gum [music] and hard rock, especially Elvis Presley," said Tommy Ramone. "I like comic books," added Dee Dee Ramone, "especially anything with swastikas in it, like Enemy Ace, which is very hard to get." In order to better define his magazine's sensibility, Holmstrom began listing important influences in the "Top 99," a parody of the record charts found in most rock magazines. The column was left open for just about anything, including current trends, TV shows and movies, and readers were encouraged to mail in suggestions. The Ramones (Holmstrom's favorite band) held an unwavering grip on the number-one slot for several years, but other frequent entries included: Lester Bangs, Dead Boys, Patti Smith, Lenny Kaye's *Nuggets*, LSD, Sex, Batman, Blondie, Alan Suicide, vodka, *The Gong Show*, Iggy Pop, Soupy Sales, *The Flintstones*, *The Three Stooges*, Richard Hell,

William Burroughs and Budweiser.

Needless to say, *Punk* magazine came as something of a shock to many East Village residents, a number of whom were aging hippies. "In the early days there were never more than twenty people at CBGB," recalls Roberta Bayley, who worked the door and later became a photographer for *Punk* magazine. "The night Patti Smith played was the big night we made three hundred dollars, which seemed like a lot of money."

A groupie scene quickly developed at the club, and many of the arrivals were refugees from earlier scenes—Max's, Mercer Arts Center, Club 82. "We knew glitter wasn't what we were supposed to be doing anymore," says Animal X, a freelance clothes designer. "But many of us were still into glamour and a lot of girls were having this problem, to find something glamorous but still tough. I used to wear a lot of leopard and '50s things. I never finished the edges and I'd tear them sometimes. I called it the just-been-raped look. I went out a couple of times with live cockroaches glued to my ears instead of earrings. We made things out of bones, animal heads. The idea was to shock people."

Several of the regulars, including Animal X and Anya Phillips, began go-go dancing and stripping at Times Square porno clubs to support their musician boyfriends. Phillips, a short, plump Taiwanese girl began dressing in black leather and studs, a look that had been pioneered by the Velvet Underground 10 years earlier. S&M attire gradually became more popular at the club. "Anya gave the impression of being a frivolous person," says Bayley. "She dressed really outrageously and seemed like a hanger-on. But she began having great tea parties for women at her apartment and I discovered she was really very talented at designing clothes."

"A lot of women didn't like Anya because she was manipulative," says Animal X. "Anya was a user, but she always gave something in return. She encouraged people to do things. I also remember she really liked LSD. One time after she took it, she crawled out of her apartment, crawled downstairs, hailed a cab, crawled into the cab and asked the driver to take her to Cuba."

In 1976, Richard Hell left Television and formed a group called the Heartbreakers with two former members of the New York Dolls. Within a few months, an enterprising clothing boutique owner from England named Malcolm McLaren (who had briefly managed the Dolls and had been hanging around CBGB) invited Hell to front a band he was forming.

Hell declined the offer and McLaren returned to England and hired Johnny "Rotten" Lydon instead. After the Heartbreakers broke up, Hell formed the Voidoids and wrote a song to sum up the spirit of the times. America had previously given birth to the lost, Beat and love generations and was now slipping into an economic depression. The country had never really recovered from losing its first war and having its President resign in disgrace. With the idealism of the '60s fading into the background, "The Blank Generation" struck Hell as an appropriate title for a punk rock anthem. "It was an assertion of the formless, inarticulate anger of ignored youth," says Hell, who adds: "I also wanted to get rich and get laid."

Amos Poe, an Israeli-born freelance photographer, became friends with Ivan Kral, a guitarist in the Patti Smith Group, and together they made a pair of 16mm films on life at CBGB. The first was called *Night Lunch* and the second *The Blank Generation*, after Hell's song. Out of synch, often out of focus, poorly edited and practically unintelligible, *The Blank Generation* nevertheless became a cult classic, probably because it was the only documentation available on the early days at the club. In July 1977, Tish and Snookie Bellamo, two sisters from the Bronx, opened Manic Panic on St. Marks Place, New York's first punk rock store. Within a few months, several other punk boutiques opened in the area.

The music world, meanwhile, was gearing up for the coming punk rock explosion. Signed by Sire Records, the Ramones quickly put out an album and toured England, where they came to the attention of several British bar bands who had been keeping a close eye on developments in New York. (Patti Smith, who had already released a record and toured extensively in both Europe and the United States, later told reporters she felt like Paul Revere, traveling through the countryside shouting at kids to wake up.) After English youth discovered *Punk* magazine, several similar English fanzines appeared, the most popular of which was titled *Sniffin' Glue*.

In less than a year, England virtually co-opted the punk rock movement, a development that was not really surprising considering that unemployment, immigration and festering social problems had created a large, disaffected teenage population in that country. Since they had less to lose, British youth were more willing to adopt a lifestyle initially viewed as too negative and extreme by many American teenagers. Much of the success of English punk rock can also be credited to the uncanny media manipulations of McLaren, creator of the Sex Pistols. Fashion was an essential component of punk and no one exploited its symbolic power with more skill than McLaren, who was operating a London boutique called Sex, a store that sold many items inspired by the owner's frequent trips to CBGB. Although nihilism was rampant in both branches of punk, the English bands tended to be more sophisticated about politics. Drinking was a far more popular topic at CBGB.

Meanwhile, events were stirring in the SoHo art district, located only a few blocks southwest of CBGB. Although the two neighborhoods were in close proximity, they were miles apart in aesthetics. This would soon change. In 1975, the art scene, like the music scene, was desperately in need of an overhaul. Painting had been pronounced dead and most dealers had shut their doors to new artists, turning their galleries into nearly impenetrable fortresses. As is often the case in such close-knit communities, the work was growing stale and tired. Minimalism, the foremost sensibility of the '60s, had been exhausted and was followed by a proliferation of mini-movements: earth art, body art, conceptual art, video art, feminist art, decorative art, fetish art and many others. Although some critics applauded this pluralism, others were clearly disappointed by a lack of enthusiasm pervading much of the work. In the mid-'70s, however, a new generation of artists emerged, one that was working on live performance instead of painting, and many critics felt their work showed considerable promise.

In 1975, the first comprehensive exhibit of this new work was organized by Edit deAk, an Albanian refugee, art critic and co-founder of *Art Rite*, an influential art magazine published between 1972 and 1978. Held at Artists Space, the show was titled Person into Persona. Because the genre didn't have a generally recognized title, deAk spent three days trying to write a press release for the event. "I finally settled on the word 'performance,'" she says. "Laurie Anderson was a very important pioneer. Her piece in the show was an extended metaphor for water. She was wearing ice skates on a block of ice, which timed the length of the performance, and she already had a voice-distortion device, but a very primitive one. Before Laurie, performance was being done by these tough guys, like Vito Acconci. It was 'hate me, hate me.' Laurie completely reversed that—she was a suction cup for love." The shows were held in the early evening and afterward everyone went to Barney's, a tiny bar in TriBeCa.

Although the English already had a long history of art students turning into rock stars (an exhaustive list that includes members of the Beatles, the Rolling Stones and Roxy Music), it wasn't until the mid-'70s that the idea seemed to take hold in New York. In 1976, three graduates of the Rhode Island School of Design performed at the Kitchen, an alternative space that was cultivating the new performance artists. The trio called themselves Talking Heads (a television term for news and talk programs). However, since rock music was still offensive to many in the art world, a catalogue published by the Kitchen explained the group's appearance in rather delicate terms: "Talking Heads is a group of performance artists whose medium is rock and roll music and the pursuant 'band' organization and visual presentation. The original music and lyrics are structured within the commercial accessibility of rock and roll sound and contemporary popular language. Described as a cross between Ralph Nader, Lou Reed and Tony Perkins, lead singer David Byrne dresses like the proletariat everyman and relies on Chris Frantz and Martina Weymouth to complete their anti-individualist stance as a group concept."

"When I came to New York I guess I was very naïve," Byrne later told a reporter for *Art News.* "I expected the art world to be very pure and noble. I was repulsed by what I saw people putting themselves through, the hustling to try to get anywhere. My natural reaction was to move into a world that had no pretense of nobility. Since I'd always fooled around with a guitar, I formed a rock band. When Talking Heads took off, I didn't have any more time for my art projects. I guess I consider the band my art project, although I hate to put any kind of label on it. Using the word 'art' tends to scare people off."

Since the members of Talking Heads weren't entirely comfortable with the art world, they migrated over to CBGB. No one knew it at the time, but they were forging a path from SoHo to the East Village which would soon be trod by many others. Once at CBGB, the group toned down its art-student rhetoric considerably. Unlike the Ramones, they didn't attract flocks of groupies, but the audience seemed to enjoy seeing a band dressed in Oxford shirts and chinos that sang songs about life in the middle class. Byrne's tortured stage persona reminded some of a suburban nerd gone mad, and the group's best song from the period had a title guaranteed to appeal to the punk sensibility in anyone: "Psycho Killer." (In writing the lyrics, Byrne may have been influenced by one of the greatest garage songs of all time, "Psycho" by the Sonics.) "Talking Heads jerry-built their own version of Top Forty bubble gum—absurd, exuberantly naïve little anthems to perseverance and confusion, mixed in with covers such as the 1910 Fruitgum Company's "1, 2, 3 Red Light," wrote music critic Tom Carson. "It was weirdly liberating."

Although some artists were switching over to rock, others were searching for new ways to raise money. Grant-raising became a major preoccupation for many. In 1977, Michael McClard, Alan Moore, James Nares and Robin Winters founded Collaborative Projects (Colab), correctly assuming they would have less difficulty obtaining grants if they applied collectively. Membership quickly swelled to several dozen. Diego Cortez, an early member, looks back on the era with regret. "As far as I'm concerned they should stop all funding for the arts," says Cortez bitterly. "Look who gets the money: the professional art administrators! I hate the whole Colab aesthetic. They were fake radicals. There was a new aesthetic coming but they missed it. So did Laurie Anderson. These people were straddling the seventies. I abandoned ship. I gave up ten years of art training and my whole career in the art business and started hanging out at CBGB."

A handful of Colab members joined Cortez at the club, including Nares, a performance artist and painter who had recently moved to New York from England. "I'd been starving for music my first couple of years in New York," says Nares. "But when I went to CBGB I got really excited about music again. I got into the whole thing very quickly—dying my hair red one week and shaving it off the next. We consciously stood against what was happening in SoHo." Cortez introduced Nares to another refugee from the TriBeCa scene, a saxophone player named James Siegfried, who had been prowling around the fringes of SoHo wearing a prominent scowl of disapproval and a full-length leather coat. Seigfried soon changed his name to James Chance and formed a band called the Contortions.

In 1977, both Nares and Chance moved into tenement apartments on East Third Street, which was rapidly becoming the center of a new scene. Tina Lhotsky, John Lurie, David McDermott, Eric Mitchell and Patti Astor were among those who had recently moved onto the block. "We were all jamming together, playing music and working on each other's Super 8 films," says Nares. When the Contortions played Max's Kansas City that summer, Chance surprised his band members by sauntering into the audience and punching a few people. It wasn't an entirely original gesture—Iggy Pop had done it several years earlier—but it made for a great show.

Due in part to Chance's well-publicized stage antics, the Contortions quickly became a known attraction in the neighborhood. One night at CBGB, Chance met his future manager and lover, Anya Phillips. "Anya was the single most important spirit and inventor of half the things that went down in those days," says deAk. "She was very influential for Deborah Harry [of Blondie], who definitely needed to punk out. Anya had the troops with her, the wild girls from the Midwest: Lydia Lunch, Pat Place, Adele Bertei. Third Street was where it was glued and blasted, even before it went to CBGB. When I think of those holy short moments when art happens—I think of that Third Street moment."

Meanwhile, the national media was relentlessly attacking and ridiculing the punk movement. Sire Records, the company that had signed many of the original groups from CBGB, began an aggressive campaign to replace the word "punk" with a less threatening term: "New Wave." However, just as this was happening, the film *Saturday Night Fever* was released. The movie launched disco as the most popular music in America, and suddenly punk-bashing became a popular sport for out-of-town teenagers visiting the East Village. "A lot of people told us to change our name," says Holmstrom. "They said the punk thing was over. The amount of anti-punk sentiment was incredible. There was a rumor that President Carter said, 'stop this punk thing' during a jazz festival on the White House lawn."

Despite these problems, Holmstrom brought out a special issue titled "Mutant Monster Beach Party," which many consider his masterpiece. The entire issue was devoted to a parody of beach party and monster movies in the form of a film script written by Holmstrom, McNeil and Joey Ramone. The cast included the Ramones, Deborah Harry, Andy Warhol, Anya Phillips, John Cale, Lester Bangs, David Johansen, Edith Massey and many others, all of whom agreed to be photographed acting out scenes from the script. "People like it now, but the issue died on the stands," says Holmstrom. *Punk* lost its publisher and was on the verge of collapse. With the end of publication in sight, Holmstrom responded in his next issue with one of his funniest cartoon strips—"Disco Maniac," *Punk*'s answer to *Saturday Night Fever*. The strip showed the interior of a disco (patterned after Studio 54) filled with bald-headed men dressed in jogging shorts, running shoes and muscle T-shirts. The issue also included a review of CBGB, which had lost favor with the magazine's staff. "This shithole sucks," wrote the reviewer. "It's been going downhill since it opened to rock. Now most people who go there are hippies, fags and heroin addicts trying to get their name in the papers."

The review was really an attack on the club's second generation of bands, a group billing itself as "No Wave." Led by the Contortions, Teenage Jesus and the Jerks, Mars and DNA, the No Wave groups were the most experimental rock bands to appear since the Velvet Underground. With songs like "I Don't Want to Be Happy," and "Contort Yourself," Chance began fusing the angry energy of punk rock with the minimalist funk of James Brown. He played howling, free-form saxophone solos and often gave electrifying performances.

No Wave was far too grating and dissonant to find a wide audience, despite the fact that the bands were taken seriously in some quarters of the art world. In 1978, deAk invited six No Wave bands to perform at Artists Space, an event that had a profound impact on artists and musicians who had not yet acknowledged the importance of punk. Soon afterward, many people began looking for signs of punk in the art world. They didn't have to look far. In April 1978, the first punk art exhibit was held in Washington, D.C., sponsored by the Washington Project for the Arts and organized by Marc Miller and Bettie Ringma with the assistance of Alice Denney.

"It was just supposed to be a collaboration between *Punk* magazine and us with some photographs by Marcia Resnick taken at CBGB," says Miller. "But the show got immense press coverage. All these artists suddenly wanted to get involved and the project kept escalating. A lot of people from New York came down to the opening." A catalogue for the show addressed such issues as, "Does punk art exist, and if so, how serious is it?", a question which was posed to such diverse artists as Neke Carson, John Holmstrom, Steven Kramer, Tina Lhostky, Tom Otterness, Alan Vega and Andy Warhol. The more intelligent answers sidestepped the issue entirely. When told that he invented punk art, Warhol replied, "No, we just knew a few drag queens."

"The punks were totally anti-art," recalls Cortez. "When Anya Phillips would introduce me to her friends at CBGB as an artist from SoHo, they would turn the other way." However, in the next three years these barriers would crumble. The most significant artists of the next generation would emerge from the clubs instead of the galleries—Jean-Michel Basquiat (Bas-ski-ya) from the Mudd Club, and Keith Haring and Kenny Scharf from Club 57.

NEW WAVE VAUDEVILLE

At David McDermott's tenement building on Avenue C there is no telephone, no electricity and very little in the way of modern conveniences. Although the apartment is cluttered with antique furniture, stuffed animals, photographs and assorted memorabilia, it's difficult to find a single object produced after 1920. The Victrola phonograph which sits in one corner dates from 1903. The walking stick with the solid gold handle mounted on the wall dates from 1880. In fact, the newest thing in the apartment—with the exception of McDermott himself—seems to be the Victorian revival wallpaper, which dates from the mid-1930s. It is April 28, 1985, and McDermott and his companion Peter McGough have just held their first painting exhibit at the Massimo Audiello Gallery. The paintings were executed on antique canvas and dated from 1884. Although the dates vary, all paintings made by McDermott and McGough are predated, usually something close to the turn of the century but occasionally as far off as A.D. 200. They think of themselves as time travelers.

McDermott enters the room and sits on a couch. He carries himself elegantly on a thin, wiry frame and his hair is greased and parted in the center. His long neck protrudes from an antique robe. Although he was a member of the original Third Street crowd, McDermott looks as if he'd be more comfortable in the pages of a novel by F. Scott Fitzgerald than hanging around a punk rock club. Nevertheless, he made his debut in the downtown scene in 1978, with an appearance in the New Wave Vaudeville show. That same year he starred in several underground films, including *Rome 78* and *The Long Island Four*. He is high-strung and excitable and speaks in a squeaky soprano voice.

"My opening number in New Wave Vaudeville had an Egyptian theme," he recalls while pouring a cup of tea. "It was a commercial attempt to cash in on the King Tut exhibit at the Metropolitan Museum. We were trying to be commercial then because we were sick of being poor. Everyone in the East Village was starving. Punk didn't work because the mechanism for failure was built into it."

Although McDermott admits New Wave Vaudeville was underappreciated and underfinanced (lasting only four performances with no one getting paid), he also believes it contributed to a shift away from the hardcore punk sensibility toward one that was considerably less destructive. It accomplished this by combining elements of pop culture, futurism, revivalism and gay cabaret, and by bringing together a wide range of performers, some of whom had only recently arrived in New York. Even more important, a few months after the show closed, the producers (Tom Scully and Susan Hannaford) teamed up with the director (Ann Magnuson) and organized Club 57, which continued exploring this aesthetic and eventually helped launch a number of important artistic careers.

McDermott was born in 1951 in Hollywood, California. He is the son of a Yugoslavian-Jewish father who survived a Nazi concentration camp and an upper-middle-class mother with roots in the Old South. The marriage dissolved soon after his birth and McDermott's mother moved with him back to New Jersey, remarried and settled in Teaneck. At an early age, McDermott developed a fascination for Nazi memorabilia. After high school, he enrolled at Syracuse University, where he developed a passion for collecting antiques. Around 1970, McDermott joined a campaign to keep nuclear reactors out of the Hudson River Valley, painting posters that depicted farmers tilling their fields with a mushroom cloud looming in the background. He was living in a small house in the country without electricity and offered to host a press conference for the cause. In preparation for this event, he put a large sign by the road that read, RURAL DE-ELECTRIFICATION PROGRAM, 1928. "I was interested in the effect of tossing an old year into something to throw people off," he explains. Later in the day, he played "You're Driving Me Crazy" by Rudy

Vallee on his wind-up Victrola. Inspired by repeated listenings to the song, he yanked down the power line to his house. "I just wanted to see the pristine beauty of the little house sitting in the middle of the land without this wire going into it," he says. "Little did I know the electricity ran like Chinese Christmas lights into my house and then back again to the next farm. Here I thought I was living like an Amish person, when actually there was this electricity radiating at the corner of my house." By ripping down the line, McDermott had unwittingly disconnected the power for an entire township. Before long the neighbors began arriving. "They came on foot, on horses, on tractors," says McDermott. "Then the police came. Even the liberals I was working with were mad at me. They said I was destroying their plan to stop nuclear power." Fortunately, the police took pity on him and dropped the charges.

While McDermott was enrolled at Syracuse an artist from New York named Richard Merkin visited the school. Merkin was a dapper dresser who wore starched collars and a bowler hat and smoked cigarettes custom-made in Turkey. "He personified what I wanted to be," says McDermott. "I had already established a little society in Syracuse, but Merkin convinced me to move to New York. 'You can be the greatest eccentric of Syracuse,' he said, 'and no one will ever hear of you in Utica.' It struck me as absolutely true, so I began putting everything into moving to New York."

He arrived in 1974 and immediately tried to join the New York art scene. Unfortunately, this task proved more difficult than he'd anticipated. "There were already too many painters coming to New York," he says. "There weren't enough art patrons to go around." To solve this dilemma, McDermott renovated a brownstone apartment on West 82nd Street, filled it with imitation Old Master paintings (which he painted himself) and began posing as a wealthy patron of the arts, although he was earning less than $100 a week as a messenger boy.

Duncan Hannah, a handsome young painter who had recently arrived from Minneapolis to attend the Parsons School of Design, toured the apartment and was so seduced by McDermott's illusion of wealth that he asked McDermott what his father did for a living. "I thought it was very rude to ask something like that," recalls McDermott, "so I told him my father was president of Chase Manhattan Bank." McDermott became Hannah's patron and gave him his first art show at the apartment, printing up invitations and altering full-dress tails for him to wear. According to the invitation, the event was staged in 1952, the year of Hannah's birth. "After the opening, Duncan told some people I was a cheapskate," says McDermott. "He said my champagne wasn't good enough." Appalled by these charges, McDermott decided to abandon his illusionary estate and move to the East Village.

"When I first came to New York, no one cared about painting," says Hannah. "Everyone was trying to get into record company parties. The entourage from the back room at Max's Kansas City held the keys to the city and glitter rock was the big thing." After Hannah graduated from Parsons, he began hanging out at CBGB, where he met the Talking Heads. One night, Warhol came to see the group perform and Hannah and the band were invited to be photographed at Warhol's Factory. "I met David Hockney at a bookstore and we became best friends for five days," says Hannah. "He came to see my work, which was kind of flashy collages, very zeitgeist and trendy. He said nothing, smoked a cigar and drank tea. There was a huge painting on the wall by Steven Kramer, who'd been in a band with me in Minneapolis. It was a portrait of Don Rickles with a knife in his head. Hockney couldn't understand how I could live with such a terrible image. He invited me to an opening and I brought Steven along. When I introduced them, Steven stabbed Hockney in the chest with a fake knife. Hockney was terrified and recoiled in horror."

That summer Hannah began conducting an informal salon for artists at his apartment in the West Village. "It was pretty wild," says Min Thometz, who was 17 and had just arrived in New York from Minneapolis. "We used to go there every day and drink. Duncan had pictures of himself with Warhol and Hockney on the wall. He also had a poster of Jean-Paul Belmondo. At night we'd go to the East Village to play pool at this seedy place called the Hollywood Bar. Now it's called Nightbirds. It was full of pimps and junkies and whores. Everyone wanted to be an artist but no one was making any money. Steven Kramer was a real strong personality. He was so reckless and funny. He was making these viewing boxes. You'd look inside and see a tiny theater filled with mice. He made one with a cat chained to the stage and when you pressed a button, the cat would move like King Kong, while all the mice jumped up and down. David McDermott tried to convince me that electricity was going to be obsolete in the future. I thought he was mad."

"We were just a group of like-minded people with a lot of time on our hands," explains Hannah. "I'd fallen in love with the Beat Generation and was drinking a lot. Steven was recognized as the primitive genius of the group. He was sort of inarticulate, so he'd express himself through absurd actions, some of which involved much risk to his life and limb. His lifestyle was chaotic, so you had no idea where his work came from. The boxes were such elegant curiosities, beautifully crafted and finished with wallpaper."

Hannah, as it turned out, was working on a fantasy life almost as complex as McDermott's: he worshiped Belmondo and often seemed to think he was a gangster living in Paris in the '50s. "I went to a Contortions gig at Max's and Amos Poe came up and asked me if I wanted to be in a movie," says Hannah. "I told him I wasn't an actor, but he said it didn't matter. I figured it was a five-minute movie, so I asked him how long it was. He said it was a feature. I asked him when he planned to start shooting and he said in two weeks. I asked him when I could see the script and he said he hadn't written it yet."

Poe eventually decided to film a camp remake of Godard's *Breathless* with Hannah playing the role of Belmondo. Deborah Harry agreed to play a supporting role. Poe needed more actors and put a casting notice in the *Village Voice*, which was answered by Patti Titchener and Eric Mitchell, two budding actors who were studying at Lee Strasberg's Actors Studio. Titchener had already changed her name to Patti Astor.

Since *Breathless* was itself a camp takeoff on Hollywood gangster movies, Poe's film, *Unmade Beds*, was almost absurdly removed from its original source material. "It may have started as camp," deAk would say later of the entire scene. "But soon everything became extended into a double take, a triple take." "We shot the movie in thirteen days," says Hannah. "Every morning, Amos would give me a bottle of wine so I could get into character. The dialogue was pasted on the walls and there were many long silences as the actors searched for their cue cards. It gave the film an even greater existential flair."

Because he'd directed *The Blank Generation*, the first punk rock film, Poe was already something of a father figure for the Third Street crowd. He found an apartment on the block and held a birthday party for his wife, Sarah Charlesworth. "It was a boring party because they were all smoking marijuana," recalls McDermott. "I got to lecturing. I was interested in organizing society and getting all our friends to function as a group. I did my impersonation of the vocal refrain over the decades, demonstrating how people's mannerisms and vocal styles had changed." McDermott lectured and sang for over two hours until he got hoarse and had to stop. Several people were impressed with the marathon perform-ance, including a friend of Poe's named Tom Scully, who had recently graduated from SVA. Scully asked McDermott for his phone number.

"Tom began calling me and making overtures about coming to a meet-ing at his house to talk about a play or a show or something," recalls McDermott. "I wasn't going to go, but at the last minute I changed my mind based on the fact I might get something to eat."

Scully assembled quite a collection of eccentrics for his meeting, but none stranger than McDermott, who had abandoned his role as an art patron and was now frequently posing as a 1930s woman living in a ten-ement slum. He dressed in period clothes, washed his dresses by hand and held elaborate tea parties for his friends, many of whom assumed he had lost his mind. "I would just cook and clean and iron clothes all the time," says McDermott. "Many of my friends rejected me and said I was being stupid." "He called himself Edith," recalls Hannah. "It was almost too peculiar. You could never figure out if it was just some sort of con-ceptual stunt. If that was the case, then David was certainly the most extreme performance artist of his generation." However, since Edith sel-dom ventured outside her apartment, McDermott appeared at the meet-ing dressed in a cotton suit, knickers and straw hat.

"Tom's idea was to do something really low, some art thing involving drag queens in a basement," says McDermott. "But I gave great speeches and convinced them to do something more ambitious. By this time, the term 'New Wave' was completely passé but we decided to pretend to be the New Wave just to get publicity."

After reading a book on Tony Pastor, the legendary king of vaudeville, Scully decided to revive the vaudeville spirit of the old East Village. "It seemed like all these kids were hanging around waiting for something to happen," says Scully. "Nothing was going on. There were still freaks and hippies in the East Village." Like everyone else, Scully felt something was needed to define the growing energy everyone felt in the air. After sever-al meetings with a variety of friends, Scully and his girlfriend Susan Han-naford appointed Ann Magnuson, a former theater student from West

Virginia, to direct the show.

Flyers announcing auditions were plastered on St. Marks Place. "There was a big controversy over the word 'punk' at the time because it had such negative connotations," recalls Hannaford-Rose (who has since married), "but I guess we were looking for punk acts. The flyer appealed to 'Nazis, emotional cripples' and any other stupid thing we could think of. We got a lot of strange responses. Just about anyone could be in it, as long as their act was under five minutes. Ann worked with them to keep it theatrical."

Legitimate theaters proved far too expensive for their limited budget, so finding the right venue for the show was not easy. "One day we saw a flyer for *Made in the USA*, which is the title of a very obscure Godard film we'd been trying to rent," says Hannaford-Rose. "We went to see if it was really the film, but it turned out to be some terrible band." The trip was not a total loss, however, for the band was playing at a Polish veterans club called Irving Plaza, a squat, unimpressive four-story building on the corner of 15th Street and Irving Place. After ascending a marble staircase decorated with neo-classical motifs, they entered a large ballroom with a pair of crystal chandeliers. It was obviously the perfect environment for their show. Until recently, the club had been empty—the Polish veterans had long since moved away. "We immediately went to the management to discuss renting the hall," says Hannaford-Rose. "Suddenly this fellow Stanley got in the way and told us if we wanted to do anything there, he'd have to have a cut of it."

An affable man who spoke English with a halting accent, Stanley Stryhaski had emigrated to America from Poland in 1972 and was working as the superintendent of the Holy Cross Polish National Church on St. Marks Place. In 1973 he had organized a Saturday night social club in the church's basement, complete with a cash bar and polka band. Unfortunately, the program was not a success. "The Polish people who make money move to New Jersey," explains Stryhaski. "The poor ones who stay here—I'm sorry to talk like this, but it's true—they drank too much and weren't too high-class. I had too many problems with them." Strangely enough, Stryhaski found the local teenagers much better behaved. In fact, his devotion to punk rockers soon became legendary in the neighborhood. "So many bands came to see me and said, we'll play for free, just let us play here. So I let four bands play one night. It was snowing and I thought nobody would come. But the basement was packed! Punks, mostly. The punks were better behaved than anyone in America. We just didn't understand them. Then I went to Irving Plaza and they gave me use of the hall for very little money. I had an agreement that only I could do American shows there." An uneasy meeting was held between Stryhaski and Scully and it was decided that Stryhaski would get the gate receipts.

A week before the show was scheduled to open, the producers decided to stage a publicity stunt. Dressed in outlandish outfits, Magnuson, McDermott and two others drove around the city in a Volkswagen convertible. McDermott shouted at passing strangers through a megaphone. As the car drove down the Bowery, McDermott began directing his comments to itinerant men on street corners. "You've been to the top!" he shouted. "You've made your millions and now you've fallen into the gutter! Well, hope is nigh... come to New Wave Vaudeville!" As the car stopped for a red light at the corner of Bowery and Houston, the driver noticed a man with a gun chasing the car. Without waiting for the light to change, he roared through the intersection. Oblivious to the incident, McDermott continued shouting through his megaphone. "We called the newspapers and told them there was going to be a punk rock riot in front of Manic Panic," says Magnuson. Actually, there was only a fire-eater, who was part of the show, but the press failed to attend anyway, with the exception of Michael Shore from the *Soho Weekly News*, who took one look at the sparse crowd and was heard to comment, "So this is the punk rock riot?"

Despite a lack of pre-opening publicity, nothing would deter McDermott's boundless enthusiasm. On opening night he rented a 1952 Rolls-Royce limousine and instructed Scully to obtain a giant searchlight for the purpose of drawing a crowd to the front of the theater. For nearly three hours McDermott drove around the city, excitedly preparing for his grand arrival. "I had free passes to the show in my pocket because I didn't want to seem uncharitable as I broke through the crowds," he recalls. "When we drove up to the theater, the marquee lights were off. The street was empty. I stepped onto the sidewalk and for the sake of my friends inside the car shouted, 'Thank you! Thank you! It's a pleasure to be here!' A bum came along and I handed him a ticket." McDermott stomped off to his dressing room in a foul mood.

Shortly before 8 P.M., McDermott peeked through the curtains and was grateful to find a modest crowd had gathered for the show. He took a seat in a rickety sedan chair and was hoisted onto the shoulders of four slaves dressed in loincloths. He was wearing a gold helmet and gold skirt. Aside from a mantle of Chiclets gum around his neck, he was barechested. In his hands were two scepters—ancient symbols for the upper and lower Nile. As the triumphant soundtrack from *The Egyptian* (a 1954 Hollywood epic starring Victor Mature) came blasting through the sound system, the litter slowly crossed the stage, passing in front of a gigantic backdrop of a Camel cigarette package.

The audience applauded as McDermott dismounted his throne by stepping on the back of one of his litter-bearers. He waved a scepter at Kristian Hoffman, his piano accompanist, who responded with the opening bars of "King of the Nile," a song Hoffman had written for the occasion. "They call me pharaoh," warbled McDermott in a trilling falsetto. "All the hieroglyphics... say that I'm terrific... just look me up in the Book of the Dead." Midway through the song, McDermott lifted his skirt and began pounding his feet on the stage. He had no training in dance, but he was wearing authentic 1920s tap shoes.

Dressed like a B-movie starlet, Donna Destri soon arrived with a placard announcing the first act. There were over 30 to follow, spanning every conceivable gamut of performance. Beanie the singing dog and the stripper who performed with a dancing bird were among the two most popular routines. Other favorites included: Man Parrish and Lance Loud, who sang a song as the Sparkelletos; Animal X, who came onstage smashing a pink guitar (a routine which later became her trademark); George Elliot, Page Wood, Jamie Kaufman and Ralf Mann, who came out with briefcases stuffed with foam guitars and performed a bizarre number called "Businessmen in Space"; and the Bellamo sisters, who sang the mystery date song, which was accompanied by a raffle in which members of the audience could win dates with two unnamed downtown celebrities. "I think everyone knew James Chance and Lydia Lunch were the dates," says Tish Bellamo. "When the girl who won Chance came up to claim him, he either bit her or hit her. She screamed and said she was going to sue." There were two intermissions, during which they showed trailers for films like *Planet of the Apes* to the accompaniment of Jimi Hendrix records. McDermott, who insisted on performing without the aid of amplification, was understandably horrified. "Acid rock!" he gasps. "I don't know what could have been on their minds!" But the crowd loved it.

Toward the end of the show, the lights dimmed and the room was filled with a thundering musical ovation. The curtains opened and the spotlight fell on a strange, unearthly presence wearing a black gown, clear plastic cape and white gloves. As the orchestral refrain from Saint-Saens' *Samson et Dalila* was played, this strange Weimar version of Mickey Mouse began singing in an angelic soprano voice. "I still get goose pimples when I think about it," remembers Joey Arias, who was in the audience that night. "Everyone became completely quiet until it was over." The act was billed "Nomi by Klaus," but the man's real name was Klaus Sperber and he was McDermott's only true competition as star of the show.

After Sperber finished the aria, smoke bombs were ignited, strobe lights began flashing and the sound of a spaceship launching was played at an ear-shattering volume. Sperber bowed and stepped backward. The crowd stood and screamed for an encore, but Sperber just kept backing up into the cloud of smoke. "It was like he was from a different planet and his parents were calling him home," says Arias. "When the smoke cleared, he was gone."

An only child who was raised by a single mother in the German Alps, Sperber had worked as an usher at the Berlin Opera in the late '60s, where he'd entertained the maintenance crew with his Maria Callas imitations. He had a striking puppetlike face, with a high forehead and sharply pointed nose. He heightened these features by plucking his eyebrows, wearing dark lipstick and combing his hair into a crown with three points. He moved into an apartment on St. Marks Place in 1972 and appeared in a camp production of *Das Rheingold* with Charles Ludlam's Ridiculous Theater Company.

A self-taught chef as well as self-taught singer, Sperber took a job as a pastry chef at the World Trade Center and later formed a freelance baking company with Kay Kattelman. "I met Klaus at an uptown disco," says Kattelman. "He was wearing a beret and a woman's jacket from the forties. I'd never seen anyone quite like him. He was so shy and quiet. We both had two different lives: a straight day job and a real nutty night life. We started going to Max's and CBGB together." Magnuson lured Sperber into New Wave Vaudeville after hearing him sing on the way home from

Max's one night. Sperber was friends with a young dancer from Chicago named Adrian Richards, who had perfected a mime-like robot dance. Originally scheduled to perform with Sperber, Richards backed out at the last minute, leaving only the name he'd invented for the act, an anagram of his favorite magazine, *OMNI*. Later on, Sperber took the name Nomi for himself.

In two short years, Nomi went from his position as a poor pastry chef to become New York's leading New Wave performer. He created a cabaret style that is still being imitated today and assembled a group of promising young artists and performers around him, a list which at various times included Kenny Scharf, Keith Haring, Jean-Michel Basquiat, John McLaughlin and Joey Arias. (It was during a period of rampant promiscuity that Arias renamed McLaughlin "John Sex.")

Arias was working at Fiorucci, an innovative clothing boutique on East 59th Street that sold disco and New Wave clothes. Born in Fayetteville, North Carolina and raised in Pasadena, California, Arias had studied art and film in California, became a member of a proto-glitter group called Pearly and performed with the Groundlings, an influential L.A. theater troupe whose members included Pee Wee Herman and Larraine Newman. He achieved a certain notoriety for being the first person in New York to dye his hair bright blue. "I was living uptown and the kids on the street hated me," says Arias. "I got into a lot of fights. Klaus was very supportive, so I started hanging out with him."

One day while working at the store, Arias spotted a young man who appeared to be a recent arrival from California. "I guessed he was new in town," says Arias. "So I invited him and his girlfriend [Kitty Brophy] to come to a fashion show at the Mudd Club." The young man turned out to be Kenny Scharf and the next time Arias ran into him, Scharf invited Arias and Nomi to his apartment. Scharf wanted to show them his paintings.

Scharf was friendly, handsome and incredibly naïve. Having recently arrived from the University of California at Santa Barbara (where he'd studied art for one year), he was studying illustration at SVA and was obsessed with television, Pop Art and outer space. He talked incessantly about his favorite TV show, *The Jetsons*. He had also invented his own religion in which he worshiped the element hydrogen as God. Nomi was impressed with Scharf's paintings, particularly with a large one of a

Cadillac flying through space. "You and I are working on the same thing," he told the young artist.

"I could tell Kenny was baffled by Klaus," recalls Arias. "We were getting really stoned and Kenny said: 'I want to be like you guys.' So we gave him a Nomi hairdo, with triangle ears and a triangle back. We took photographs of it and Kenny was so excited. He felt like a Nomi person. I put on shoulder pads under my shirt and Kenny put on a space helmet. Klaus thought it was great. He wanted us to be in his next show."

The next scheduled performance was at Max's Kansas City, where Nomi had been invited to open for the Contortions. Arias and Scharf appeared as go-go dancers. "We painted our faces green," says Arias. "We were completely puffed up with green helmets and shoulder pads. Klaus sang, 'The Twist,' 'Falling in Love Again' and his aria. I was into the robot dance, while Kenny was more into just go-going. People went completely crazy over the act."

Arias introduced Scharf to the managers at Fiorruci, who organized an exhibit titled Fiorruci Celebrates the New Wave, which combined an art show by Scharf with a performance by Nomi. Scharf created a series of paintings detailing the misadventures of a jet-set woman of the future named Estelle. The next-to-last painting showed Estelle seated inside a spaceship, looking at a TV set that showed the Earth exploding from a nuclear bomb. "She looked really pleased because she was the only survivor," recalls Scharf.

"Around this time Klaus and I decided we were the future," says Arias. "We formed the Nomi family. We lived as if we were on the space shuttle. We ate little bits of food—space food." The lifestyle added a lot to the shows, which were becoming an increasingly stylized mixture of New Wave, Kabuki and Bauhaus. Scharf's dancing no longer fit in with the style and he was booted out of the group. One night at the Mudd Club, Nomi met his idol, David Bowie. After discovering they had mutual friends in Germany, Bowie invited Nomi and Arias to appear with him on *Saturday Night Live.* Soon afterward, Nomi signed a record deal with RCA.

"Then Klaus and I had a falling out," says Arias. "I was writing songs on my own and Klaus got pissed about that. He said, 'You're starting to do your own thing and I think you should move out.'" As his self-importance increased, Nomi began alienating many of his former friends. He dissolved his group and hired a professional band to back him. His first album was released in 1981, and it sold poorly.

MUDD CLUB

January 23, 1985: For the past two years, Jean-Michel Basquiat has lived in a two-story brick building on Great Jones Street owned by his friend Andy Warhol. The first floor is divided into two areas: a large open loft space that serves as a painting studio, kitchen and dining room, and a slightly smaller back room where completed paintings and drawings are stored. It is four o'clock in the afternoon and Basquiat has just gotten up for the day. His second-floor bedroom is clean and sparsely furnished. The walls are white; the floor is covered with gray industrial carpeting. His bed faces a large projection TV. Nearby is a bookcase filled with hundreds of movies on videocassette. Dozens of records are stacked next to a stereo system. On top of the stacks are albums by Maria Callas and Dinah Washington. Two works of art hang on the wall: a painting by Andy Warhol and a photograph of Williams Burroughs, pictured aiming a gun.

In a relatively short time, Basquiat has become one of the most celebrated artists in America. His face has adorned the cover of the *New York Times Magazine,* his work has been purchased by many leading museums, including the Whitney and the Museum of Modern Art, and his paintings have been sold to some of the world's most prestigious collectors for upward of $25,000. Much of Basquiat's notoriety results from his lifestyle, which more closely resembles that of a jaded rock star than an artist. His racial heritage has also been a factor: he is the first black artist to achieve anything close to blue-chip status in the contemporary art market.

Basquiat takes a seat in a Mission chair and opens a bottle of first-growth Bordeaux. He is dressed in a blue shirt and black paint-splattered jeans. He has a handsome face dominated by a fleshy nose. His hair is disheveled in a nappy snarl. "What am I going to do?" he says with a smile. "If I tell the truth I'm going to sound like an egomaniac."

As it turns out, Basquiat is reluctant to discuss his childhood influences or his days as a graffiti writer. After a few questions, he abruptly stands and leaves the room. "I just can't confide into a tape recorder," he says when he returns. "Who have you been talking to about me? A lot of people are going to say they know me." He takes a sip of wine and gradually delivers a few autobiographical sentences in a painfully slow monotone. "My father is a businessman... My mother went crazy as a result of a bad marriage—to my father. They've been separated since I was eight. I'd say my mother gave me all the primary things. The art came from her. I can't describe my mother. It would take too long... My childhood was really ordinary... I left home when I was fifteen and lived on the street for a while... Then I went back to school... Later I made postcards and sold them on the street... I did some postcards with John Sex. He had a really great mind. Still does."

"What about Kenny Scharf?"

"I knew he was going to be famous the minute I met him."

"But you had a falling out because you felt Kenny's parents had too much money?"

"We didn't have any falling out," he says. "I don't know why these things happen... It's just that... aesthetically I really hated Club 57. I thought it was silly. All this old and bad shit. I'd rather see something old and good."

"The Mudd Club was better?"

"It was the same attitude... There's not enough black people downtown in this... whatever it is, pseudo-art bullshit."

The phone rings and Basquiat answers it. He reaches over and turns off the tape recorder. "I'm doing an interview but I'm saying too much," he says into the phone. Shortly after he hangs up, Basquiat ends the interview. "I don't know if I want people to know these things about me," he explains. "It's like the end of mystery. You know what I mean?"

Basquiat was born in Brooklyn in 1960 to a black Haitian father and Puerto Rican mother. He had a turbulent childhood. At age seven, he was hit by a car and critically injured. His spleen was removed, and during his convalescence his mother gave him a copy of *Gray's Anatomy* to study in the hospital. His parents divorced the following year.

His artistic side emerged early, though it often manifested itself in strange forms: in the third grade he was filling his notebooks with drawings of guns and sent one to J. Edgar Hoover, who did not reply. Other favorite subjects were Alfred E. Newman, Richard Nixon and Alfred Hitchcock. He also drew a lot of cars, mostly dragsters. His father (who remarried in 1977) is a successful accountant who worked his way through night school. Today his father plays racquetball, drives a Mercedes Benz and owns the building in which he lives.

In the ninth grade, Basquiat took a class in life drawing, which he failed. Then, at age 15, he dropped out of school and left home. He hung around Washington Square Park for a year and spent most of the time dropping acid. "Now all that seems boring—it eats your mind up," he told an art critic. When he returned to school, he entered City As School (CAS), an experimental high school exploring innovative concepts in education, one of which was to send students to work in the community instead of keeping them in the classroom. Although founded with the best intentions, CAS provided an unstructured environment that was easy to abuse, especially for someone like Basquiat. He soon found someone who shared his enthusiasm for delinquent behavior, a young Puerto Rican named Albert Diaz, who had grown up in the Jacob Riis Projects in the East Village. Diaz had been an early member of the graffiti subculture that started in New York in the late '60s. His tag was "Bomb 1."

Through CAS Basquiat became involved with a drama group on the Upper West Side called Family Life Theater. While working with the group, he concocted a comical character who made a living selling a fake religion he called SAMO. "Jean started elaborating on the idea and I began putting my thoughts into it," recalls Diaz. "We Xeroxed a pamphlet and handed it out on the street. It had pictures of people from around the country with little quotes like: 'I tried it. It changed my life.' We decided to start leaving these cryptic messages around: SAMO is coming... SAMO is here... SAMO as an alternative to ego." The messages were written in magic marker or spray paint, but they represented a conceptual leap forward from subway graffiti, which often had no more motivation behind it than self-aggrandizement.

On the eve of Diaz' graduation, Basquiat and Diaz began discussing the possibility of throwing a pie at their principal during the ceremony. "It became a dare," says Basquiat. "This girl said, 'Are you really going to do it? It would be great.' I bought some whipped cream and tried to fill a box, but it didn't work. Then I tried a can of shaving cream." It worked. Just as the principal finished his speech, Basquiat snuck up behind him and dumped the box of shaving cream on his head. "He was wearing a white jacket," recalls Basquiat, "so it looked like a magic trick. When the box fell off, there was no reaction from the audience. They were supposed to applaud the speech, but they didn't want to do that, and they didn't want to laugh either." Basquiat didn't wait for a reaction. He went flying out the side door and never returned, even though he had another year to complete before graduation. "There didn't seem to be much point in going back," he says.

Basquiat and Diaz began spending most of their time in SoHo, probably because Basquiat had already decided on a career as an artist. For a while he had been painting in a psychedelic style reminiscent of Peter Max, but he quickly abandoned it and began painting T-shirts and postcards with drips of spray paint. It was the first attempt at marketing a combination of graffiti art and abstract expressionism. He hawked this work in Washington Square Park, SoHo and outside the Museum of Modern Art.

"Jean was a film buff," says Diaz. "He could tell you who the star and director of almost any movie was, but he was really into sixties films like *The Wild Bunch*. We were also big *Eraserhead* fans. Even before the punk thing started, Jean would splatter a lab coat with paint and walk across the Brooklyn Bridge with his face painted green and a Nosferatu haircut. He was a real attention-getter. One night we were at a party with these West Village kids. When we left, we took all these seltzer bottles with us and went into a cosmetics store on West Broadway. We said, 'All right, everybody in the back.' The people in the store screamed and ran to the back as if we had guns under our coats. We sprayed the entire store with seltzer and left. That's what it was like—total amphetamine madness. I remember one morning we were up all night on acid and Jean said to me, 'I know I'm going to be a star. I know it, Al, I really know it.' We had a mutual back-patting committee going and were getting more and more indulgent and egotistical. I think he cooled out a bit, while I sort of lost it and became a nasty kid for a while."

Meanwhile, Basquiat and Diaz were secretly spray-painting SAMO sayings all over SoHo:

> *SAMO as an end to mindwash religion, nowhere politics, and bogus philosophy*
> *SAMO as an escape clause*
> *SAMO saves idiots*

"We became self-appointed critics, telling everyone what their problems were," says Diaz with a laugh. (They hadn't heard of the Diggers of San Francisco, but the SAMO sayings were in much the same spirit as the anonymous broadsides handed out on the streets of Haight-Ashbury during the mid-'60s. The mimeographed sheets ridiculed merchants, tourists, drug dealers, gurus and anyone else who offended the Diggers' anarchist sensibility.)

Basquiat began sneaking into SVA and marking the halls with messages like "Stop running around with the radical chic playing art with daddy's dollars" and "SAMO as an end to playing art." The authorities put a guard at the door with instructions to find the culprit and keep him out. Since he didn't have a student ID, Basquiat was unable to enter the school. He showed up and asked the first person he could find to walk him past the guard as a guest. That person happened to be Keith Haring. "I liked SAMO but I didn't know who he was," says Haring. "But later that day I saw all these fresh SAMO pieces in the hall and I knew it was him."

While hanging out in the SVA cafeteria, Basquiat met Kenny Scharf and John Sex. "Jean-Michel showed me a color Xerox of John and Jackie Kennedy with their faces shattered," recalls Scharf. "I thought it was really good. I went out writing graffiti with him a couple of times. He would write his SAMO thing and I'd borrow his marker, draw the outline of a TV set and write 'The Jetsons' inside. But then one day he got mad at me and didn't want me writing with him anymore."

"Jean-Michel had shaved his hair into a real severe 'V' like Klaus Nomi," adds Sex. "We weren't punks but we had a very punk attitude. We were into outrage. We used to make postcards together. Once he bought some supplies for a painting. I think he paid $11.95 for them. I told him he should paint $11.95 on the canvas. So he painted that and then he wrote some other stuff. We were standing on the street corner and I said, 'You know what you should do now? You should throw it under that truck.' He flung it into the street like a frisbee. I fell on the ground laughing."

Basquiat retrieved the painting and took it to Fiorucci in hopes of getting an exhibit similar to the one they had given Scharf. The managers of the store weren't interested, so he deposited the painting in the garbage can. He also stopped speaking to Scharf.

People around town began wondering who SAMO was, and the *Soho Weekly News* ran a series of pictures of SAMO-marked walls, pleading with the artist to come forward and identify himself. A reporter from the *Village Voice*, the *Soho Weekly News*' competitor, found Basquiat and Diaz first and offered them $1,000 for an exclusive interview. The story ran on December 11, 1978. "Later I heard the *Soho Weekly News* was really pissed about it," says Diaz. "But we needed the money.

They were photographed leaning against a wall splattered with their graffiti. Basquiat insisted on disguising himself by drawing a pair of round, oversized sunglasses over his face. "The stuff you see on the subways is inane," Diaz was quoted as saying. "SAMO was like a refresher course because there's some kind of statement being made. It's not just ego graffiti."

"We were smoking some grass one night and I said something about it being the same old shit," said Basquiat, "Sam-o, right? It started like that—as a private joke—and then it grew... this city is crawling with uptight, middle-class pseudos trying to look like they have money they don't have: status symbols. It cracks me up. It's like they're walking around with price tags stapled to their heads. People should live more spiritually, man. But we can't stand on the sidewalk all day screaming at people to clean up their acts, so we write on walls."

Shortly after the article appeared, Basquiat and Diaz had a falling out. Basquiat began writing "SAMO is dead" and then stopped writing SAMO altogether. Instead, he concentrated on his postcard and T-shirt business. One day, while standing outside the WPA restaurant, someone told him Henry Geldzahler and Andy Warhol had just gone inside for lunch. "It took me about fifteen minutes to get up the nerve to go in," Basquiat later told Geldzahler in *Interview* magazine. "I went in and [Geldzahler] said 'too young.'" Warhol, however, seemed intrigued and bought a postcard.

While Basquiat was trying to get his art career going, New York's underground film scene was receiving some outside recognition. Amos Poe returned to New York City from France in 1978, and found himself penniless and without a place to live. *The Blank Generation* and *Unmade Beds* had been surprisingly well received in Europe, and Poe had been heralded as the first punk director (a title he detested), but he was still a nobody in New York. However, Poe received an unexpected offer his first week in town: someone named Steve Mass called him up and invited him to dinner.

Although Mass had been hanging around the fringe of the downtown scene for several years, he remained something of an enigma to those who knew him. Born in Macon, Georgia in 1942, Mass had majored in philosophy and art history at Northwestern University and attended the creative writing workshop at the University of Iowa for one year. Afterward, he'd helped edit two independently published books, but he made his living by providing inexpensive ambulance transportation and basic medical services for elderly people living in the outer boroughs of the city, a business he'd inherited from his family. By 1978 Mass had grown tired of this and was looking for something more stimulating. He was one of the few people living in the East Village who had money.

When he'd first come to New York, Mass had worked briefly with the experimental filmmaker and performance artist Jack Smith, who became Mass' most important influence. In the late '50s, Smith pioneered a wacky, Beatnik, drag-queen aesthetic that glorified the B-movies of Maria Montez. His underground films were inspirational to a young unknown artist named Andy Warhol, and his most famous film, *Flaming Creatures*, prompted several essays by Susan Sontag, including "Notes on Camp." In 1978 Smith was living and occasionally performing in the East Village, and Mass correctly perceived that Smith's sensibility could be updated for the '80s, especially after Mass visited the lower-middle-class homes of Brooklyn and Queens. "It could be very surrealistic going into those homes," says Mass. "I saw how far removed artists and intellectuals were from real life."

When Mass called Poe, the impoverished filmmaker jumped at the opportunity for a free meal. "He wanted to talk because he was interested in making a punk film," recalls Poe. Mass was living in a duplex on Eighth Street. Since the upstairs was empty, he offered it to Poe free of charge. "Every night we'd go to dinner and he'd drink lots of vodka while milking me for ideas," says Poe. "We decided to form a film company called Mud Films because a critic had written that my films looked like mud. Every night I'd get real excited and say, 'Okay, tomorrow we start work.' But the next morning Steve would be too hung-over to do anything. After a few weeks of this, I got real frustrated and fed up. I told him he really didn't want to make a movie. Later, he bought five thousand dollars worth of equipment just to show he was sincere. By that time, I'd introduced him to Diego Cortez and Anya Phillips and he'd decided to make a movie with them."

In the winter of 1978, Mass packed his 16mm film equipment into an ambulance van and set out for Memphis, Tennessee with Phillips and Cortez in tow. "Diego wanted to make a film on Elvis," he explains. "He was obsessed with Elvis." When the trio arrived at Graceland, however, they found the estate closed to the public. A group of Veterans of Foreign Wars from Tupelo, Mississippi happened to arrive the same day to award Elvis a posthumous medal. By posing as a camera crew for ABC television, the trio managed to join the veterans for an audience with Elvis' father, Vernon. "After a while the guards began to look at us suspiciously, especially after Anya began sitting in Vernon's lap and he seemed to be taking an unusual interest in her," says Mass. When their true identities were revealed, they were unceremoniously booted off the estate.

From Memphis they drove to Chicago, Cortez' hometown, where they visited the first disco to start playing punk rock. Located in a working-class neighborhood, La Mere Vipere was crowded with prototypical punks in torn shirts, dyed hair and hard hats. "They looked like some underground species that had survived a nuclear holocaust," recalls Mass. Cortez and Phillips had been trying to get Mass to open a punk rock club for months, but it wasn't until he visited La Mere Vipere that he knew the concept would work.

When they returned to New York, Cortez approached the artist Ross Bleckner, who owned a building at 77 White Street, two blocks south of Canal and within easy walking distance of TriBeCa. "I told Ross we wanted to open an artsy cabaret with Laurie Anderson-type performances. He didn't want any loud music," says Cortez. "As soon as the contracts were signed, we brought in the big speakers. Brian Eno helped design the sound system."

Cortez and Phillips wanted to name it the Molotov Cocktail Lounge but they soon had a falling out with Mass, who renamed it the Mudd Club. Originally conceived as a parody of disco culture (Studio 54 was approaching its heyday), the club was put together with the crudest and cheapest materials available, using surplus goods purchased at discount stores along Canal Street. The plastic bar was covered with airplane maps and Mass spread the rumor that the club was a former hangout for a drug smuggler, probably an homage to *High Times* founder Tom Forçade, a mysterious and legendary figure of the New York underground scene who had recently died. Pre-opening nights were attended mostly by the

Third Street crowd: Chance, Astor, Mitchell, Phillips, etcetera. "They were completely dressed up and ready to go," says deAk with a smile. "But there was nothing to do and no one else was there." On opening night, Mass threw a party for the staff of *Punk* magazine. "Steve really wanted to ground the place with the *Punk* magazine people," says Cortez. "I think it was a commercial ploy to assure a large drinking audience." The magazine, however, was destined to fold within a few months.

It didn't matter. Word about the Mudd Club was already spreading through the city and a wide variety of people were showing up, including TriBeCa performance artists and '50s-style greasers from New Jersey. Mass had a talent for picking out creative ones and putting them to work. "Steve was trying to create a new scene. He wanted to be the new Warhol," says writer and underground filmmaker Tina Lhotsky. "The early crowd was one-third CBGB punk, one-third art scene and one-third uptown elite. A lot of new fashion ideas were popping up and a lot of personality cults were developing."

Mass began renting limousines and parking them in front of the club so people would think celebrities were inside. Robert Molnar, a freelance fashion designer who had been operating the coat check, was put in charge of the door. "People would line up outside and I was supposed to pass out poker chips to those who should get in," recalls Molnar. "I felt really guilty about turning people away and Steve was always changing his mind about the door policy. One night he told me just to let in downtown artists. The next night he'd want punk rockers. The next night he wouldn't want anyone in a leather jacket. One night he told me not to let in any more Hell's Angels. But after I turned one down, they all came back. I left eight huge security guards in charge and went upstairs to hide. Somehow they got past the guards, came upstairs, smashed the door down and punched me out in front of everyone."

It didn't take long before a rigid code of behavior was established at the club. "It was a very strong, self-policing policy of what was cool," says Carmel Johnson-Schmidt, an early regular at the club who later briefly owned an East Village boutique. "There seemed to be a definite fear of the future. People gave up on planning things. It was all for that moment, that night. People barely even fucked. I mean, they did, of course, because it was the beginning of the scene and a lot of people met that way, but it was more like... blasé. You did it in the bathroom. There seemed to be a lot of bitterness in the air. It very quickly became a drug club. A lot of down drugs were being used—heroin, Quaaludes. You could wear the grubbiest thing, but you had to style it. There was a definite dislike for anything unstyled. The fifties were popular because they were cleaner, more defined. I think we were attracted to the geometric shape of the fifties clothes. I remember a fashion show during the winter of 1978 that was an odd combination of some SoHo fashion, which was immediately dropped, and some fifties cocktail dresses. I was a model and we went out in whiteface, like zombies, with plastic roses. It was ridiculous, but it was fun. By the summer of 1979, you created a character every time you went out. The girls got fanatical about clothes and makeup. Everything had to be original from the fifties."

Nares, Mitchell and Becky Johnston opened a small theater called the New Cinema, which was designed to showcase films made by the Third Street crowd. The project was funded by a grant from Colab, and the theater was located on St. Marks Place. Strongly influenced by the European avant-garde (Mitchell was French; Nares, English), the New Cinema group filmed in Super-8, which was transferred to video for editing, a process which gave the films a distinctive washed-out texture. "They dressed forties American," says Cortez. "The baggy pants, grays and browns. Real *arte povera*." Aside from the original three, the movement attracted a number of other budding filmmakers including Charlie Ahearn, Vivian Dick, John Lurie, Jim Jarmusch and a couple who billed themselves as Beth and Scott B.

"Like the makers of Hollywood's old two-reelers, the New Cinema crowd churned them out, picking the subject, shooting the film, and showing it as fast as possible—like a Movie of the Week," wrote deAk later. "The emphasis on action and expedient production technique ran counter to the contexts of art film and independent cinema. Music was the mercury which floated everything. Jamming became an almost obligatory social ritual, an indispensable social skill." Unfortunately, many of the films were technically crude, sometimes virtually unintelligible, and the ultimate significance of the films probably resides not with the directors or scriptwriters, but with the actors, who comprised a post-Warhol generation of self-made stars.

Patti Astor and Tina Lhotsky, two of the leading actresses associated with the New Cinema, created similar archetypes: blond bombshells in the B-movie mold. Astor's character, however, was pure glitzy Hollywood, while Lhotsky's was more East Coast and intellectualized. Lhotsky became increasingly involved with activities at the Mudd Club and eventually crowned herself "queen" of the club at a coronation ceremony she organized at the Cathedral of St. John the Divine. "Tina could be pretty cold to the outside female," remembers Johnson-Schmidt. "It was the typical female-to-female thing in a club—she wanted all the men to be nuts about her. But she was a really good writer and part of her was very spiritual. Her character was part of the basic underlying agreement of the club—that everything was false, that nothing mattered and that nothing was going to last."

"Everyone was making a movie and everyone was in a band," recalls Haoui Montaug, a poet who later became a doorman at several downtown clubs modeled after the Mudd Club. "Things were evolving into the cold, modern look. Eventually, everyone would just stand around and look aloof."

A radio deejay from Atlanta, Georgia named Anita Sarko visited the club during the winter of 1979. "I thought the music was going to be amazing," says Sarko, "but I walked in and they were playing New York street music—a lot of New York Dolls. Then I went upstairs and found 'April Love' by Pat Boone on the jukebox—a song I played in Atlanta. That's when I knew the mentality was the same—very reactionary. I gave the doorman a tape and within a month I was working there. Steve literally slapped me into being a New Yorker. At the time there was a heavy clone scene going on. You had your Bowie clones, your Johnny Thunders clones, your soul boys, your fifties rockabilly types, your sixties revivalists. I played a lot of Zombies, Petula Clark, Beatles and Kinks for the sixties revivalists. I played Motown one night at four A.M. and everyone just died. They loved it. If I put on something electronic, the soul boys would leave the floor and the Bowie clones would come on. If I played a rockabilly song, the Bowie people would leave and the fifties people would come on. It was great watching all this commotion. A lot of celebrities began showing up. You'd turn around and Bowie, Jagger and Iggy would be in one corner, and Roxy Music would be in another. Jean-Michel Basquiat was one of my regulars. His group would come in at three A.M. and dance all night. I started mixing the new electronic music coming out of England with old funk. Being a very good dancer, Jean caught on to that right away."

"Jean-Michel, Michael Holman and Vincent Gallo became the baby crowd at the club," says deAk. "They were gorgeous, extremely stylish and danced fantastically. They were also the biggest prima donnas I ever met." The trio formed a group called Gray, a noise art band similar to the ones already created by Glenn Branca and Rhys Chatham (both of whom were working on updated versions of the No Wave movement). "I played a guitar with a file, and a synthesizer," Basquiat told a reporter for the *New York Times Magazine*. "I was inspired by John Cage at the time—music that isn't really music. We were trying to be incomplete, abrasive, oddly beautiful." Since Basquiat didn't have a fixed address, he showed up at the club every night hoping to find someone to take him home. Several regulars recall him saying he was going to be a famous artist someday, but few believed him.

As the Mudd Club got famous and hordes of people descended on the place, it got increasingly difficult to get inside. Mass replaced the velvet rope used at the door of Studio 54 with a more punkish metal chain. He refused to cater to uptowners who arrived by limousine, often making them endure long waits in front of the club before allowing them entrance. "The club started as a toy for me to play around with," says Mass. "But the crowds made it more costly. I needed more security, sound engineers, air conditioning, bathrooms. The toy became a business."

Since entry to CBGB or Max's had never been based on one's appearance, the institution of a door policy at the Mudd Club had a profound effect, dividing the underground into those who were eligible to enter the club (meaning they dressed in the latest style), and those who steadfastly refused to become fashionable, a schism that was notable within the Colab group. "The chic ones in Colab got into the club, but the rest were left out," says deAk. "It caused a lot of problems." Before long, Mass was branded an elitist and his female patrons were charged with anti-feminism because of their affection for makeup and cocktail dresses.

In the spring, Colab and Jenny Holzer organized The Manifesto Show on Bleecker Street. Crammed with posters and polemics, it was the first indication of the seething energy building on the fringe of the art world, energy which would explode in Colab's Times Square Show during the summer of 1980. Like SAMO, Holzer had been working anonymously in the streets, putting up posters filled with provocative and ambiguous statements, such as:

Abuse of power should come as no surprise.
Humanism is obsolete.
Morals are for little people.
Murder has its sexual side.

When they first appeared, the posters had a great deal of shock value. No one could be sure if the author was serious. "They were pretty scary," admits Keith Haring, who attended the exhibit and was becoming interested himself in putting work on the streets.

"The Lower East Side was the Hollywood studio supplying all the actors, musicians and fashion designers," says deAk, "but the Mudd Club was the office. No one had telephones, so everything was arranged at the club. It was a post-midnight office. You could always tell what kind of movie was going to be shot next because the wishful starlets would change their looks to suit the style of the movie, hoping to get noticed by the director. The style was monstrous, tasteless and morbid, but it had that art drama, that anything-for-the-cabaret attitude."

The art establishment slowly began taking notice of the club. For the most part, they didn't like what they saw. *Village Voice* critic Lucy Lippard labeled the current style "retrochic" and became its most outspoken opponent.

"Punk artists—retro and radical—trace their bloodline back to Pop Art and Warhol (though the latter epitomized the scorned sixties), and to Dada (though it's not fair to blame a partially socialist movement for its primarily reactionary offspring)," wrote Lippard. "The real source of retrochic is probably Futurism, which made no bones about its fundamental fascism and disdain for the masses. Violence and bigotry in art are simply violence and bigotry, just as they are in real life. They are socially dangerous, not toys, not neutralized formal devices comparable to the stripe and the cube."

Despite what Lippard thought, artists were becoming infected by a new zeitgeist (a word suddenly in popular usage). At first, the most noticeable change was a shift away from abstract art toward more recognizable imagery. "The idea of performance art was already getting close because you had the image of the artist on a shallow, nonexistent stage," says deAk. "But it was undefined and didn't gel until later. In 1976 you could have beat people over the head with the biggest club saying 'return to imagery' and they could not have come up with anything." Susan Rothenberg's large heraldic horses comprised some of the earliest attempts at forcing recognizable images into abstract art, but there were others working along similar lines. One of them was a young painter named Julian Schnabel, who, because he was good friends with Ross Bleckner, knew about the Mudd Club early on and never had any problems getting inside.

Schnabel's second solo show, held at the Mary Boone Gallery in November, included several paintings covered with shards of broken dinner plates. They were not his first "plate" paintings (the first had been purchased by art dealer Annina Nosei for $3,250 in 1978), but the idea suddenly came into vogue. Although Schnabel admitted he'd been inspired to make the paintings after a disastrous breakup with a girl-friend, he denied any autobiographical connotations in the work—as far as he was concerned, the plates were just a means for building up the surface of his canvas and were not to be considered as subject matter in themselves. For whatever reason, there was no doubt the broken plates evoked psychological reactions in some viewers. Schnabel began paint-ing on black velvet, which led to the speculation he was pursuing a "kitsch" aesthetic, a charge the artist vehemently denied. Interest in Schn-abel's work spread quickly, and his reputation began taking off faster than anyone could have thought possible. Initially mistaken for a "punk" artist, Schnabel, a masterful manipulator of his own career, began to bill himself as the next Jackson Pollock.

Some would describe the dominant mood of the Mudd Club as stylish nihilism, but a band calling themselves the B-52's arrived early on and began swinging the pendulum in a completely different direction. Although the band was based in Athens, Georgia, two of its five members were from New Jersey, including Fred Schneider, the group's lead singer.

Schneider was a devoted fan of science fiction novels, '50s monster movies, and Martha Reeves and the Vandellas. He'd moved to Athens to study forestry at the University of Georgia. After joining the campus film society, Schneider had brought several John Waters movies to Athens. "I liked his crazy humor even though I wasn't into some aspects of his work, like the violence," says Schneider. "One night my friends and I went to a house with all these instruments and started jamming. We wrote a song called 'Killer Bees.' Then we played a Valentine's party. We sent a tape to Max's Kansas City in 1977 and they invited us to come up and play. We were petrified. We'd never played in a club before."

The group arrived in New York in December and began playing fun, upbeat dance music with lyrics that parodied beach party movies and science fiction novels. Their most popular song was "Rock Lobster." The band came as something of a shock to the punk crowd at Max's. "Everyone was dressed in black leather," says Schneider. "We couldn't afford anything but thrift shop clothing. I would wear horrendous polyester things that didn't match. The girls wore big beehive wigs from the sixties. We started dancing away in our rainbow polyester outfits and everyone just stood and watched. At the time it wasn't cool to dance in rock clubs. I think we made seventeen dollars that night. Later on we played CBGB and Hurrah. We knew something was happening when we looked out the window at Hurrah and saw a line around the corner."

Although the Mudd Club had been originally conceived as a disco, Mass invited the B-52's to perform at the club the first night he saw them. Their inaugural performance was so hastily arranged that Mass didn't even have time to build a proper stage. Animal X opened as a solo act and remembers the concert well. "They were introduced by their manager, who came out wearing a bathing suit, a swim cap and a rubber ducky," she says. "The band came out dressed in girdles from the fifties. On the first song they held a laugh box to the mike after every chorus. They were the only band around with a sense of humor."

"The stage wasn't even finished," recalls Schneider. "There was a big hole in the middle of it. This guy showed up in a giant lobster outfit and wanted to dance with us. We told him there wasn't room." As soon as the band started playing "Rock Lobster," the giant lobster jumped on stage and disappeared into the hole.

Mass asked Schneider to throw a party at the club, and with '60s beach movies in mind, Schneider selected a Hawaiian theme. "I thought a cheezy luau would be fun," he says, "so I went out and bought all these tacky Polynesian records and Hawaiian party store decorations." Little did they realize that theme parties at the Mudd Club would turn into highly conceptualized events that would eventually rival the be-ins and happenings of the '60s.

The first '60s revival party was organized by the Bellamo sisters from Manic Panic. "Steve wasn't sure it would work because it was too recent," recalls Tish Bellamo. "He felt it was kinda too close to home because a lot of people still looked like hippies and he didn't know if they would get the joke. But he finally let us do it in April, 1979. We divided the club into the bad trip side and the good trip side. On the good side were nice posters, flowers, pretty stuff, with 'love' and 'peace' painted all over the place. The bad trip side had rubber spiders hanging from the ceiling and all this bad stuff. We put sugar cubes on the bar."

"Upstairs we had the recovery tent for freak-outs," adds Snookie. "We brought pounds and pounds of clothing to give to people if they weren't dressed properly."

It was Lhotsky's parties, however, that became the most famous, especially her Joan Crawford Mother's Day Celebration, which featured a large Carvel cake topped by a baby doll tied to a bedpost. Other Lhotsky parties included the Blonde Night, the Pajama Party, the Monster Party and the Cha Cha party. Her most lavish celebration was a tribute to dead rock stars which reportedly cost Mass over $10,000 to produce. "I rented all the trappings of a professional funeral home," says Mass. "It wasn't just stage crap, we had real caskets, an organ and four limos to deliver the caskets. I had tremendous losses on these parties because they were held on Sunday nights and the people who came were the same ones who always got in for free."

"The club changed constantly," says Lhotsky. "I tried to make it as chic as possible but Steve always wanted to cover everything with Scotchgard and Hamburger Helper, if you know what I mean. During the summer of '79, everyone was wilting around the jukebox listening to Marianne Faithfull's crackly voice of doom on 'Why'd You Do It?' I think a lot of Warhol's dark glamour bled into the club. I always liked the way Warhol put everything into an erotic nutshell. He used to show up at some of the parties, sniffing out his past sensibilities. But when he came, it was generally a nose-up-in-the-air kind of thing."

"Nobody cared about Warhol," says Sarko. "He was part of Studio 54 and we were a joke on that whole thing. It always seemed to me Warhol was like Klamm in Kafka's *The Castle*. He was somebody you knew you were supposed to meet. But when you'd see him, you couldn't understand what was so great about him and for the life of you, you couldn't figure out why you were supposed to meet this person."

Warhol's major representative at the club was probably Glenn O'Brien, the music critic for *Interview* magazine. In December, 1978, O'Brien had begun hosting a cable TV show called *TV Party*, which, along with the Mudd Club, quickly became a focal point for the emerging underground scene. Co-hosted by Chris Stein, songwriter and guitarist for Blondie, and occasionally directed by Amos Poe, the hour-long show lasted for four years and set a standard for infantilism, chaos and insanity that will probably never again be equaled on television. (David Letterman frequently cites it as his favorite program.)

One show opened to the strains of "Mr. Lucky" by Henry Mancini, while the camera panned a minimal set composed of a few folding chairs and a blackboard. Taped to the blackboard was a large photo of Lenin, whose forehead was inset with a gleaming third eye. In the background anxious voices could be heard inquiring as to O'Brien's whereabouts. The host was finally located sitting in a corner rolling a marijuana cigarette and wearing dark sunglasses. (Just about everyone on the show smoked pot and wore dark sunglasses.) "Welcome to *TV Party*," said O'Brien. "The show that's a cocktail party, but which could also be considered a political party."

No two shows were alike, but O'Brien frequently began with a rambling stream-of-consciousness monologue. On one program he urged forgiveness for artists who had benefited from the patronage of the Shah of Iran (a large and somewhat embarrassing list), while on another he praised Muammar el-Qaddafi's decision to give automobiles to his subjects. Afterward, guests might be introduced, but they were seldom formally interviewed. Walter Steding was the leader of the house band, and a photographer from *Interview* named Edo operated the camera. Later on, a young black man from Brooklyn named Fred Brathwaite also became a camera operator. The structure of the show was borrowed in part from Hugh Hefner's short-lived talk show, which allowed guests freedom of the set. Phone calls from viewers were usually taken at some point.

Basquiat began showing up each week and was eventually invited onto the show. "I always knew he'd make it," says O'Brien. "He used to come over to my apartment, lay on the floor and draw with crayons. It was fascinating just to watch him work. He was always trying to get me to take him to meet Andy Warhol."

CLUB 57

TV is capable of inspiring at least as much cynicism as docility. The viewer who can transform that cynicism into critical energy can declare the war with television over and instead savor the oracular quality of the medium. As Roland Barthes, Jean-Luc Godard, and the French devotees of Jerry Lewis have realized for years, television is American Dada, Charles Dickens on LSD, the greatest parody of European culture since "The Dunciad." Yahoos and Houyhnhnms battle it out nightly with submachine guns. Sex objects are stored in a box. Art or not art? This is largely a lexicographical quibble for the culturally insecure.
—David Marc, *Demographic Vistas*

After the close of New Wave Vaudeville, Scully and Hannaford found out about the church basement on St. Marks Place where Stanley Stryhaski had held his unsuccessful polka parties. Scully suggested they use the space to show grade-B horror movies—a concept he felt would appeal to the young punks in the neighborhood. They cleaned and painted the room and began showing films on Tuesdays starting in May, 1979. *Invasion of the Bee Girls, She Demons* and *Hercules in the Haunted World* were among the early offerings. The room also had a jukebox, which Scully programmed with a combination of punk, reggae and Motown classics.

Since East Village apartments were too small for parties, people hung around long after the movies were over. Scully suggested they turn the basement into a club and open it during the rest of the week. Stryhaski hired Magnuson to act as manager and they named it the East Village Students Club. The official name never caught on, however, because the locals already knew the basement as Club 57. (The building was located at 57 St. Marks Place and the address was prominently displayed above the door.)

"It was pretty ugly and creepy before we moved in," recalls Hannaford-Rose. "There were these drunk foreign guys around that would always try to grab the girls. But then a bunch of neighborhood kids began showing up, like Keith [Haring], Kenny [Scharf], John [Sex] and Drew [Straub]. Drew was my personal favorite because he would always heck-

because I wouldn't let him in for free. He was completely gone on TV and pop culture. Tom [Scully] always wanted the films to be taken seriously, but I just wanted to dress up, decorate the club and make it a party place. Ann and I would think of the victim in the movie that week and dress the part."

Since he was living two doors away, Sex became a frequent visitor. "The movies were so bad that people sat around making fun of them," he says. "That's how it started—with a bunch of witty people tearing apart a really bad movie and acting out the roles. Sometimes I'd go in and only three people would be there. Other times it would be packed. There was a tiny sign by the door that said 'East Village Students Club,' but it was so small you couldn't even see it from the sidewalk. Everything was done the Polish way. If a leg fell off a chair, Stanley would go searching for a piece of fruit crate to hammer on it. If a bulb went out, he'd put any old bulb in. Maybe that's how the black light got there."

Sex had arrived in the city in 1979, accompanied by his girlfriend Wendy Andreiev. Both came from Centerport, Long Island, where Sex had performed with a local rock band. Once in the city, Andreiev shed her Long Island persona by bleaching her hair and cutting it short. Her boyfriend, however, wasn't interested in adopting a new look. "I had a real stubborn streak," he says. "I wasn't into change at all." Around SVA, he had a reputation as an expert on the Dada movement, and classmate Bruno Schmidt recalls him lugging a huge portfolio filled with illustrations for Ezra Pound poetry. Sex met Scharf, who introduced him to Nomi and Arias. Before long, he began undergoing a slight shift in attitude.

"Klaus Nomi lived on the same block as me and I was really shocked the first time I saw him," recalls Sex. "I'd seen London punks, but he was so much older and wore so much makeup. He was also in spikes and leather. I didn't know how he had the nerve to walk down the street. When I met Kenny, he tried to get me to put on makeup before going to the Mudd Club. He told me I should pluck my eyebrows. I got into a big fight with him. I said, 'I don't want to put on makeup and I don't want to pluck my eyebrows! That looks effeminate!' I was really insulted." Later that year, however, Sex decided to change and speedily surpassed even his wildest classmates. The following September he arrived at SVA with a blond pompadour and Day-Glo pants and began silkscreening Pop-influenced posters.

Magnuson, meanwhile, organized 15 women into the Ladies Auxiliary of the Lower East Side, which she envisioned as a sort of warped version of the Junior League. "I was obsessed with the late fifties and early sixties," she says. "I was collecting all the magazines from the period. I loved the graphics. I was really into the Donna Reed look." Magnuson circulated a calendar of events and newsletter for the club, both of which were painstakingly edited. The calendar was filled with '50s and '60s imagery. The newsletter featured a logo designed by Scharf depicting a TV set with the words "Club 57" on the screen. Under the channel dial was an atomic symbol and the word "Fun."

The Auxiliary's first official event, a slumber party, was held in August. It started out with a game of Mystery Date and a pillow fight. "By the time I got there, everyone was tripping on hash brownies," recalls Dany Johnson. "We had three male go-go dancers, Kenny, John and Shawn [McQuate]. Other boys weren't allowed in. I didn't want to stay overnight—that floor was disgusting. But Ann locked the door, punched me and pushed me under a bench." Tish and Snookie Bellamo arrived with their hair in rollers, wearing baby-doll pajamas. Sex removed his pants because his underwear lit up better under the black light. Lisa Baumgardner, editor of *Bikini Girl Magazine*, walked by and stuffed a dollar bill into his jockey shorts while he go-go danced. "I couldn't believe it," says Sex. "I was having fun and getting paid at the same time."

A few weeks later, Magnuson arranged for representatives from the Mary Kay cosmetics company to give a sales demonstration at her Avenue B apartment. Two salesmen and a photographer arrived expecting to find a group of middle-aged housewives. Instead, they found a motley crew of young punkettes. They sensed something was wrong, but dutifully went ahead and outlined "the seven steps to beauty" while passing out makeup samples. "Everyone started doing these slut makeup jobs," recalls Johnson. "The guy was going 'No, no, no, that's too much over there.' He kept calling us girls and we finally told him we wanted to be addressed as debs."

The highlight of each meeting was the reading of the Secret Boy File, a collection of index cards containing various data on members of the opposite sex. Submitted anonymously, the cards were stored in alphabetical order and typically read aloud, a ceremony conducted, according to

Magnuson, "to the sound of much cackling." Many struggling artists received their first reviews in the file, the contents of which remain a closely guarded secret. "Most of it was just important information every girl needs to know before she goes out with a man," says Magnuson. "Like, does he spend money on you? Is he a good kisser? Does he have the crabs?"

In September, 1979, Scharf was given the first art exhibit at the club and showed several of his "space" paintings, including Nomi's favorite, the Cadillac painting, which was subsequently exhibited at the Xenon disco, where it was stolen. Scharf had given up painting and was wandering the streets looking for broken TV sets, which he'd reassemble and paint in crazy colors. He had a large collection of toy dinosaurs, which he'd glue onto almost anything, including his broken TVs and his sunglasses. He built a miniature city, modeled after *The Jetsons*, and fell in love with glitter, plastic baubles, beads and bangles. Needless to say, the faculty at SVA was finding it increasingly difficult to take his work seriously.

Inspired by the antics at the Mudd Club, Club 57 began throwing their own theme parties. However, since their parties were staged on negligible budgets, they relied more heavily on imagination and resourcefulness. In The Model World of Glue, Hannaford handed everyone a plastic model, glue and a paper bag (for sniffing). A few weeks later, The Putt-Putt Reggae party, staged by Johnson and Magnuson, featured a miniature golf course built out of cardboard boxes and designed to resemble a Jamaican shantytown. Although an immense amount of work went into the parties, they were often attended by only a handful of people.

By 1980 it had become noticeably more difficult to draw a crowd into a club. The success of the Mudd Club had caused a proliferation of similar places and the competition among them was intense. Even the Mudd Club began to founder after a new club called Danceteria opened farther uptown. A year earlier Hurrah and the Mudd Club were the only two dance clubs in the city playing rock music, but now new ones were sprouting every week.

Understandably, a certain amount of tension, jealousy and snobbery divided the various scenes. The original Mudd Clubbers, the most established group, were older and more influenced by European culture than the emerging younger generation. The Club 57 crowd was more interested in the sort of sensibility embodied by the B-52's. Scharf, Haring and Sex had been attending every local performance by the band, and Scharf later described himself as a B-52 groupie.

"I always separated the two camps into cool and groovy," says Magnuson. "The Mudd Club was cool and we were groovy. It can be tough doing anything when there's too much of that cool business infiltrating you. You start to feel hesitant. I don't think you should be intimidated to try anything."

"The Mudd Club was a business and Club 57 wasn't," adds Haoui Montaug. "That was the essential difference. Club 57 was more like a fun, drug-crazed clubhouse. It had a Mickey Rooney-Judy Garland let's-put-on-a-show feeling."

Not everyone approved of what was happening at Club 57. As the club descended deeper into American pop culture, the Mudd Club crowd last interest. A few of the New Cinema directors screened films at Club 57, but it was obvious the two cliques had vastly different sensibilities. "For a while, Club 57 was the most uncool place in the world," says Dany Johnson. "I was fascinated by the whole Mudd Club thing, so it took me a while to figure out what Club 57 was doing," says Carmel Johnson-Schmidt. "They would take mushrooms and play Twister, rolling on the floor, screaming and laughing for hours. Sometimes they were so ridiculous you just wanted to wring their necks."

The club's first fashion show was held in January 1980. Titled "The Amazon School of Modeling," the event was organized by Stacy Elkin and Terry Parson. Min Thometz came down the runway wearing a plastic garbage bag for one outfit and two lamp shades for another, setting the tone for an event that was more parody than real fashion show. "I started with the idea of showing these clothes I'd made," says Elkin. "But I gave the models free reign to do whatever they wanted. It turned into a joke and I didn't care." In later fashion shows, Ande Whyland would administer a shaving cream enema to Sex, while Johnson would glue hair on her chest and wear every outfit backward.

By this time, Johnson had emerged as the club's deejay. A fan of the B-52's and the Cramps, she began devoting much of her time to ferreting out strange kitsch records from the '60s. "I'd buy anything that looked weird," she says. "I played a lot of raunchy disco music. Everyone had their favorite song. John Sex liked the theme song from *The Vindicators* by the Fleshtones. Kenny Scharf loved the *Batman* theme. He even made up a dance called the Batusi."

While Club 57 was presenting its criticisms of society in the form of satire and parody, a more straightforward radical viewpoint was simultaneously being expressed by the older generation, the Colab artists. On January 1, 1980, Colab illegally occupied an abandoned city-owned building on Delancey Street with the aim of staging The Real Estate Show. The following day, the exhibit was closed by the Department of Housing Preservation and Development (HPD), which locked the artists out of the building. A '60s-style confrontation ensued, highlighted by the arrival of Joseph Beuys, an event met with much the same reverence as David Bowie's arrival at the Mudd Club. A few days later, Colab reached a compromise with HPD and the show was moved to 175 Delancy Street.

"The intention of this action," wrote the participants in their manifesto, "is to show that artists are willing and able to place themselves and their work squarely in a context which shows solidarity with oppressed people, a recognition that mercantile and institutional structures oppress and distort artists' lives and work, and a recognition that artists, living and working in depressed communities, are compradors in the revaluation of property and the 'whitening' of neighborhoods."

(Although the Colab artists were certainly driven by sincere motivations, the tone of their manifesto seemed like old news in 1980.)

The following month, Magnuson staged a Valentine's Day Love-In, the first of many '60s revival parties at Club 57. Haring and Scharf showed videos made at SVA; *The Trip* and *The Wild Angels* were screened; and Edward Bryezinski, Paul Bridgewater, David McDermott and Duncan Hannah scheduled an exhibition called Painting: The New Wave. "The art world was on Geritol and had just discovered the term 'New Wave,'" explains Bryezinski. However, Hannah and Bryezinski decided to go one step further and retitled the exhibit Beyond the New Wave, a change which caused McDermott to withdraw angrily from the exhibition.

In March, several Doris Day films were shown; Manic Panic sponsored the first glitter-rock revival party; *Beyond the Valley of the Dolls* was screened; and Lance Loud hosted a punk rock quiz show, Name That Noise. In April, Min Thometz and Bradley Field staged a bizarre tribal rite called Bongo VooDoo; John Holmstrom gave a slide cartoon show; and Kenny Scharf hosted a Salute to NASA. One quickly got a crash course in New York's underground scene by hanging out at the club. John Waters, Amos Poe, James Nares and Nick Zedd were among the film-makers who came by to show movies. Ondine, a Warhol survivor, screened *Chelsea Girls*, and Jack Smith was also known to drop in occa-sionally. Many of these filmmakers were introduced to the club by Bill Landis, who was the resident expert in sleazy exploitation films. Landis later wrote a short play titled *Burr*, which was inspired by Gore Vidal's biography of Aaron Burr. However, when the audience arrived they dis-covered the play was actually about the actor Raymond Burr.

The club's most significant event probably occurred in April, 1980, when Sex initiated a series of performance nights entitled Acts of Live Art. "It was a real turning point—a lot of people got their performance careers started that night," says Shawn McQuate. "Dany put on some really loud punk music and came out in a wheelchair. She went around having con-vulsions and screaming. It was really striking." Sex, who already had a reputation for removing his clothes in public, performed a Spanish mata-dor burlesque dance, his first in a long series of stripteases. Haring also disrobed, but came out wrapped in clear plastic and recited a rap song. Scharf did a caveman dance called The Bertha Butt Boogie. McQuate made a salad using the name Shawn Salad. Performing for the first time in years, Magnuson put on a majorette outfit and did a tap dance, baton twirl and juggling act to "Hot Stuff" by Donna Summer.

"We got into the goofiest stuff," says Sex. "Kenny was a big part of that because he was into silliness and it rubbed off on all of us after a while. We were pretty silly to begin with, but Kenny was super-silly."

By this time, Haring had decided the best work by young artists was appearing not in the galleries but on the streets of the Lower East Side. He developed a deeper appreciation for graffiti. "I was immediately attracted to the subway graffiti on several levels," he wrote later, "the obvious mastery of drawing and color, the scale, the pop imagery, the commitment to drawing worthy of risk, and the direct relationship between artist and audience." Haring was a fan of SAMO, and when "SAMO is dead" began appearing on the streets of SoHo, he performed a eulogy in SAMO's honor at Club 57.

One afternoon, while visiting the Strand Book Store on Broadway, Haring and Sex found a book published in 1940 titled *Sex Guide to Mar-ried Life*. "There was a chapter on homosexuality and it was so absurd," recalls Haring. "It had really funny descriptions of typical male and female homosexuals. Like, 'big hips for men.'" They bought the book and spent the rest of the afternoon on a stoop on St. Marks Place reading it aloud. Since Gay Pride Week, an annual event in the West Village, was coming up, they decided to make 500 posters of the homosexual descriptions and post them in the West Village. "We did it as a joke," says Haring. "But some people didn't think it was funny. It was the first time I got to see how something on the street could really affect people. They were freaking out and ripping it off the wall."

Once a haven for bohemians, the West Village had long since become overly commercialized, overpriced and overcrowded. East Village gays like Haring were growing increasingly worried about the possibility of a West Village invasion into their neighborhood. "One of the earliest signs of gentrification was that it was safe for the gay clones to come over here," says Haring. To thwart this development, Haring began stenciling the words "Clones Go Home" in orange Day-Glo paint at every entrance to the East Village from the west. He signed the stencil with the letters FAFH, which stood for Fags Against Facial Hair, an imaginary gay group. While Haring was spray-painting this message, David McDermott happened to walk by.

"I didn't know Keith, but I thought he was doing the greatest thing," says McDermott. "A lot of East Village gays were dressing up like clones at night and going over to the West Village. It was the first time anyone had said anything against the macho image of the clones." A few weeks later, McDermott was inspired to write an article attacking the clones in the *East Village Eye*. "First of all the whole Gay lifestyle is an anachronism left over from the year 1972," wrote McDermott. "The Gay West Village and its representatives in the neighborhoods throughout Manhattan, and in cities of America from San Francisco to Syracuse, is as relevant to the present as a Pierre Cardin suit and a wide tie."

Sex, in the meantime, had achieved a reputation as the leading poster artist of the East Village. During the summer a collection of his work was put on display at a short-lived neighborhood gallery called The Second Wave. However, just as Sex became known for the posters, he abruptly stopped making them. "I got sick of doing posters for other people," he says. "Sometimes the band didn't have a logo or anything and I'd make up the whole image. I was getting real frustrated. I always had my name real big on the poster anyway—like half as big as the band. So, I decided to put the whole thing to work for myself. I started making posters of myself and putting them on the street."

That summer, Club 57 reached a frantic peak of activity. Membership had risen to 119 and Magnuson was booking wacky parties every other night. "I hated it when I had to go home for vacation," says Stacy Elkin. "I was afraid I might miss something." A Father's Day celebration was held for Stanley; *Las Vegas Hillbillies* and *Loves of Hercules* were shown as a tribute to Mamie Van Doren and Jayne Mansfield; a tribute to Lawrence Welk was held; Elkin and McQuate staged another fashion show; *Cobra Woman*, Jack Smith's favorite movie, was screened; Acts of Live Art continued with parts two and three; and reruns from the *Monkees* TV show were shown. At the end of the month, the Monster Movie Club went on a field trip.

They gathered early in the morning and boarded a rented bus which took them to an amusement park in New Jersey. Almost immediately, they realized they'd made a mistake. Everyone at the park thought they were freaks. To make matters worse, Nomi and Arias had decided to come along wearing long blond wigs. "We wanted to be like surfers at the beach," recalls Arias. "Everyone wanted to kill us. We got on one ride and the man said, 'Look at the faggots.' He kept the ride going until we got sick. They were laughing and pointing at us. We stayed in the Haunted House. We liked it in there because it was cool and dark. The kids would walk by and scream when they saw us. They thought we were the monsters."

Everyone was creating new personas to complement the parties at the club. Incorporating elements from Liberace, Tom Jones, Mamie Van Doren and Paul America, Sex gradually evolved into a glitter Las Vegas version of the all-American kid—a handsome, fun-loving sex maniac with a foot-high shock of blond hair. His former girlfriend, Wendy Andreiev, transformed into Wendy Wild, the mushroom queen, while Katy Kattelman (who had been introduced to the club by Nomi) became Katy K, a New Wave Dolly Parton. Scharf and Straub became the Batusi Brothers. Magnuson, however, never seemed comfortable with any single identity and kept putting on new ones at every event.

Before long, outsiders began to notice what was happening at the club. Tseng Kwong Chi, a Chinese photographer raised in Canada and educated in France, arrived and began documenting the parties. "I got the impression every time Ann did a performance it was like a purge for her," he says. "She seemed to be pouring out all these things from her childhood. In the early days it was like they were spilling their guts. And I think it was totally subconscious."

Kwong Chi brought a friend, an art director named Dan Friedman, who was also struck by the energy of the scene. "They had an incredible amount of playfulness," says Friedman. "Even if you weren't formally involved in putting the shows together, you could instantly slip into a role. It was an organic transformation of people into a living theater. They were expanding their boundaries, altering and pushing them around by creating fantasy environments. They were also the dearest, sweetest, most decent people I'd ever met. It was almost like they were good Americans in a classic sense."

In August, 1980, the Colab artists occupied a former massage parlor near Times Square and converted it into a temporary art museum. Fashion Moda, a gallery in the South Bronx that had been cultivating graffiti-based art, also participated in the show. Scharf heard about the event from the sculptor John Ahearn, who had been visiting Club 57. Scharf arrived the next day and began painting fuse boxes and water coolers in the building. He quickly became embroiled in a series of arguments with artists who felt he was "invading their space."

"That was the first time we were confronted with Colab," says Haring. "The show was supposed to be an alternative space but everyone had these old ideas about territory. Kenny just wanted to paint fixtures and make them fun. But the day after he painted the water cooler, this guy came in and built a wall out of sheetrock right in front of it because he wanted a clean room for his installation." Haring hung a Xerox drawing next to Scharf's water cooler. Basquiat painted a wall and wrote "Free Sex" outside the entrance. "It was already getting heavy in there," says Haring. "All these winos and prostitutes were wandering in and nobody knew if they could keep it under control."

The exhibit received tremendous press coverage, including a cover story in *The Village Voice*. Even Lippard was impressed: "As a whole the show did successfully appeal to a fairly varied audience—locals as well as disillusioned sophisticates, cynical radicals and chic seekers," she wrote. "This accomplishment can't be underestimated."

In his review in *Art in America*, Jeffrey Deitch called it "a sort of art fun-house," and singled out Basquiat's contribution: "A patch of wall paint-ed by SAMO, the omnipresent graffiti sloganeer, was a knockout combi-nation of de Kooning and subway paint scribbles." A consultant and art buyer for the Citibank Corporation as well as a critic, Deitch subsequent-ly bought five drawings from Basquiat for $250. Basquiat was either unconcerned with his first sale or he put on a good acting job. "Jean kept on working as if I was interrupting him," recalls Deitch.

At the same time as the Times Square Show, Haring began curating art exhibits at Club 57, the first of which was an invitational that included a hundred local artists. He later staged a somewhat controversial erotic art show. "The day of the show, I went out to buy some supplies for the bar," says Magnuson. "When I got back there was a huge picture of a cock on the wall. I thought, if the people from the church ever see this... Lo and behold, Bishop Jacubik walked in with some people. We got into a little trouble, but Stanley always straightened things out." (During a church meeting, a member of the congregation wanted to know why such decadent people were allowed in the basement. Bishop Jacubik reportedly replied, "This is exactly where evil people belong—in a church.")

On August 16, Magnuson staged the Elvis Memorial Party, which fea-tured an Elvis shrine made by Katy K, a look-alike contest and the screen-ing of a film Magnuson had made in college. "I had a ton of makeup on and my hair was done up all high," says Sex. "And I had the heaviest eye-brows, like Groucho Marx." The basement was always a sweatbox when crowded and it was particularly packed that night. There was one air conditioner in the room and it had been going full blast for hours when some neighborhood kids began throwing beer on it. Sparks flew off, igniting the soundproof paneling on the back wall. The fire spread quick-ly and the room was filled with black smoke. Everyone screamed and ran for the door. "I pushed some girl," says Sex. "I said: 'GET OUT OF MY WAY! I'M NOT GETTING TRAPPED IN THIS!' I remember Jean-Michel was standing in the corner smoking pot. He was the only one who was-n't moving. He was laughing."

By the time the fire trucks arrived, everyone was in the street. The fire-men sealed off the block. A searchlight was turned on and a crowd of Elvis look-alikes immediately ran into the pool of light. The fire was already out (someone had taken off a jacket and smothered it), so the firemen stayed around and joined the festivities. "I grabbed April Palmieri and started having a big pose-a-rama in front of the fire trucks," says Sex. "But then the police arrived and they weren't much fun at all."

Despite the constant activity, Club 57 was always running out of money and never seemed to get the recognition it deserved. The regulars kept wondering when Warhol was going to show up and make them famous. But Warhol never came. "I sat at the bar thinking, yeah, no one's coming here," says Magnuson. "And no one writes about us. But in five years, they'll probably want to know all about it. And that's exactly what happened."

NEW YORK, NEW WAVE

It's 1985 and Keith Haring is working in a large loft on the corner of Broadway and Houston. The studio is neat and orderly—almost obsessively so by painters' standards. A small stack of finished paintings, each one carefully wrapped in plastic, leans against one wall. Four recently completed canvases hang on another. The paintings have an appealing directness, a result of Haring's mastery of universal sign language. He doesn't work from preliminary sketches or drawings, but prefers to let these images pour directly from his imagination onto a canvas. Although thoughtfully composed, the work retains an element of improvisation.

A long platform in the center of the loft is covered with books, catalogues and press clippings. Haring is seated at a desk, talking on a Mickey Mouse telephone. He is wearing a T-shirt, shorts and tennis shoes. He has closely cropped hair, blue eyes and a round, boyish face. At 12:45 P.M., Kenny Scharf arrives, announces it is a beautiful day and complains the room is too stuffy. He walks to a window, throws it open and breathes a sigh of relief. (In less than five minutes, Haring will ask his studio assistant to shut the window.) Scharf runs his hand across the surfaces of Haring's most recent paintings and inquires what type of paint was used. He is wearing a T-shirt, pegged pants and black Beatle boots. He has long sideburns and a jagged front tooth. Scharf and Haring studied together at SVA and lived in the same apartment for nearly a year. They continue to speak daily and consult each other before making even the most trivial decisions. Not since Jasper Johns and Robert Rauschenberg have two famous American artists formed such a close bond at such an early age. In the cutthroat environment created by the current art boom, alliances between powerful artists are common. Friendships like theirs, however, remain an oddity.

"I remember going to Club 57 when it was just a bar," says Scharf. "We would hang out and listen to the jukebox. Ann [Magnuson] asked me to do an art show there and I remember thinking, this girl is kind of interesting, but she's so demure. Later, we began to realize how incredible she was and how many different personalities she could portray."

"It was the best when Ann was managing the club," says Haring. "In the beginning, it was Susan Hannaford, Tom Scully and Ann. Other important people were Dany Johnson and Drew Straub."

"And John Sex," says Scharf.

After being pressed for more names, Scharf adds Shawn McQuate to the list. "He was part of it," says Scharf. "We used to do weird religious things—chant and make noises. Everyone would be spellbound. 'Who are these people? What are they doing?' Shawn started off sort of New Wave, but by the end he was getting really tribal. He did some incredible fashion shows—very avant-garde. I mean, even for today. No one will ever catch up with his fashion shows. The major thing about Club 57 was that everything had to be entertaining. Like, you could do something serious, but it had to be fun."

"There was a lot of recycling trash and satire on the sixties," says Haring. "Everyone was in the same boat then. No one was jealous of anyone. As soon as I started to make money, all those people on the borderline couldn't handle it." Haring talks briefly about the store he plans to open in the spring and holds up a Smurf radio as an example of the type of object he will be selling. Because it is a blatantly commercial venture, the store is a controversial project. But Haring's primary appeal has always been to the mass market and he has no intentions of making any changes in this regard.

"He knew everyone," says Scharf, nodding at Haring. "I used to walk down the street with him and he was like a politician. He was nice to everybody. I didn't have the patience. Like, I'd say, 'Why are you talking to this person?'" Scharf turns to Haring. "You should run for mayor."

"Run for mayor?" says Haring while setting down the radio.

"You're still nice to people," says Scharf. "I'm trying to get into this new movie—*The Jetsons Movie*. It would be a dream come true. Then I could say goodbye to the art world and only do movies." Scharf waits for a reaction. "Not really," he adds finally.

Scharf was born in Hollywood, California in 1958, a month after the launching of the first Sputnik, This fact is mentioned only because space travel became a recurring theme in his work, an obsession that may have been nurtured by the urban landscape of Los Angeles, where car washes and coffee shops can resemble space stations. His parents are transplanted Jews from New York. Scharf's father worked briefly as a Catskills comic in his youth. Later, he founded and ran a successful women's knitwear business in California. Scharf was the baby of the family and had two older brothers much closer in age. "He had an imagination that just wouldn't quit," says his mother, Rose. "He never shut his mouth and he always had something going on."

The arrival of a color television set at his parents' home in the San Fernando Valley provided Scharf with one of the happiest days of his life. Although only six at the time, he still recalls the incident with vivid detail. "The first color sets had colored dots on a black surface," he says, "so if you looked really close, it was like hallucinating. I watched everything. If you were that close, it didn't really matter what you watched. But Saturday morning was the most fun time of the week, when my favorite shows came on: *The Jetsons*, *The Flintstones*, and *Felix the Cat*."

When he was 15, Scharf's parents moved to Beverly Hills, primarily so their son could attend the richest high school in California, an institution with its own oil well, TV station and observatory. Coming from the less pretentious and more plebian San Fernando Valley, Scharf had trouble adjusting to the school. "I hated it," he says. "It was full of the worst brats. Everyone had a Porsche and I drove a Capri. I got into a groovy cocaine and Quaalude set when I was sixteen, but I always felt I was playing with it, almost using them. They were so spoiled. They'd smash up their car and Daddy would buy them a new Ferrari."

Scharf had been painting seriously even before entering high school, but it was at Beverly Hills High that he developed his affinity for Pop Art and surrealism. He painted several Rousseau-style jungle scenes and some outer-space vignettes. By the time he entered the University of Santa Barbara, in 1976, his own aesthetic was emerging. It was surprisingly mature for a freshman. In 1977, he produced *Barbara Simpson's New*

Kitchen, a small acrylic painting that showed a suburban housewife standing proudly in her kitchen next to a small dragon, whose tail looped over the counter and disappeared into the sink. Scharf took an art history class with Eileen Guggenheim, who told him about the SoHo art scene. In 1978, he moved into an apartment on 55th Street and Seventh Avenue.

During the summer of 1980, when Club 57 was reaching its peak, a painter named Jonny Rudo invited Scharf to share a cavernous two-floor apartment that was wedged between a pair of skyscrapers on Sixth Avenue between 39th and 40th Streets. (The loft actually belonged to photographer Jimmy DeSana and Rudo was subleasing it.) Shortly after Scharf moved in, Rudo met David McDermott and Peter McGough at an art opening. McDermott visited the loft and convinced Rudo to let them move in as well. "The upstairs was very old," says McDermott. "It was the perfect place for us to establish our time machine. When we arrived we found piles of plastic stuff and junk all over the place. The refrigerator had toy men glued to it. We scraped them off." They found an antique tea set in a closet and set the table for a tea party. When Scharf came home, McDermott approached him and announced: "We're here to kick you out."

It was clear McDermott and Scharf could never get along. While Scharf was propelling his environment into the future, McDermott and McGough were putting an equal amount of energy into the past. McDermott scraped plastic toys off the appliances, while someone burned some antiques in the fireplace. Rudo unhappily found himself trapped in the middle of an ongoing feud. "David went through all my clothes and threw out anything modern he didn't approve of, including a lot of expensive items," recalls Rudo. "After that I recovered my senses and asked David and Peter to leave." A few weeks later, Rudo found an apartment in the East Village and moved out. Finding himself alone, Scharf invited Keith Haring to move in.

Also born in 1958, Haring was raised in Kutztown, a sleepy, picturesque town in the rolling hills of eastern Pennsylvania. Located two and a half hours from New York, Kutztown is a clean, orderly, Pennsylvania Dutch community. Haring's ancestors—all Germans—stretch back several generations in the state. His father, an avid cartoonist in his spare time, works for the Western Electric Company. The oldest of four children,

Haring has three sisters. "He was always unselfish," says his mother. "In the third grade Keith donated money from his paper route to buy art supplies for underprivileged kids in a nearby city. We didn't ask him to do things like that. He just did them on his own."

In high school Haring began drifting away from his family. He grew his hair long, took LSD and attended Grateful Dead concerts. "I wanted to be a hippie," he says. "But it was already too late for that scene." After graduating, he followed the advice of his guidance counselor and went to Pittsburgh to study commercial art. Six months later he quit and hitchhiked to San Francisco. Within a year he was back in Pittsburgh, working a CETA job at the Pittsburgh Center for the Arts. In 1977, he attended a Pierre Alechinsky retrospective at the Carnegie Institute. "Alechinsky's work was similar to what I was doing," says Haring, who was making large, abstract, Dubuffet-like drawings with tempera paint on paper. "I was getting into the Eastern idea of calligraphy and drawing self-contained shapes that got energy from themselves." When the director of the center saw Haring's work, he was sufficiently impressed to arrange a solo show for him, held in the summer of 1978.

Later that year, at age 20, Haring moved to New York. Drew Straub, a friend from Kutztown who had been commuting to CBGB for over a year, also quit school and went with him. Haring enrolled in SVA and Straub got a job as a gallery assistant in SoHo.

In December, while living in the West Village, the two attended the Nova Convention, the first mingling of the old avant-garde with the new generation, an event held at Entermedia Theater in the East Village. The convention featured performances by such venerable masters as John Cage, Merce Cunningham, William Burroughs and Jack Smith, along with relative unknowns like Laurie Anderson and the B-52's. "We just stumbled into the theater while walking down the street," says Haring.

"The crowd that night was eagerly awaiting the promised arrival of Keith Richards and/or Patti Smith," wrote Robert Becker in *Interview*. "Philip Glass' organ recital wasn't greeted with overwhelming enthusiasm. Out came Laurie Anderson with fellow performer Julia Hayward to the shouts of 'rock'n'roll,' armed only with a slide projector, a violin and a microphone. But by the end of their short performance, having used Laurie's tape-bow violin, a synthesizer of some sort which sent their voices from Mickey Mouse to Louis Armstrong, and a series of images that enticed the whole audience, groupies and St. Marks poets alike, the artists had mesmerized and aroused everyone and left the stage to a spirited ovation."

Haring, however, was even more moved by the poetry readings, especially those by Burroughs and Brion Gyson. Within a few weeks, he and Straub left the West Village and moved into an apartment on East Second Street. Haring began writing verse, dressing in a black beret and black clothes, and describing himself as a "terrorist poet." Straub dyed his hair bright blue and started wearing a fluorescent yellow raincoat.

While walking home from school one day, Haring discovered a roll of photographic backdrop paper in a garbage pile. He dragged the paper back to a small, vacant room in the school and covered the walls and floor with it, converting the room into a private drawing studio. "I was getting into Burroughs a lot—making videotapes that experimented with his 'cut-up' technique," he says. "One of the tapes showed me drawing in the room with a soundtrack by Devo."

"The best thing about Keith is he could go ahead and do things without verification from anyone," says Samantha McEwen, a fellow SVA student. "The school had a sculpture studio on Twenty-second Street with a loading dock and huge garage doors that looked out onto the street. One day Keith was drawing on the backdrop paper in front of the doors. He was using Chinese drawing ink and he was so pleased when he discovered that ink because it could cover large areas really fast. People walking by would stop and talk to him and he had a series of incredible conversations with them. One woman thought the drawing looked like Noah's Ark. Another guy started talking about the war, saying it looked like machines and guns. I think Keith started working out the idea that he wanted his art to be a part of these people. Of course, Keith and Kenny moving in together had a lot to do with what happened later. When you get two people like that together, they attract so much. Their place didn't function like an apartment—it was more like a nursery. A lot of people were up there all the time. Kenny had a long fringe of blond hair that he'd jelled to stick straight out. I remember him showing me his refrigerator. He was so proud of it. He kept sticking his palettes on the fridge. This was his main piece of art—the ongoing saga of the refrigerator. There was a funny abandoned room on the top floor. It was really just a closet that had never been redecorated. Kenny cleared it out and started painting the walls with fluorescent paints. He thought it would be a perfect place to take mushrooms. He'd get high, go in there and paint for hours. One morning he insisted on taking a vacuum cleaner he'd painted for a walk—as if it were a dog."

"It was the beginning of the whole black-light era," says Brathwaite. "Everyone would take mushrooms, go in Kenny's closet and bug out. Kenny would play psychedelic music and Keith would bring out paper and say, 'Let's draw.'" Scharf painted a fluorescent orange and blue spiral on the ceiling and discovered if he stared at it long enough, he could experience out-of-body voyages. "I'd leave my body, go into the spiral and fly around in space," he says. "It was the most uplifting experience." After it happened once, Scharf made sure he stared at the spiral every time he took mushrooms.

Haring, meanwhile, stopped making abstract drawings and began work on a new style. A few months earlier, he'd been cutting up headlines from the *New York Post*, rearranging the words, Xeroxing them and posting the results on the street: "Pope Killed for Freed Hostage," "Mob Flees Pope Rally," "Reagan Death Cops Hunt Pope." He also began tampering with billboard ads in the subway, drawing flying saucers and other objects on the ads with a magic marker. However, after noticing the city was covering unrenewed ads with black tar paper, Haring began drawing on the tar paper with chalk. It was illegal, so the drawings had to be simple enough to execute quickly. He developed a complex vocabulary based on easily identifiable symbols—babies, dogs, angels, snakes, pyramids, etc. Although instantly recognizable, the images were put together in ambiguous narratives. The result was a synthesis of most of the important styles of the period, one that embraced graffiti, the new imagery of SoHo, semiotics and the political activism of Colab. Somehow, Haring had taken the branches of pluralism and united them in one simple cartoon style. For freehand drawings, the work was amazingly uniform: Haring could draw an endless series of crawling babies and each one would be virtually identical in size and shape. He became fanatical about the drawings and began putting them everywhere.

While Haring was chalking up the neighborhood, Scharf was "customizing" everything in sight, especially televisions, radios, toasters, blenders and telephones. After gluing plastic baubles on the appliances, he'd paint them with colorful decorations and goofy cartoon faces. "The telephone became another ongoing saga," says Samantha McEwen. "It was constantly being repainted and you could never tell what number you were dialing." One morning Scharf asked Haring for his glasses and those were customized as well.

Every morning Scharf walked to a dingy coffee shop called the Hippodrome, where he ate breakfast. The interior of the shop was painted an electric yellow and the window booths were lined with plastic hanging plants. One day Scharf asked if he could customize the plants. "He painted them bright pink and blue," says McEwen. "The chef thought it was really cool."

In September, the Club 57 crowd was invited to throw a party at a bar called Nobodies. Scharf went in a day early and painted a mural of an atomic explosion with the word "fun" emanating from the center. During the party, Magnuson performed as Penelope and the Exploding Mind Dimension and the Batusi Brothers sang "For Your Love." "Everyone took acid," says McQuate. "We crawled under a canvas and body-painted each other. Later on, we went to Kenny's and tripped in his psychedelic closet. I remember standing in one spot for over an hour because I felt I'd finally discovered the way we were meant to stand. I was sure that primordial man had stood this way. Keith went off and read a book about Andy Warhol, which I thought was a strange thing to do on acid."

There were two developments in the underground film scene that year: Eric Mitchell released *Underground USA* and Glenn O'Brien began work on *New York Beat*. *Underground USA*, the most ambitious film to come out of the New Cinema movement, was shot in 16mm and starred Patti Astor, Rene Ricard, Cookie Mueller, Taylor Mead and Mitchell, who also directed and wrote the script. The film opens with a long pan of a West Side street lined with homosexual hustlers, one of whom visits the Mudd Club and picks up a jaded rich girl. The rest of the film revolves around their passionless love affair—which lasts only a few days. Although the film takes place in the late '70s, it seems closer in spirit to Warhol's movies of the mid-'60s. The crucial difference, however, is that Warhol stars always played themselves, while in *Underground USA* Mitchell and Astor, the two leads, often seem to be mimicking characters out of a Warhol film. The movie had some funny moments, but it was not the commercial success Mitchell was hoping for. It did, however, attract a cult following in the East Village, where it had an extended run on St.

Marks Place.

Although not released until 2001 (under the title *Downtown 81*), *New York Beat* was also inspired by the downtown scene. The project began when Edo, a photographer for *Interview*, and Maripol, art director of Fiorucci, told O'Brien that Fiorucci had found a potential backer for a New Wave movie. "I wrote a scenario in one day and they gave us $250,000," says O'Brien, who must have been a little surprised considering he had no film experience. A union crew was hired and O'Brien and Edo co-directed. "The script was an exaggerated fairy tale based on a day in the life of Jean-Michel," says O'Brien. "It started with him being released from the hospital, getting kicked out of his apartment and trying to sell a painting to a rich model. We came up with a lot of excuses to throw in bands like the Contortions, Kid Creole, Tuxedomoon and Gray. David McDermott, Chris Stein, Deborah Harry and Amos Poe all had bit parts. Jean-Michel was a really good actor, although he mumbled a lot."

Basquiat lived in the production office during the course of the shooting, his first stable living environment in months. He had stopped writing SAMO at this point and was drawing primitive, expressionistic images—mostly with crayons on notebook paper. Although Basquiat retained his penchant for words and phrases, the neat SAMO-style lettering had given way to childlike scrawls. He was aware of important developments taking place in SoHo: Schnabel's unprecedented success had been accompanied by the arrival of the Italian painters, Clemente, Chia and Cucchi (known as the three C's), who were being packaged and promoted by Zurich art dealer Bruno Bischofberger. More than any other dealer, Bischofberger was setting the trends for the '80s. He was already Schnabel's representative in Europe, and was orchestrating an international wave of neo-expressionism. Hilton Kramer, a conservative art critic for the *New York Times*, had already thrown his support behind the movement.

"Bruno conspired the whole phenomenon of new painting," says Diego Cortez. "He had a very eighties approach that was popular with the artists. He would buy everything up front, taking the risk himself. He supplied eight-by-ten color transparencies for all the magazines and made beautiful, expensive books. He got out of the cheap attitude that paralleled the alternative spaces." Bischofberger also had a flashy, international style which impressed many young artists.

In the fall of 1980, Cortez was putting together an exhibition of current American art that was supposed to travel to Europe. "It was going to Bologna," says Cortez. "That fell through and then it was supposed to go to Florence. That fell through and then it was supposed to go to Rome. By that time, I'd gotten into the graffiti thing, and it had developed into a larger project—three or four exhibitions." P.S. 1, the alternative space in Queens, agreed to mount a portion of the show, which Cortez titled New York/New Wave. While scouting material for the show, Cortez arrived at the *New York Beat* production office and asked to see Basquiat's current work.

"When Jean-Michel and Fred Brathwaite started coming into the rock context, it was the greatest period for me," says Cortez. "One reason I left the art scene was because it was so white. You'd go to openings and find white walls, white people and minimal white art. Now there was finally starting to be a cultural mix. I'd met Jean around 1979 when he had his Mohawk. That attracted me to him immediately—the fact he was black and had a Mohawk. I would see him in SoHo all the time. He was always asking me for money. When I came to visit him, I saw he was doing some fantastic things. I started to sell some of them right away. Chris Stein and Deborah Harry bought a large piece on raw canvas."

Organized in part around documentary photos of CBGB and the Mudd Club, New York/New Wave opened in February 1981 and included 20 artists associated with Club 57, murals by a dozen graffiti artists, photography and artwork by four rock stars (David Byrne, Chris Stein, Brian Eno, Alan Vega) and drawings by several dozen children between the ages of six and 14. (It also included a memorial to John Lennon.) Widely misunderstood and misinterpreted, the show never attracted the praise showered on the Times Square Show, even though history has proven it to be a far more seminal exhibition. It was the first exhibit to acknowledge the importance of the Mudd Club and Club 57.

"Warhol's influence is the most pervasive," wrote Richard Flood in *Artforum*. "He's the model and the master. What Warhol signifies is the ability to make it in both worlds—art and commerce—and make it big. He has promoted himself as a franchise that is the art world's answer to McDonalds."

"No one seems too clear about what constitutes 'punk art,'" wrote Kay Larson in *New York* magazine. "Is it truly a style, or just the look-alike product of a bunch of young music lovers with safety pins in their ear-lobes? A calm, rational assessment might have provided a good opportu-nity for clarification. Unfortunately, this fevered exhibition looks less like an explanation than an advertisement for a Club Med-Mudd Club Party."

"One of the functions of the show was to document the rock scene, which I considered to be over at that point," explains Cortez. "People said, 'We've already seen these pictures.' But the reason I wanted them was to end it. Jean had fifteen pieces in the show. He was the only one I thought was so fantastic that he had to have paintings on canvas. I think some peo-ple were expecting an introduction to neo-expressionism, but the show wasn't about painting at all. It was really a neo-Pop show."

The critics didn't like it, but Henry Geldzahler, former curator of the Metropolitan Museum, certainly did. "Henry fell in love with the show," says Cortez. "He told me it was just like the one he did at the Met [in 1969]. We became good friends."

Sandro Chia, one of the Italian neo-expressionists, wanted to buy the most important Basquiat painting from the show and was willing to pay $1,000 for it. Cortez wanted more. A few days later, Christophe de Menil, a well-known collector from Texas, bought the painting for $2,500. Emilio Mazzoli, an Italian dealer, came to see Basquiat's work and immediately arranged his first solo show, which was held in Modena, Italy. Annina Nosei was interested in representing Basquiat in New York. Cortez was leaving for Europe and told Nosei they would discuss Basquiat's future when he returned.

"By the time I got back, she'd given him a few thousand dollars and he was in her gallery," says Cortez, who, as Basquiat's informal dealer, was still holding 100 drawings and 20 paintings. Cortez discovered that Basquiat was working in the gallery basement. "Who ever heard of an artist working in the basement of a gallery?" he says incredulously. "Peo-ple can joke about it now, but it's the kind of thing that could kill some-one off. It's bad taste. People refer to it as the dungeon period."

No one was really sure what was going to happen to Basquiat in 1981. Was he a teenage prodigy or a novelty folk act? Would a black artist be accepted by the upper-class elite? SAMO had toyed with radical politics, but Basquiat the painter dropped most of his overt political content, sub-stituting diagrams and phrases lifted from old medical journals. Ele-ments from the old days were retained, most noticeably the crown, a graffiti symbol for a "king" of a subway line. Basquiat also included a few skelly courts (chalk diagrams used by children in street games). Super-heroes and black celebrities (especially boxers and musicians) became favorite topics, perhaps reflecting the artist's own quest for fame. Certain words appeared often in his paintings: tin, asbestos, mud, oil, ribs, pork, tar town. These words were often repeated many times, crossed out or partially erased. Although many theories existed on the paintings, there was little consensus. DeAk felt the constant repetition stemmed from school punishment, while Cortez saw something shamanistic about Basquiat's "scratching of the surface." Other critics felt the crossed-out words merely reflected Basquiat's frustration with the inability of lan-guage to accurately express emotion. (As in: "This isn't the right word, but it's as close as I can come.") Most of the paintings did not depend on content anyway—Basquiat's strangely elegant sense of color and compo-sition was enough to keep the work selling. Before long, unsettling crea-tures with black faces, black bodies, white almond-shaped eyes and no hands began appearing in many of the paintings.

"Jean knew how to pick things," says his old friend Al Diaz. "He'd write down really funny Spanish curses you'd hear from the old people in the neighborhood. He knew how to put things together to remind you of something else."

"When I met Jean-Michel, it seemed to me that he was always being run out of those residential hotels," says Nosei. "He was very disorderly and very fertile in drawings and his work reminded me of Cy Twombly. It had a quality you don't find on the walls of the street—a quality of poetry and a universal message of the sign. It was a little bit immature, but very beautiful. When I started to work with him, I had to call a hotel to give a deposit for him to sleep there. He worked in my basement because he didn't have a space to paint. It seemed he liked to come here and have breakfast with my secretaries and see people. He was very enthusiastic and friendly. His father and his sister came. He talked about his mother as all very angry adolescents do, as if she'd left him. The paintings he made downstairs were fantastic. Major artists came and seemed to be ready to learn from those canvases. The people who know about art were completely taken by the simplicity and directness of his images. Collectors were fighting to have this painting or that painting. It was an incredible phenomenon. The money affected him because of drugs. He could afford drugs."

By this time Nosei realized Basquiat had an important career ahead of him and that his early work was very valuable. She asked Cortez to return all the paintings he was holding. Cortez refused and Nosei served legal notice against him. Basquiat, Cortez and Nosei had a meeting at Nosei's office to settle the matter. Cortez asked for $30,000. Nosei pretended to be appalled and accused him of extortion.

"The only reason I made a figure like that was because she was making me so angry," says Cortez. "I subsequently sold almost all the work to Bruno."

When Basquiat's friends discovered Nosei was paying top dollar for his early work, they flooded the gallery with scraps of paper, refrigerator doors—anything with a SAMO tag. When an artist presents someone with a present of his work, it is not considered polite to turn around and sell it a few months later, so Basquiat could not have been very happy. He visited a few people just to paint over every mark he'd left behind. Alienated from former friends, he was being surrounded by leeches, many of whom were feeding his ego in return for free drugs. Everyone was giving him career advice.

Haring's career was also taking off, but in a much different fashion. Cortez had only sold one Haring drawing from the P.S. 1 show—for $350. But while Basquiat was courting rich collectors, Haring was becoming a hit with the lower-middle class. Although the vast majority of subway riders hated graffiti on subway cars, they fell in love with Haring's chalk drawings. Even the graffiti writers (a difficult audience to impress) showed remarkable respect for Haring's work by leaving it untouched. Before he was known to the art world, Haring earned his reputation on the street.

His work was also showing remarkable growth. After being exposed to radiation from a spaceship, the crawling baby became a "radiant" baby. Dogs began barking, snakes came out of the trees and atomic bombs began going off in the background. "One can be tempted to analyze Haring's images from a semiotic point of view," wrote Jeffrey Deitch in "Why the Dogs Are Barking," the best essay on Haring's early work. "The stubby crawling baby, for instance, reads not just 'baby,' but such things as human vulnerability, a sense of unfettered freedom associated with a baby's developing consciousness, and a polymorphous sexuality. One could make a similar analysis of Haring's entire image vocabulary. His images are insightfully chosen and carefully worked out with a sensitivity toward layers of meaning and sexual connotation…. Haring's image of an outsized atom bomb bouncing across the screen of a TV set illustrates our strange situation particularly well. Life is still full of fun on the surface, but underneath it all, the specter of nuclear destruction creeps closer and closer. We can still frolic around like Haring's little babies, but the barking of the dogs becomes louder and louder."

Haring was reaching a vast new audience and exposing them to art in a daily, intimate manner. Since the work was unsigned, everyone started to wonder who was doing it. Many bizarre theories were invented to account for the sudden appearance of the drawings. It was only a matter of time before the newspapers, TV stations and magazines interviewed Haring. Not long after, the collectors began appearing at his apartment on Sixth Avenue.

Haring graciously made a point of showing the visitors his roommate's work, but no one seemed interested in Scharf, who had just graduated from SVA. Faced with daily rejections, Scharf grew depressed and wouldn't get out of bed until late afternoon. It was also getting difficult for him to paint. He was happy for Haring, but their friendship was put under considerable strain. In an attempt to get some publicity for his own work, Scharf wrote an article for the *SoHo Weekly News* about an artist named Van Chrome. "Tired of the same old appliances?" wrote Scharf. "Pop a little zip in your life and treat your everyday electrical appliance to Van Chrome's functional home-improvement idea: customizing!… Bored with television? Hire Van to make your TV experience incredible. With Van Chrome's expertise, you'll have things to watch even if the set is turned off! Best of all, when your electrical energy runs out, you don't have to throw your appliances away; they become art objects reminiscent of the prosperous electrical age we've come to know and love. Van Chrome will customize anything and everything—appliances, bicycles, eyeglasses, bodies, closets, cars, coffee shops. Just ask him and he'll do it." Scharf listed his phone number, but the article disappointingly produced only one phone call.

Haring was not naïve about dealers and galleries. He had worked for a few months for a dealer named Tony Shafrazi, who was getting ready to open a new gallery in SoHo, and Shafrazi had already expressed interest in representing his former employee. But so had others, including Brooke Alexander, Hal Bromm and Nosei, who included Haring in her group show Public Address in 1981. Haring, however, was having trouble making the transition from public graffiti artist to the more commercially minded gallery artist. "There was a philosophical purity and excitement about the drawings in the subway," says Dan Friedman. "It was a very clear alternative to what artists were doing in galleries. So when Keith wanted to show in galleries, it became a philosophical dilemma for him. He visited me one day and I asked him to draw on a big vase I had. I think that was the first object he drew on that wasn't paper and I think it opened up a lot of possibilities for him." One thing became clear when Haring entered the studio: he did not intend to hide his sexual identity. Several of the studio paintings contained openly homosexual references.

In 1981, Steve Mass unexpectedly began showing up at Club 57. The first night he appeared, Mass took a seat at the bar and Johnson crawled up to him on her hands and knees and began barking at him. Anita Sarko, Mass' deejay, also began attending the club's parties. "They gave me heavy attitude at the door because they considered the Mudd Club so chic," says Sarko. "People give you attitude if they expect attitude back. One night I was there, they were doing a spoof on the New Romantic look from England. Now, I wasn't part of that. I always dressed the same way I would down South. If anything, my look was Southern Belle. But Dany [Johnson] was wearing a big hat like mine and they thought I'd be upset, but I was honored. They made fun of Steve and he took it the same way."

Mass began hiring the Club 57 crowd in the hope they could revitalize his dying club. Haring was one of the first to be employed. "I didn't even have a job title," says Haring. "He just wanted me there so my friends would come. There was an empty room on the fourth floor, so I thought, what the hell, I'll make this a late-night art gallery." For his first show, Haring hung the work of more than 100 artists, including everyone who had ever shown at Club 57 as well as the graffiti writers he'd met through New York/New Wave. The second show was an exhibit of photographs by Tseng Kwong Chi. Beyond Words, the third show, was co-curated by Fred Brathwaite and Lennie McGurr, who were known by their graffiti tags, Fab Five Freddy and Futura 2000. A week before the show opened, Brathwaite went to a cocktail party where he met Patti Astor, the star of Underground USA.

214 • ADVENTURES IN THE COUNTERCULTURE

"I'd seen the movie and Patti was my favorite star," says Brathwaite. "So I asked for her autograph." Astor signed a scrap of paper and then kissed it, leaving a perfect lipstick imprint. Brathwaite invited her to attend the opening party for Beyond Words. He also told her about a film Charlie Ahearn was writing, producing and directing called *Wild Style*. It was going to be the first feature film on the graffiti subculture.

Through his contacts in both the downtown scene and the South Bronx, Brathwaite was one of the first to realize something few New Yorkers knew: a complex subculture had blossomed in the South Bronx between 1974 and 1977. The subculture had its own music (rap), its own form of dance (breaking) and its own art style (graffiti). Collectively known as "hip hop," this subculture also had striking parallels with the East Village punk movement: both were reactions against disco, both had affectations for S&M leather gear, both had musical styles derived from late-'60s records, both were youth movements despised by the middle class. In fact, CBGB had a parallel club in the South Bronx called The Black Door. Even more remarkable, the two scenes knew next to nothing about each other. Edit deAk, the first person in the art scene to draw a connection between the two worlds, invited a group of South Bronx rappers to appear at the Kitchen. Astor also realized what was happening and immediately decided she had to have a part in *Wild Style*.

FUN GALLERY

There is the new movement. There always has been the new movement and there always will be the new movement. It is strange that a thing which comes as regularly as clockwork should always be a surprise. In new movements the pendulum takes a great swing, charlatans crowd in, innocent apes follow, the masters make their successes and they make their mistakes as all pioneers must do.

—Robert Henri, 1915

In the spring of 1981, the New York art scene was thrown into a tizzy with the opening of Julian Schnabel's joint exhibition at the Mary Boone and Leo Castelli galleries. Although Schnabel's work was by no means universally praised (most critics found something negative to say about it), the stamp of approval of SoHo's leading art dealer elevated the young painter into another league entirely. Castelli had not taken on a new artist in 10 years and the addition of Schnabel to his highly regarded stable gave the budding neo-expressionist movement one of its first signs of credibility. A smart businessman, Castelli knew something was happening and wanted to get in on it. *Exile*, Schnabel's most popular painting from the show, had already been sold for a reported $20,000; in fact, every painting in the exhibit was sold in advance, mostly to well-known, influential collectors. Everyone knew this was true because the buyers' names had been conspicuously posted on the wall next to each painting. Almost overnight, Schnabel became a rich man.

Suddenly, it was no longer fashionable to be a starving artist living in an East Village garret. Artists saw the future and it was painted with neo-expressionist brushstrokes and illuminated by neon dollar signs. Many of the TriBeCa performance artists, who had struggled for years making very good work on virtually no pay, gave up performance and picked up paintbrushes. Hundreds of neo-expressionist paintings appeared in the galleries with impressive speed.

But then, the following fall, Keith Haring emerged. And when Haring held his first solo show at the Tony Shafrazi Gallery in October 1982, it was in many ways an even bigger triumph than Schnabel's. Not only was the opening packed with collectors, reporters, rock stars and famous artists, it was being taped for network television. Haring wasn't commanding prices equal to Schnabel's, but one had to consider that Haring took only a few minutes to complete a painting. Besides, Haring was already more famous than Schnabel and fame was just as important as money. To achieve this notoriety Haring had employed marketing techniques similar to those used by the rock industry: he gave away 10,000 posters during his show (most of which were handed out at an anti-nuclear demonstration in Central Park) and distributed free buttons covered with his distinctive imagery. Not long after his success, dozens of struggling artists covered the streets of the East Village with a shower of New Wave graffiti. Some worked on semiotic-influenced pictograms, while others borrowed spray-can techniques from the original graffiti artists.

Midway between the Schnabel and Haring openings, Patti Astor and Bill Stelling opened the Fun Gallery in the East Village. Underfunded, operated by a pair of novices who had never sold a painting before, the Fun quickly became the most influential gallery in New York by staging

Kenny Scharf's second solo show, held in September 1982, and Jean-Michel Basquiat's second solo show, held the following month. By illuminating the links between the East Village and the South Bronx, the gallery staked out an important aesthetic at a time when most SoHo galleries were loading up on neo-expressionism. Inexplicably, the Fun struggled along for four years, never making much money, and finally closed in July 1985.

Patti "Astor" Titchener grew up in Cincinnati, wanted to be a ballet star and got as far as the junior company of the Cincinnati Ballet before it became obvious she wasn't built for the job. At 16, she had a body like Jayne Mansfield and a face to match. Both parents were psychiatrists, so she was expected to be somewhat odd, but still—she was a bit much for a gritty steel town on the banks of the Ohio River. She drove a 289 Mustang convertible with a stickshift and a Harley Davidson motorcycle. Everyone assumed she was a bad girl.

"She wasn't really," says Janet Borden, her best friend at the time. "Patti was always very sweet and protective to me. Even in high school she was wonderfully exotic and flamboyant. She had really long hair, wore very short miniskirts, and looked very up-to-the-moment. There was an area in town where the flower children lived and we always tried to hang out there, although Patti was always much better at it than I was."

In her junior year, Astor's high school advisor told her that based on her grade-point average, the only college likely to accept her was the Colorado State Institute for Women. Astor studied like mad, beefed up her activities and scored well enough on her SATs to get accepted into several Ivy League schools. She chose Barnard because it meant moving to New York City. "It was terrible," she says. "They expected you to stay in your room and memorize for a good three or four hours every night. All I wanted to do was drop acid and listen to Jimi Hendrix." Manhattan youth culture at the time was essentially divided into two wings: The East Village was headquarters for the more frivolous, fun-loving set. On the weekends this crowd dropped acid and went to rock concerts at the Fillmore. The Motherfuckers, a local streetgang that employed radical politics to intimidate merchants and tourists, were a visible force on St. Marks Place. (To their credit, they briefly kept the Fillmore open for free one night a week.) Barnard, on the other hand, was located on Manhattan's Upper West Side, a neighborhood that housed a larger and more serious group of radicals. It was toward this group that Astor gravitated. When the SDS formed its affinity groups and went underground to start the Weathermen, Astor joined a separate but equally extreme organization known as the Running Dogs. "We were hardcore and fought police," she says, "but we didn't want to be associated with the Weathermen. They were such ridiculous rich kids. They were into a sickening, self-hate thing." Astor was arrested and jailed three times and was once beaten so badly by riot police that she had to be taken to Bellevue Hospital.

In 1973, Astor moved to San Francisco and found a job as a receptionist at a recording studio. After a few weeks, she met Eric Mitchell, who had just arrived from France. Both were expecting the city to be wild and exciting, but they were quickly disappointed. The hippies had long since moved to the country and those who remained had become pacified by the California welfare system. Astor called her grandmother and requested funds for a European adventure. She spent six months living in little hotels in Paris, hanging out alone, until she decided to move back to New York.

She arrived just in time for a brief flowering of the East Village underground filmmaking scene. Mitchell, who was also interested in a film career, arrived from San Francisco. In 1976, they answered Amos Poe's ad in the *Village Voice* and were cast in *Unmade Beds*.

"It was shown at the Deauville Film Festival," says Astor. "Eric was in his punk rock period. He'd been hanging out at CBGB and dancing the pogo. He refused to speak French because he wanted everyone to think he was an American. It was a bit ridiculous."

A slew of films followed: *Snakewoman, The Foreigner, Rome 78, Kidnapped, Long Island Four* and *Underground USA*. In 1978, Astor dyed her hair platinum and began cultivating the bombshell image. She could walk into any art gallery in town and within minutes be surrounded by adoring fans. They didn't know who she was, but they knew she had charisma. "Duncan Hannah had all this upward mobility and wanted to be in the swinging New York art scene," says Astor. "We were just his swarmy friends who would show up at all the parties with him."

Steven Kramer, a promising artist from Minneapolis who played keyboards in the Contortions, had a reputation for life in the fast lane that rivaled even Astor's. When the two were married in 1978, they seemed a perfect, if somewhat self-destructive couple. Their traditional Southern wedding was held at Astor's home in Cincinnati. "The marriage just never worked out, for all the usual reasons," says Astor. "One night Steven was tap dancing on a ledge at a party and pretended to lose his balance. Then he really lost his balance and fell. Fortunately, he hit a roof two stories down. Otherwise he would have gone nine stories." Kramer's face was flattened and a wire cage had to be built around his head to hold the broken bones in place. He was in the hospital for three months. When he got out, he began drinking heavily and using drugs. After he stopped painting, Astor divorced him. Kramer survived two heroin overdoses and finally admitted himself to the St. Mary's Rehabilitation Center in Minneapolis.

In 1981, Astor was cast as a reporter in the first hip hop film *Wild Style*. "It turned out to be the worst filmmaking experience of my life," says Astor. "I was always sitting in the freezing cold with no nifty van to get into. The actors were all nonprofessionals, except me, so I had to do all the waiting. But I'm certainly glad I made the film because that's where I picked up all my inside knowledge on graffiti. All these writers were sitting around with nothing to do but tell stories."

During the filming, Astor was working for Bill Stelling. One day Stelling mentioned he had a studio in the East Village he wanted to convert into an art gallery. It didn't seem like a very commercial idea—a couple of galleries had opened in the area only to close after a few months. But Stelling wanted to know if Astor could recommend some artists. Astor immediately mentioned Kramer, who had just started painting again. She also told Stelling she knew a lot of graffiti artists.

"Patti was a big film actress, so I was totally intimidated by her," says Stelling. "Izzy Brinkly, a friend of mine from school, was running the gallery with me. But after the first show, Patti decided she wanted to get involved and Izzy bowed out."

Ever since he'd met Haring at the Times Square Show, Fred Brathwaite had been hanging out at Club 57. He brought Astor to the club and she organized a film series titled Classics of the New Cinema. That summer, Astor threw a barbecue party at her apartment on Third Street to celebrate a mural Futura 2000 had painted in her living room. "That was Patti's first art presentation," says Stelling. "Diego Cortez and Duncan Smith came." So did the graffiti artists. A month later, Steven Kramer's exhibit opened at the gallery and instantly sold out, mostly to friends.

The next show was given to Scharf, who was asked to think up a name for the gallery. He suggested "Fun." Astor planned to change the name every month, but later decided it would cost too much to have new stationery printed. Since he'd already shown his customized appliances at a Club 57 opening, Scharf decided to start painting again. Drew Straub had given him a Jetson comic book and, inspired by the book, Scharf made several small paintings of the Jetson characters. None of the paintings sold.

In March, Basquiat had his first solo show at the Nosei gallery. Julian Schnabel was not particularly impressed with Basquiat's work, but showed up anyway to take a look. Basquiat recognized Schnabel and approached him. "I asked him if he wanted to spar," says Basquiat. "I figured even if I lost, I couldn't look bad." Schnabel declined the offer but the story passed through the gallery grapevine, adding to a growing list of Basquiat's pranks. In his review of the show, Jeffrey Deitch made what turned out to be a prophetic statement. "Basquiat is likened to the wild boy raised by wolves, corralled into Annina's basement and given nice clean canvases to work on instead of walls. But Basquiat is hardly a primitive. He's more like a rock star." Shortly after the show closed, Basquiat announced his intention of leaving the gallery. Nosei tried hard to keep him, but he was determined to find another dealer. Before leaving, he went into the basement and destroyed several of his own paintings.

Meanwhile, an unprecedented social synthesis was taking place around the corner from the Fun Gallery at a tiny club called Negril, where rap acts and break dancers from the South Bronx were performing for an audience of downtown artists and musicians. The fashion, music and art styles of both worlds were to intermingle. Astor recruited many of the most promising graffiti artists for her gallery, a list that included Brathwaite, Futura 2000, Lee Quinones and Dondi White.

There was a disappointment that first season: Quinones left the gallery and went to the Barbara Gladstone Gallery. In addition, competitors were appearing in the neighborhood. In December, a gallery called 51X opened on St. Marks Place. The following spring, Civilian Warfare, the East Seventh Street Gallery, Gracie Mansion and Nature Morte opened. Joanne Mayhew-Young, the founder of Gracie Mansion, proved to be the area's most aggressive self-promoter. She mailed out letters describing herself as "New York's second-most-talked-about contemporary personality," sold art out of a trunk of a car in SoHo and staged exhibitions in her East Village bathroom.

In July 1982, an article titled "Another Wave, Still More Savagely than the First" by Nicholas Moufarrege appeared in *Arts* magazine. Orginally from Lebanon, Moufarrege arrived in the East Village with a master's degree in economics from Harvard University. He became enthralled with the emerging art scene. "Everything is moving so much faster: waves, volcanic eruptions, high-voltage currents," gushed Moufarrege. "The East Village, Manhattan, where different drummers unite in a Zeitgeist despite their varying and very personal rhythms. The need to communicate is overwhelming; in more important ways than literally, the boundaries of art have gone beyond the stretcher and the canvas. The spirit of the age is apparent in the melange of people that live in the neighborhood, a neighborhood that encourages one to be the person he is with greater ease than other parts of the city." In the first five paragraphs the article mentioned 36 East Village artists and reiterated Deitch's comparison of artists and rock stars. Until the article appeared, the East Village was in danger of becoming a sort of farm league, with important artists moving immediately to SoHo or 57th Street. Moufarrege encouraged the dealers to aim for higher sights and become independent of SoHo. Of course, if this goal were realized, he'd become an important art critic. A talented artist himself, Moufarrege began exhibiting his own work in group shows. A lot of money could be made in the current art boom and the stakes got higher every year.

Astor decided to move into a bigger space and located a small one-floor building on East 10th Street. The building had an interesting pedigree: during the '70s it had been converted into a theater by performance artist Jeff Weiss and during the previous decade the Diggers had used it as a free store.

While Astor was moving, Scharf was taking lessons from a graffiti writer named Haze on how to paint murals with spray paint. He'd learned how to use an airbrush at SVA, but painting with spray cans was even faster. He began spraying Flintstone and Jetson characters in the street. Although Scharf's graffiti phase lasted only a few weeks, it helped his painting style considerably. After working on the limitless canvas of the city walls, Scharf became more expansive with his imagery and less concerned with microscopic details. Scharf began altering the Hanna-Barbera characters, adding his own inventions and calling the result "Pop surrealism." When Scharf's next show opened at the Fun in September, his paintings had gotten bigger, bolder and more confident. *Whooaa Nelly*, the show's most impressive piece, showed the Flintstone family trapped in a purple whirlwind with a menacing snakehead looming above Fred's head. A television set was blowing away in the distance. At six by nine feet it was Scharf's biggest canvas to date, and Astor was a little shocked when Scharf told her he wanted $5,000 for it. It was the highest-priced painting the Fun had shown.

The real centerpiece of the show, however, was a black-light room similar to the one Scharf had built in his apartment. Scharf partitioned off half the gallery and spent one week painting atomic symbols, Eastern mandalas, graffiti tags and cartoon faces on the walls in fluorescent colors. He glued automobile parts, fragments of old televisions, plastic dinosaurs and jet airplanes everywhere. Black lights were installed on the ceiling. After this show, Scharf was no longer content to make paintings. Now he wanted to build environments that would literally pull his audience into his aesthetic. (Apparently, the strategy worked too well. Two years later the East Village went Day-Glo crazy and dozens of artists were making Pop-surrealist paintings.)

In November, *Artforum* published an article on the Fun Gallery by Rene Ricard, who had already written influential essays on Schnabel and Basquiat. "Patti Astor is a beautiful example of what John Ashbery would call 'An Exhilarating Mess' in operation," wrote Ricard. "She isn't a businesswoman: She's currently starring in Charlie Ahearn's movie *Wild Style*, and the opening of the gallery coincided with (or caused) a definite shift in the social pattern of the last two years. The underground movie scene played itself out. The rock scene, sperm of the great club period of the second half of the '70s, has run to water, losing the music war and now, except for a few skinhead arsenals, barely exists. Painting became big news."

"The article legitimized us and made people in the business take us seriously as an art gallery on par with SoHo or Fifty-seventh Street," says Stelling. It also helped create the phenomenon of the art dealer as the star of the East Village scene. In the near future, Astor would be a much-imitated role model. More important, Ricard convinced Basquiat to show at the Fun.

Meanwhile, local residents hardly knew what to make of the changes in their neighborhood. During the last days of Group Material's short-lived gallery on East 13th Street, Tim Rollins interviewed a man named Richard who had lived in the neighborhood for 18 years. "When you first opened up here with that first big art exhibition, everybody on the block came and sat on the sides of the cars in front of the building and just stared at all the white people coming in," said Richard. "Now, like, nothing like that had ever happened on this block! I mean, we were all just trying to figure out what the fuck was going on. We saw the posters and we all knew you during the summer when you were fixing the place up. But still it was real strange to see when it happened."

The following year, 10 more galleries opened in the East Village: Piezo Electric, New Math, Oggo Domani, Sharpe, C.A.S.H., Christminster, International with Monument, P.P.O.W., Sensory Evolution and Pat Hearn. One might have thought this was the saturation point, but it was actually just the beginning. Twenty more would open the following year and after that even the local art critics would start losing count. For the most part, the galleries were opened by young professional dealers hoping to discover the next Basquiat or Haring, not by locals who had emerged from the club scene. After four galleries opened a block from the Fun Gallery on East 10th Street, Astor wrote "Yankee Go Home" on their windows.

Group shows were held everywhere as arriving artists jockeyed for position in the better-known galleries. A few of these shows were curated by Carlo McCormick and Walter Robinson, two writers for the *East Village Eye* who were jointly promoting the scene. "Taken as a package, the East Village art scene is so much a 'ready-made' that it seems uncanny, a marketing masterpiece based on felicitous coincidences," wrote the pair in *Art in America*. "Besides having its own artists, neighborhood, art press and distinctive gallery names, the East Village scene has its own day (Sunday) and its own gallery architecture—small tenement storefronts, with no back room and no storage."

Suddenly, all conversations in the East Village seemed to revolve around money. "The whole dialogue of painting seems to be lost," moaned David Wojnarowicz, one of the few artists who wasn't caught up in the prevailing spirit of the times. The infusion of so much new capital into the neighborhood pushed storefront rents to unexpected levels. Local Polish and Ukrainian shops were driven out of business with alarming speed as chain stores moved in. New restaurants opened almost daily on St. Marks Place, but the established punk boutiques like Manic Panic could no longer afford the rent.

The rapid gentrification of the neighborhood was largely blamed on the art galleries, but they probably played only a minor role in a process that had been taking place throughout the city for over four years. A new white-collar labor force had moved into the city, a group dubbed the yuppies, and in order to make room for them the city was driving the lower class out of the inner city. Before long, the police launched a campaign to displace the East Village drug trade (a major source of youth employment in the area). Titled Operation Pressure Point, the program was widely seen as an important step in making the neighborhood safe for yuppies.

With all the changes taking place in the East Village, a few people began wondering what had happened to the original CBGB and Mudd Club crowd, especially since so many of their concepts were being recycled on canvas. Sadly, Anya Phillips had died of cancer in 1981, long before her effect on the scene was widely acknowledged. "I think about clothes worn by people so recently and yet how long ago it seems that Anya would show up in those cocktail dresses and, of all things, a Chinese girl in a blonde wig," wrote Rene Ricard in *Artforum*. "And now, all the girls in their cocktail dresses who never heard of Anya and how quickly each generation catches the look of its creators and forgets the moral underneath."

Drugs, always readily available at the clubs, provided an explanation for what had happened to many people. "Eventually drugs and drinking get to almost everyone," says Anita Sarko. "But that's New York, right? New York offers you everything you have never experienced before. Most people just keep taking and taking without realizing it's just a big joke New York plays on them." Heroin addiction had taken the heavist toll. A few artists continued to celebrate the junk lifestyle, but it was increasingly viewed as a downwardly mobile dead-end. "The people who glamorize heroin are the true pornographers," says Rockets Redglare, an early regular at CBGB. "They're the ones who get kids to move to New York and throw their lives away. No one perpetuates their own slavery like the junkies."

Unfortunately, in 1982, another plague appeared, one even more deadly than heroin. Acquired immune deficiency syndrome, or AIDS, had been spreading anonymously for several years, primarily through the gay population. The disease was barely identified when Klaus Nomi was diagnosed and hospitalized. "They made me wear a plastic bag when I visited him," recalls Arias. "I wasn't allowed to touch him. After a few weeks, he seemed to get better. He was strong enough to walk around. So he left the hospital and went home. His manager was making him sign all these papers, like we'll give you $500 if you sign your life away one more time. He developed kaposis [lesions associated with Kaposi's sarcoma, a rare skin cancer linked with AIDS] and started taking interferon. That messed him up real bad. He had dots all over his body and his eyes became purple slits. It was like someone was destroying him. He used to make fun of it. He'd say 'Just call me dotty Nomi.' Then he got real weak and was rushed back to the hospital. He couldn't eat for days because he had cancer in his stomach. Herpes popped out all over his body. He turned into a monster. It hurt me so much to see him. I talked to him on the night of August Fifth. He said, 'Joey, what am I going to do? They don't want me in the hospital anymore. They pulled all the plugs. I have to stop all this stuff because I'm not getting any better.' I had this dream of Klaus getting strong and singing again—only he'd be a little deformed, so he'd have to stay behind a screen or something. 'You'll be the phantom of the opera.' I told him. 'We'll do shows together again.' 'Yeah, maybe,' he said. But Klaus died in his sleep that night."

In retrospect, it's unfortunate Nomi's career began before the rise of MTV. At the time of his death, he was just getting established in Europe and with the help of MTV videos, he certainly could have pushed into the American market. His first album contained an interesting mix of '60s pop, opera and ethereal space music, but if fell between so many stylistic cracks that it had difficulty finding an audience. (A year after Nomi's death, however, Malcolm McLaren successfully released a dance-rock version of an aria from *Madame Butterfly*.)

In 1981, the Ladies Auxiliary formed a band called Pulsallama. "It was really an anti-band, a parody of groups like Bow Wow Wow," says Magnuson. "We'd take mushrooms, run around screaming like banshees and beat on pots and pans." Shortly after the group formed, Magnuson left her position as manager of Club 57. A few months later she was cast in a film with

David Bowie titled *The Hunger*. She dropped out of Pulsallama and began concentrating on her performance career. After shedding several other members, Pulsallama went on tour with the Clash. "We were fun to watch but we sounded like a train going through a tunnel," says Dany Johnson. "Other bands would fight over things like drugs or money, but we'd fight over things like: 'You're not going to wear that ugly wig on stage! What do you think this is, a clown show!?' After we got a look at ourselves on cable TV we realized, yes, we were a clown show." The group released two singles before disbanding, "The Devil Lives in My Husband's Body" and "Pulsallama on the Rag." Unfortunately, the breakup of the band also spelled the end of the Ladies Auxiliary.

As a solo act, Magnuson became a leading East Village performer, pioneering a style later called "pop performance" by *Drama Review*. "I've always felt my performances were similar to what Kenny does in his paintings," said Magnuson. Most of the shows were satires constructed around characters like Tammy Jan, a Moral Majority evangelist, Anoushka, a Russian pop star, or Mary Margaret McKeon, a wealthy East Village art dealer. She also created more elaborate productions, including a parody of a heavy metal group called Vulcan Death Grip, in which she played Raven, the group's lead singer. "Our first gig was on an abandoned floor of Danceteria," she says. "We had two smoke machines and lots of people with snakes and lizards." The group performed a heavy metal medley of "Smoke on the Water," "Purple Haze" and "Five to One," while Magnuson presided over a black magic incantation. (Coincidentally, a film with a similar concept titled *Spinal Tap* was released the following year.) Later on, Magnuson began performing a series of collaborations with Joey Arias, one of the most popular of which had Arias playing a demonic Charles Manson to Magnuson's servile Squeaky Fromm. "Magnuson's knack for concise comic characterizations puts me in mind of Lily Tomlin," wrote Don Shewey in the *Village Voice*. "But she has enough wit and imagination, combined with Southern charm and lurid sex appeal, to establish her originality as a writer/performer/conceptual comic."

In the spring of 1983, Steve Mass sold the Mudd Club. A few months later, after being investigated for income tax evasion, he was accused of attempting to bribe a city tax auditor. Mass paid several fines, dropped out of the underground scene and began putting his money into real estate. Tina Lhotsky moved to Hollywood to pursue a film career. In May, Club 57 closed. This was perhaps the saddest blow of all. Essentially a nonprofit laboratory for experimental art and theater, the club had been an invaluable resource for young artists. Each year a new generation had taken over the club. In 1981, Scott Wittman and Marc Shaiman, both of whom had formerly worked with Bette Midler, staged several camp musicals at Club 57, including *The Sound of Muzak, Peter Pan* and *Trojan Women*. The following year the pair wrote and produced an original musical titled *Living Dolls*. Based on a combination of '60s beach movies and Barbie dolls, the musical received lavish stage productions in both New York and Los Angeles. However, bad management and mounting fines for sound violations eventually killed Club 57. In 1983, the church rented the space to a mental health clinic.

What was left of the Club 57 sensibility moved into other nightclubs opening in the neighborhood, the first of which was the Pyramid Cocktail Lounge, a club booked by manager Bobby Bradley. Within a year, several other clubs opened, most notably the Limbo Lounge and 8BC. Along with Magnuson, Sex and Arias, these clubs featured performances by such talents as Eric Bogosian, Tony Heiberg, John Kelly, Phoebe Legere and Wendy Wild. They also attracted a few cabaret artists who had been performing sporadically since the '60s, the most influential of whom was the multitalented Craig Vandenburgh (who had created kitsch parodies of Las Vegas lounge acts long before Club 57 was founded).

In September 1983, a new club called Area opened in TriBeCa and quickly became New York's most successful night spot since Studio 54. Inspired in part by the Mudd Club, the owners redesigned and redecorated the club every six weeks around such themes as "War," "Elements" and "Confinement." *New York* magazine did a cover story on Area and photographed the four youthful owners (average age 27) wearing identical Brooks Brothers suits. "If there's a precedent for Area, it's the Mudd Club," observed David Hershkovits in *New York Beat*. "Today, some of the same faces can still be seen roaming about, but times have changed. Back then, it seemed all you needed was a liquor license and a sound system and you'd have a packed house. Open to new experiences, people flocked to meet their kindred spirits, exchange ideas and phone numbers, maybe hook up together on a project. There was no East Village art scene, so many of the new young artists currently making their mark first got their exposure at the Mudd. Area is a fixture of the Reagan '80s. The conservative government has ushered in a conservative lifestyle as well. It is no longer acceptable to lose oneself in music, to walk about unshaven and disheveled, to make a lot of noise, or to act in an eccentric manner. In response to the subdued, upwardly mobile character of its clientele, Area provides a dash of excitement for humdrum lives obsessed with dressing for success."

The East Village art scene continued to mushroom and the number of galleries peaked at 60 before attrition set in. In 1984, both the University of California at Santa Barbara and the University of Pennsylvania staged exhibitions devoted to East Village art. McCormick, who was rapidly becoming a leading expert on the scene, wrote essays for the catalogues of both shows. "The East Village's growth, a meteoric rise of galleries and artists, is a particular manifestation of art marketing today," wrote McCormick. "The mass co-opting of the most avant-garde and intentionally offensive developments of Modernism by an art-market industry that is as corporate as any bureaucratic structure, bred a peculiar reaction to Modernism. In the vague, general atmosphere we have labeled Postmodernism, we must account for the personality of careerism in the visual arts. The East Village is right at the cutting edge of this commodity-based enterprise. It is the locus of creativity for what we must call the most truly capitalist art ever produced. While most critics attack this generation on these very grounds, few can deny the cultural significance of an art which cannily transforms inspiration to commodity and willfully avoids the hypocrisy of denying its materialistic value."

In his essays, McCormick frequently exposed a theory popular with many East Village artists, one that professed it was far more noble to be openly avaricious than to work for nonexistent higher motives. This attitude was probably displayed with greatest zeal by Mark Kostabi, who, in imitation of Warhol, continually flaunted his overwhelming desire for fame and money. "Amateurs imitate—professionals steal," Kostabi was fond of saying. "My paintings are doorways into collectors' homes." Although he was accused of pandering to the marketplace, the charge only served to make Kostabi more of a local celebrity. However, East Village galleries were not exactly catering to New York's most discriminating art collectors. Instead, many were selling primarily to novices who wanted to get in on the "new movement." Descending on the East Village in droves, these collectors often appeared in tour groups sponsored by adult education classes. Although their guides knew little about the history of the East Village scene, they did know the names of a few prominent artists and were anxious to promote the work. (It was not unusual for guides to request a commission for work purchased by members of their tour.)

When the Whitney Biennial opened in March 1985, art world observers were waiting to see if the museum would validate any of the work from the East Village. They were not disappointed. Scharf, who was selling as well as Haring, obviously had to be part of the exhibit, but the curators also included Rodney Alan Greenblat, Sherrie Levine and David Wojnarowicz, as well as two artists' collectives from the East Village, TODT and Group Material. "I always get irritated by this emphasis on the East Village," said Whitney curator Richard Marshall. "It's just such a vague category. You can make generalizations about the work there. It seems to be rawer, it has more cartoon imagery, more political content. But the category means absolutely nothing."

Nothing in the Biennial demonstrated the rise of the East Village club sensibility more than a room curated by the Marxist art collective Group Material.

"Pictures of all kinds were hung edge to edge, floor to ceiling," wrote Gerald Marzorati in *Art News*. "Drawings, packages off supermarket shelves, magazines opened and mounted, book jackets, posters and photos and paintings. Four Norman Rockwell commemorative plates were mounted together on one of the walls... A big part of this installation was a black and white console TV: always on, it relayed endless stories..." The Biennial received mixed reviews, but many critics recognized Scharf as its star. Not only did he have the most impressive painting in the show (*When the Worlds Collide*), but he'd taken a long hallway between two bathrooms and converted it into his seventh psychedelic closet. Scharf had also recently displayed his most elaborate cutomized appliance to date: the *Ultima Suprema Deluxa*, a Day-Glo 1961 Cadillac covered with cartoon faces, streaks of spray paint and plastic dinosaurs.

By the time the Biennial opened, Haring, Scharf and Basquiat had divorced themselves from the East Village. They didn't speak out publicly, but were obviously upset over the blatant plagiarizing of their work. When *Arts* magazine wanted to take photographs of East Village artists,

Haring, Scharf and Basquiat refused to pose with the others, but agreed to be photographed as a trio. (As usual, Basquiat overslept and the photo was never taken.) "The East Village artists excommunicated us," says Haring. "We are SoHo artists to them. I accept the tag. I don't mind being a SoHo artist."

As the East Village became increasingly commercialized and success-oriented, even Nicholas Moufarrege, the neighborhood's original booster, reached his limit of endurance. "The local ruling that no art is unshowable has, I think, done nothing for the meaningful, the powerful nor the beautiful," wrote Moufarrege. "The boys and girls are gone hog-wild with liberty and the effect is not of shock but of something dangerous: 'tedium.' It is easy to follow, difficult to lead. Too often, in the East Village, originality is smothered in the fashionable neoexpressionist bouillabaisse. True, mediocrity has always dominated the scene in every age, that is beyond dispute; but what is also true as it is distressing is that the reign of mediocrity is stronger than ever, to the point of triumphant obtrusiveness." It was to be his last essay. Tragically, Moufarrege died from AIDS in 1985, shortly after his first solo exhibition opened at the Fun Gallery.

The biggest irony of all came in May, 1985, when a new club 10 times the size of Area reopened. It was called the Palladium, the creation of Steve Rubell and Ian Schrager, the same pair who had founded Studio 54. After being indicted on charges of income tax evasion in the late '70s, Rubell and Schrager had cooperated fully with federal prosecutors, turned state's evidence against their former clientele and served reduced sentences. Four years after their release from prison, they moved downtown and swallowed the art scene whole, commissioning Basquiat, Haring, Scharf and others to create paintings and installations for a new club on 14th Street. By this time, however, few people could remember that the Mudd Club had begun as a statement against the Studio 54 mentality. It seemed as if the East Village was turning into everything it had once stood against.

The Fun Gallery, meanwhile, was foundering. Always distracted by her film career, Astor had never invested much money back into her gallery and had been unable to find a financial backer. In July, she held a "Sink or Swim" party in which she practically begged collectors to support the gallery so she could afford the ever-accelerating rent. Nothing sold. A few weeks later, the gallery closed, even though it still had many highly-regarded artists on its roster, including Fred Brathwaite, Arch Connelly, Dan Friedman, Futura 2000 and Keily Jenkins. (One of the Fun's final exhibits had been a solo show of paintings by Steven Kramer. David Hockney dropped by and purchased one without realizing it was the same Kramer who'd stabbed him in the chest with a rubber knife seven years earlier.)

Astor told reporters she let the gallery close because it no longer fit in with the East Village scene. The Fun was always a bit seedy around the edges and collectors favored galleries that were cleaner and less dangerous (meaning they weren't filled with black and Hispanic teenagers). East Village artists sold well, but not the graffiti artists, who had been exploited by Hollywood and misunderstood by the police and the press. Although the graffiti artists had fed considerable energy into the East Village scene, few galleries were interested in their work. They had inspired many artists, including Basquiat, Haring and Scharf, but few could play the art game with the aplomb of those three. The Whitney Biennial ignored graffiti art, as did every other important American museum. Consequently, graffiti-based paintings never sold particularly well, except in Europe.

In October 1985, Haring opened a sculpture exhibit at the Castelli Gallery; Scharf and his wife, Theresa, left for a world tour; and Basquiat and his mentor Andy Warhol collaborated on a show at the Shafrazi Gallery. Funded by Bischofberger, the Basquiat-Warhol exhibit was a disaster. "Art historians may be able to relate this manifestation to the automatist poetry that certain Surrealists wrote collectively," wrote Vivien Raynor in the *New York Times*. "They may even invoke Robert Rauschenberg's erasure of a de Kooning drawing and the mustache Duchamp added to a Mona Lisa reproduction. Anything is possible. But here and now, the collaboration looks like one of Warhol's manipulations, which increasingly seem based on the Mencken theory about nobody going broke underestimating the public's intelligence. Basquiat, meanwhile, comes across as the all too willing accessory." The pair produced 70 paintings, only a few of which sold.

While the critics were turning on Basquiat and Warhol, East Village artists seemed to reserve their greatest disdain for Haring, who was attacked by some of them while standing in front of the Shafrazi Gallery prior to the opening of his 1985 painting exhibition. Haring escaped unharmed, but the attackers had come prepared to tar and feather him. Their vehemence seemed strangely misplaced. Haring, the most compassionate of the artists who had emerged from the club scene, had devoted considerable time and money to political causes, had supported the careers of many artists around him and had brought a new populist fervor to the art world. He had opened doors for many others, but those still left out in the cold were howling mad. Haring's growing isolation and unhappiness with the current scene was evident in his work: one painting in the exhibit showed a giant, swinish creature with bloodshot eyes devouring a green bile of computers, tape decks, TV sets and clocks, while a dozen gray forms fed off its bulging nipples.

That same month, the *East Village Eye* officially announced the end of the East Village art scene. "We, who were the first to take credit for the birth of East Village art, now want to be the first to take credit for killing it," wrote McCormick. "But this is what the East Village has always been about, taking credit for other people's work and ideas. After two years of intense coverage of the scene, the *Eye* has officially run out of gimmicks to repackage the same old drivel."

"The history of modern art is also the history of the progressive loss of art's audience," wrote Henry Geldzahler in 1965. "Whether this situation is ideal or necessary is a matter for speculation. It is and has been the situation for several decades, and is not likely soon to change." Twenty years later, Haring, Scharf and their contemporaries in the East Village had done much to reverse the trend. Instead of cloistering themselves in self-referential academic communities, they had created work that could be understood and appreciated by a massive new audience. Some saw it as a healthy sign of the public's growing interest in contemporary art.

Built by an unstable coalition of gays, blacks, rock musicans, Super-8 filmmakers and art students, the East Village scene lost much of its vitality when the neighborhood became overly commercialized. By 1985, the coalition had disbanded and the scene splintered into separate fragments. After years of poverty, some East Village bohemians made money a primary objective, and once this goal was realized there seemed to be little else to strive for. Even so, the impact of their scene was considerable. For decades the art world had been dominated by a handful of artists and dealers. Compared with the plight of artists in the '70s, those arriving in

New York in the '80s found it relatively easy to get shown in a gallery. Middle-class collectors, many of whom had been intimidated by the galleries of SoHo and 57th Street, also found life much simpler in the East Village, where buying a painting was as painless as getting a loaf of bread from the supermarket. The art market had changed and people wondered if it would ever be quite the same again.

THE FUN VIBE

There are a lot of vibe trails, good and bad, but the fun vibe is the best. It's a delicate trail, easily lost. Sometimes it can disappear for decades. As legend goes, Neal Cassady surfed the hum of a gear-shift, scouted the fun vibe and gave it to the Beat Crew. The Pranksters got the trail from Cassady and shared it with Jerry Garcia, Timothy Leary and the Beatles. Some people dream about being a rock star, but I always dreamed of being a Merry Prankster and riding *Furthur*'s top deck with Cassady at the helm.

In 1997, *High Times* began advertising the first Hemp World's Fair in Oregon, just a few miles from where Ken Kesey, Ken Babbs and the Merry Pranksters were living. Our hope was to combine forces with the best vibe scouts we could find, hold a sacred ceremony and find the center of the true fun vibe.

Early in the spring, I flew out to Oregon and met Ken Babbs and the owner of a possible 15-acre site. Well, the site looked good and plans were going great. The focal point of the event was going to be a silent meditation on Sunday, from dawn until noon, followed by an OM. Babbs gave the event its name (WHEE!). But we hit a glitch as the Pranksters unexpectedly pulled out.

"We have to do a July tour in Europe for our record company," said Babbs sadly over the phone. But we still had Stephen Gaskin, Paul Krassner, John Trudell, Dennis Peron and a bunch of other good scouts. It was too late to call WHEE! off.

After months of preparations, I arrived to start construction. Although the main stage was built and water and power lines had been dug for some booths and kitchens, it was really just a barren field with a two-story high pile of twisted metal, rotten wood and garbage piled in the center. About 40 people were camped around the property. Six22, Zero and Roberto rode into camp with me.

Just looking at the pile of garbage made me dizzy. The Oregon sun was blazing. The only shade was a grove of pine trees way over in the parking lot. I knew the crew would melt down quick unless they got a steady supply of food and water. Fortunately, Sun Dog Kitchen was on site, straight from the nearby Rainbow Gathering.

I entered the Sun Dog camp and immediately caught sight of some freshly born pups.

"Aww, puppies," I said lurching forward.

Like a fearless Zen master, the mom darted out from a picnic table and sunk two teeth into my Levis at the knee.

"Damn," I said, "You just ruined my best rainbow-stripe jeans." Meanwhile, I'm thinking what a bad omen this is. After I customize my jeans, I tend to get overly attached to them.

I fingered the hole and noticed the strike was surgical, not a mark on my flesh. The Sun Dog crew jumped out of the corners to get between me and the angry mom.

"There's no dogs... supposed to be here," I snarled.

Roberto appeared. "I have a dog," he said wistfully. "Look, there're dogs all over the place." As he swept his hand across the horizon, I noticed three or four more dogs scampering about.

Lee, Stevie D's straw boss, let me know he was vexed by the mission of preparing 3,000 free meals over the next week.

"Whatta ya need, Lee?" I said. "Give me a wish list."

I walked out into the field and called council. Mostly young brothers came, many of whom seemed to be from One Love Zion Train, a tour group sponsored by Universal Life Church of One Love. They handed me an envelope filled with flyers and propaganda on their noble quest to scout the vibe all summer.

"Come on, boys," I shouted. "We're on a sacred mission to build hippie Disneyland! And we only got six days to do it!"

"What do you want us to do?" asked five voices and 40 faces.

"First, we gotta get rid of that pile of trash!"

In a matter of seconds 80 hands hit the garbage pile.

"Come on Stoney," I said walking toward the rented Ford pickup. "We gotta make a supply run. Where's that wish list?"

Before the day was through, Stoney and I visited every discount center in Eugene, and that Ford was filled with enough food and drink for 50 people for three days, along with every other type of supplies we might need, including 20 pairs of work gloves and a precious erase board and five fluorescent erase markers.

At sundown, after we made it back to the site, the garbage pile was half gone. A gorgeous sunset cloud formation appeared over the stage, while behind us, an almost full moon rose over the mountains. A dozen geese flew past in V formation. "Squawk, squawk," said Alpha Goose as they whooshed toward the sunset. I felt their bird energy as they scouted their vibe trail. Sun Dog blew the conch for dinner. We circled up, held hands and did an OM, followed by everyone throwing their hands in the air and yelling, "Whee!"

July 14

"We believe in doing what is right and respecting others, with no judgments or dogma, only true love and respect for all living beings," read the flyer from the Zion Crew. "All faiths are connected to the One and the One is connected to us. The train is an ongoing experience for the caravaners of voluntarily spreading the unity love vibrations that make this the 30th anniversary of the Summer of Love."

I was sitting in the back of an RV parked next to the stage, where we'd set up Mission Control. The radios arrived late, so it was hard to get the crews properly coordinated. So far, we had 14 members of Sun Dog and 73 other assorted volunteers on site.

Garrick Beck rolled in, set up his tipi and split. Garrick, Plunker and John Buffalo were crew chiefs on the Temple Dragon Crew (TDC), which was supposed to handle people problems inside the venue and protect the ceremonial spaces.

Hippie security is a little-known art form that has been evolving inside the counterculture for over 40 years. Groups like the Diggers in Haight-Ashbury were among the earliest proponents of this art form. Whenever anything bad would happen on the streets of the Haight, local residents would try to handle the problem using nonviolent persuasion. For example, if some brother disrespected a sister, that person would suddenly find himself surrounded by people wanting to discuss, in a quiet, rational manner, why the brother felt it was okay to be disrespectful. The fact no one would resort to anger or violence would usually throw the perpetrator so off-guard that he'd end up analyzing and apologizing for his inappropriate behavior. Techniques of nonviolent communication were eventually perfected even further by the Merry Pranksters, who knew how to "create a movie," pull a person into that movie and alter the perceptual frame of reference of a situation to their own benefit.

Many professional security guards rely on telepathic hostility and thinly veiled threats of physical harm to enforce rules. But hippie security never resorts to hints of violence. Every security situation is unique and negotiable. Over the past 30 years, the Rainbow Family Gathering has been a superb training ground for people interested in studying non-violent security techniques. The Shanti Sena (peace eyes) is the name that has evolved for this group.

Fortunately, Amazin' Dave, one of the best of the Rainbow Shanti Sena, showed up, and I hired him on the spot. He moved into the Mission Control RV with me to handle the late-night problems. Six22 was handling all medical problems. His cat Ganja moved into the RV with me and Dave. By the end of the day, the garbage pile was gone and the fence was ready to go up.

July 16

The professional, licensed and bonded company we hired for 24-hour security had rolled in and set up on the 15th. I explained we had our own internal security crew. I wanted the professional crew to work the perimeter and guard the fence, but I didn't want them to deal with people. That was for TDC. If we had serious problems, we could always call in the professional security guards. But I was confident TDC could handle the job.

However, during the night, the professionals suddenly packed up and left without so much as an explanation. I stayed up all night at the front gate without a single security guard on duty, feeling like Michael Corleone at the hospital in *The Godfather*.

John Buffalo arrived early in the morning and I explained the situation. "I'm making you crew chief of TDC, and you have to coordinate all security," I told him.

Meanwhile, Diego's bus rolled in to set up the Gypsy Village, and Felipe's bus rolled in to set up Family Village. The site map had changed drastically already, so I drew the current map on the erase board and discussed possible locations. Both crews picked new sites and started putting up tents and tarps. The Gypsies brought a huge circus tent for workshops and seminars.

We had a fence crew, sign painting crew, vendor staking crew, carpenter crew, fire pit crew, kitchen crew, Gypsy crew, tipi circle crew, stage crew and Family Village crew all working feverishly by mid-afternoon.

The biggest change in the map came when I staked a huge area overlooking a small pond as Doggie Village. There were supposed to be about 50 vendors on that very spot, and I was already wondering how I was going to explain this to people who had paid for those booths.

July 17

The vendors started arriving early in the day, and most were shocked to find the site map wasn't the same anymore. Beth, who had been recently hired as vending director of the Hemp Expo, was greeting vendors as they rolled in. Poor Beth was engulfed by hysteria. I could identify with her situation and tried to help. The most remarkable thing about the whole event was the way Beth kept her head together and never melted down once.

Most of the vendors were actually quite nice and friendly and easy to deal with once the new site was explained. However, we had a few problem cases, like the Babylon vendor, who was selling Pepsi and hot dogs out of an RV with a generator. I put him in Bus Village, where he belonged. He happily took that spot, but by the end of the day, he tore down the fence separating Bus Village from the site and demanded to be moved inside. Garrick moved him to the Gypsy camp, but the Gypsy crew exploded after he turned on his generator. The fumes were blowing right into the Casbah Tea House. So we moved him again, this time right next to our beautiful fire pit, where his exhaust blew into the amphitheater. Even so, he kept complaining about all the money he was losing.

"Nobody wants your Babylon food," I said finally. "Why don't you go solar and sell organic food, or better yet, pack up and leave?" Of course, he was making plenty of money and had no intention of leaving.

Around this time, most of the *High Times* staff were arriving for the first time and there was tremendous confusion between the property owner, the Rainbows and the newly arrived HT staff. This was my fault for not holding an orientation meeting, but everyone was working so hard, I didn't want them to stop. Some people continued to be confused because the site had changed from the original map. There were over 30 radios on site, plus a large number of CB units, and Thursday was the day of radio screaming. If the slightest problem came up, meltdowns would start yelling on the radio.

Plunker saw me starting to melt down, came in, led a silent meditation circle, and we went back to work.

Plunker had taken charge of the fire pit. Fire was a real hazard, due to a lot of dry straw on the ground. Plunker is the best firefighter I know. I served under him during the Great Wyoming Rainbow Gathering Fire, when several thousand Rainbows stomped out a three-acre blaze which topped the trees and threatened to destroy an entire national forest.

The final fire pit was heart-shaped, facing the Gypsy stage, with four rows of amphitheater seating carved out of the mound of earth displaced to make the pit. It was so beautifully constructed I almost burst into tears just looking at it. Felipe came down from Family Village to lead a service and sanctify us with sage as we lit the ceremonial flame at sundown.

That night, the vendor crew stayed up until 3 A.M. leading convoys of vendors into the site, making sure their vehicles were parked safely.

July 18

On opening day, the medical crew that had agreed to work the event did not show. Another crew, led by midwife Daphne Singingtree, came in on an hour's notice. Daphne had been lobbying hard for the job for three months, so I was happy to see her roll in with an entire medical team.

Meanwhile, some of the crew were jumping around with big knots on their third eye, all frantic, unable to make clear decisions. I sometimes had two or three meltdowns standing around yelling at the same time. No logic worked on those minds. I'd already lost my voice from having to talk to large crowds for six days, so I tried to stay low-key and not let their energy penetrate me.

"Listen," I said softly, "I've got an important mission for you. I want you to go to Sun Dog, pour yourself some fresh lemonade and wait until I get there."

Commander Gorman had taken over Mission Control, just like at the Cannabis Cup. Early in the day a few people ran up on him with requests over the radio he didn't feel like dealing with just that second. In retaliation, they changed the name of his post to Mission Impossible. The new name stuck for the remainder of the event.

The parking lots were in chaos, but inside the fence was peaceful hippie heaven, with lots of good food at low prices. The stage was even running close to schedule. The 420 Show with the Cannabis Cup Band rocked and was the main event of the day. Engineer Charlie sculpted a wonderful sound. A crew meeting was scheduled for 11 P.M., just after the main stage closed.

Since I could barely talk above a whisper, Garrick was crew chief on the meeting. I drew a map on the erase board to show how the site had changed and where the new fire lanes were. Then all hell broke loose. Everyone was pissed about the problems in the parking lots (which were being operated under the supervison of the property owner), and the lack of laminates for free food. For about an hour there was a lot of hot air, but no solutions. Then Gideon spoke. Gideon is not the sort of brother who does a lot of talking at council. Although he's a big bear of a man, he scouts a very mellow vibe. But Gideon was all fired up, like Crazy Horse talking to the Lakota warriors before the Custer fight. He laid out a plan and offered to hold down the night gate himself. Then he led the crew in a chant of "Break even, break even."

July 19

I drove into camp around 8 A.M., having spent the night at the Ramada Inn. Gideon was still on the gate, a big wad of cash in his fanny pack. I parked and walked around camp, moving signs to their proper locations, stocking the info booth that hadn't quite happened yet and checking the fire lanes.

While I walked TDC on the backline, I pulled up on a huge spotted male dog, who could have been cast as White Fang in a Jack London movie. The dog held a long stare on my eyes, and I stared back while I reached for my radio mike.

"Mission Impossible, we got a big Alpha off its leash."

"This is Doggie Village, what's your twenty?"

"Between Doggie Village and Gypsy tent."

"We'll pick up the dog."

"Ten-four. Over and out."

It was amazing how fast the radio could fix things. It was like a magic wand that made energy clouds appear like so many tornados.

Later that day, I got a big surprise when Ken Kesey and the Pranksters, all wearing green masks, pulled up in front of Mission Impossible in a white Cadillac convertible. Babbs jumped out of the back seat and showed me his watch.

"Look," he said triumphantly, "it's exactly 4:20!"

"Commander Gorman, get this crew on stage immediately!" I shouted.

"Ten-four," said Peter.

Babbs handed me a green hemp scarf with rainbow stripes. It had two holes cut for my eyes.

There was a lot of noise and chaos. Everybody was pressing toward us because they wanted to meet the Pranksters. But I had a telepathic moment with Babbs, when time slowed and the background faded. He spoke to me in a silent way only Kenmasters know how to do.

"If you put on this magic mask," he said, "you'll become invisible."

A flock of geese flew overhead and burst our bubble. Everything sped up and got crazy again.

Next thing I knew, I was on stage wearing the mask, being introduced by Fantuzzi as Phoenix 420.

"One week ago, I fell asleep in the back of a car after a party," I said. "When I woke up, the car was parked in the center of this field. Only it didn't look like this. There was no hippie Disneyland. There was only a two-story pile of twisted metal, wood and garbage. And forty hungry, homeless hippies! And the next day we were a hundred homeless hippies! And we built this New Jerusalem! I guess they wanted me to say this because I was one of the crew who worked so hard! So let's hear it for the crews, who worked for free!... In case you don't know, WHEE's name came from Ken Babbs. He's one of the Merry Pranksters, the greatest vibe scouts of our time. The Merry Pranksters couldn't be here because of some Babylonian record-company tour. But we do have the Green Vipers, so let's have a warm welcome for the Green Vipers!"

And out walked Kesey, Babbs, Mountain Girl and their crew.

Meanwhile, I melted into the crowd to explore my newfound invisibility.

Just then the strangest thing happened. I began reading auras for the first time in my life. The overwhelming majority of people at the event were radiating happy vibrations. But there was a very small minority with darker emanations. Instead of walking around the site, I found myself seated on the ground in a hidden spot with a clear view of the kids' playground. I was convinced an evil force was watching the children and I began paying close attention to a tall, middle-aged man with a military haircut who was hanging out at a vending booth next to Family Village. He was watching kids playing on the swing sets and jungle gyms we'd erected. I noticed the man did not have a wristband, indicating he had not paid to enter the venue. I decided to work my best Temple Dragon magic on him, so I walked up with a big smile on my face.

"Howdy, brother," I said, "are we having fun yet?"

He eyed me suspiciously and gave no comment.

"Hey, where's your wristband?" I continued. "Everybody's got to have a wristband."

He smirked but said nothing.

"I've got some extra wristbands if you need one," I continued, reaching into my purple hemp fanny pack. "You should put one on so security doesn't kick you out. If you can't afford to pay the admission fee, that's no problem, I'll give you a wristband anyway. But if you can make a donation, we'd really appreciate it because we didn't break even on this event. In fact, we've lost thousands of dollars. So if you could afford a small donation, we'd really appreciate it."

"I don't haf any money," he said with a thick German accent.

"No problem," I said putting the band on his wrist. "Why not just open your wallet and show me? And if it's empty, then you don't have to pay anything."

There was a long pause and I watched him take mental notes on my Temple Dragon belt, with its radio, flashlight, medical supplies and various Batman-like emergency tools. He knew he was dealing with someone who could call in reinforcements. Although I was all smiles and happiness, inside I was beaming telepathic messages that I knew what he was all about and I could read his mind like a book. Rather than show me his wallet, he reached in his pocket, pulled out a wad of cash and handed me a 20.

"Gee, thanks," I said.

Just then Plunker and Felipe walked by and I made a big deal of introducing them to the stranger. But he abruptly broke off from us and walked away without telling us his name.

"There's something funny about him," I said. "He's been staring at the kids and I don't like his vibes."

Plunker and Felipe nodded their heads and agreed he seemed a bit out of place at the event. We began spreading word among the TDC to keep an eye on him.

But he must have known something was up because he left the site within an hour and never came back.

July 20

By 8 A.M. it was apparent Sunday was going to go into the high 90s with high humidity. A silent meditation was planned for the main meadow. We made a supply run for ice, water, soda and coolers. As we passed Family Village, the "no smoking of any kind" zone, Felipe, the ceremony crew chief, emerged.

"We better postpone that ceremony until sundown," I said. "Otherwise people will be fainting out there. We also need a pole for people to circle around."

"I'll work on that," said Felipe.

On the way back to Mission Impossible, I changed the daily event sign at the entrance to read: "OM at Sunset."

I rode the TDC vibe for the rest of the day, cruising in Gideon's golf cart. "This is more fun than golfing," I told everyone. I found two kids at Family Village who wanted to see their mom at Doggie Village. "Wanna go for a ride? Only if Felipe says OK."

I took the back fire lane so they had a great view of the pond on one side and the dog run on the other. All sorts of dogs came out to greet us as we cruised past, some staked and some running free. When we got to the corner, I noticed the big Alpha I'd seen on the trail, all fenced in tight by himself with a sign reading "Doggie Jail."

"Why is that doggie in jail?"

"Because he's not a nice doggie."

"Can we go inside Doggie Village now?"

"Yes, here's your mommy."

As I drove off, I heard the kids shouting, "Mommy, there's been a mistake! This is not a bad doggie!"

The kids tore down the jail and the Doggie Village crew came running.

"Mission Impossible, we got a jailbreak at Doggie Village. Two dangerous suspects from Family Village, about four feet high, just tore down the walls of Doggie Jail."

But that Alpha walked out so meek and gentle and grateful to those kids, that the Doggie Village crew never put him back in Doggie Jail again. Isn't it funny how adults can learn from kids?

Mission Impossible called me on the radio to tell me that a Krishna crew wanted to come into camp for free. I drove to the gate to greet them and make sure they were comfortable. "Be sure and catch the OM at sunset," I told them.

Backstage, there was the typical moment of confusion because I always insist the ceremonies be as spontaneous as possible, with lots of improvisation and no script. Naturally, this drives the tech-heads up a wall! And the ceremony crew gets blamed for ruining the clockwork machinery of their rock show.

But because it was Sunday, the stage manager Alvin gladly powered up the wireless so Felipe could scout the vibe by the sacred Peace Pole that had been hastily erected. An old, well-traveled pole it was, with lots of carvings and a purple quartz crystal on top. Gaskin, Plunker and many others started to form the circle, but the circle got confused because there were too many people for just one circle in such a small space.

A Japanese monk jumped on the line and began spiraling it toward the center. Everyone got involved in the spiral hand-dance. When it ended, everyone was holding hands. A call went out for the crew to come to the pole. Gaskin and I walked slowly to the pole and were actually the first to get there. I hugged the pole while the entire 300-person crew hugged me. Tear ducts burst open in every eye, like waves in a sports stadium. My heart opened and I sobbed with joy from the telepathic energy.

Then came the WHEE! OM.

"Whee cranked the vibe," I said while hugging Gaskin.

July 22

Babbs came out to the Ramada to meet the clean-up crew. Six22, Zero, Tammy, Donna Eagle, Alvin, Edison, G. Moses and me. We held a playful ceremony upon his arrival and Babbs was so honored he made up a little song on the spot just for the crew's pleasure.

When is it all right to be too tight?
I can think of one extraordinary night when it was all right to be too tight.
I was so drunk
I couldn't even stand up

I fell asleep on the riverbank.
The cops came and arrested everybody else and they never got me.
So it was all right to be too tight.
But you still… can't… roll… the joints… too tight.

"Thank you, thank you," said Babbs. "That was a spontaneous song I've been practicing for the last twenty-two years and this was the first time I've had a chance to sing it. I want to thank you for lasting through the whole thing."

After the song, I filled Babbs in on the baby girl that had been born in the pine trees at 2:22 Monday morning.

"There was a cry in the woods of 'help me, help me,' and TDC came running fast 'cause we thought a sister was being raped. Her cousin was with her and said, 'Calm down, everybody. Jamie's just having a baby.' The cousin caught the baby coming out, and was assisted by a former EMT medic named Sunray. The baby was named Cassady Sunflower Phoenix. The cord was tied with Amazin' Dave's hemp twine. Garrick and Six22 were on the scene. I rolled up just as the baby popped out and interviewed everyone involved. Daphne Singingtree was there, too. It was a real warrior birth. That child might be a great leader some day."

"It just shows to go you that when things happen, they come into a lot of minds at the same time," said Babbs.

Babbs wanted drink, but the crew kept feeding him water and pizza. "Don't end up like Jack," I said. "Don't melt down and stay melted. *Big Sur*, that was his best book. He could've called it *Big Meltdown*."

"Kerouac, Ginsberg, they died relatively young," said Babbs. "It'd be great if they were still around. Cassady was unique. All the factions of the Beat crew revolved around Cassady because he knew what they were all talking about. They all strove to be like Cassady. You know what it was? Cassady really dealt on the lag. The one-thirtieth of a second between when you think of something and when you say it. He was always trying to beat the lag. So what he said had to do with what was happening right then. That was Cassady's thing. And he was always working on it as an artist. And at a certain point he knew that's what he was doing. But it was such a dangerous thing because speed freaks would try to emulate him, to be rapping all the time, but they weren't talking about anything, whereas Cassady was really talking about something. He was the true

Avatar. The True Seeker of the Vibe."

Then the crew introduced Babbs to Cassady the dog, the same dog the kids had busted out of Doggie Jail.

"He was abandoned on the site," said Six22. "He's my dog now."

The evening turned into a fun ceremony while Babbs relayed details of staying on the vibe trail. I caught on right away it was wrong to say "we crank the vibe." The vibe cranks itself. You have to be humble when you scout the vibe. Babbs put this information across in such a gentle manner everyone knew it was truly so.

"Hail the fun vibe," said the crew.

"I pulled a prank with the Merry Pranksters," I said to Babbs, falling to my knees. "Can I be a Merry Prankster, too?"

"Sure," said Babbs. "Let's go out in the moonlight and do the induction right now!"

Since the Ramada was located inside a freeway cloverleaf complex, the crew was reluctant to set foot off motel property, but Babbs led us through some bushes and we unexpectedly popped out on a river bank near a rose garden.

"Everyone take a big whiff," said Babbs, while pointing at the rose blossoms with a large speckled hawk feather. The feather shimmered and sparkled in the moonlight.

I got sleepy right away and lay down on a grassy knoll. The full moon had an orange glow around it, with psychedelic trails busting out all over.

There was a roar of thunder and a cloud of dust, and *Furthur*, the original psychedelic bus, pulled up with Ken Kesey at the wheel. Babbs led the crew up the back ladder to some seats on the roof.

The bus blasted off toward Interstate 5, and actually left the ground and flew into a dark, angry twister that looked about ready to touch ground and create all sorts of havoc.

When the black smoke cleared, the bus was cruising through a hundred miles of hempfields on both sides of the road. The plants were lush with birds of all colors and descriptions which flew up to us in great flocks and sang about how much fun it was to live in a hempfield, with endless food in all directions.

Furthur stopped on a cliff overlooking a lake with a view of the sunrise. There was a bonfire party going on. Krassner and Gaskin were there. So was Patti Smith talking to Bob Dylan. Julian Beck, Judith Malina, Joan

Baez and the Tin Man were having a conversation with Jack Herer! But the most amazing thing was that all four Beatles were listening to Neal Cassady, who was hanging onto a gearshift knob with one end in the fire. And Cassady was *talking about scouting the vibe!*

I found myself walking between Kesey and Babbs, headed straight for the fire. "We noticed this with Cassady," whispered Kesey. "The gearshift is the chord. The crew harmonizes because everyone is on the same gearshift chord." Kesey stopped and turned to me as if to say something really important. "Strong pot without a message is just a buzz. If you take cocaine, you'll often pick up a real bad vibe because it's traveling through those hands. Real nice dope, there's nothing wrong with it... doesn't have to be strong. You can tell how important it is by how much energy is raised to fight it."

"Is this when I get inducted?" I asked.

"Don't you know?" laughed Cassady, slapping me on the chest. "You've always been a Merry Prankster in your heart."

Everyone laughed because I had what I'd wanted all along and never even knew it. I also felt embarrassed because I'd been so overly caught up with the money situation during the event, just trying to break even somehow. I felt if the event lost too much money, I'd end up losing my job at *High Times*. But now I instinctively understood if you want to hold a true counterculture ceremony, admission must always be free.

Next thing I knew, I was asleep on the riverbank near the rose bush, almost alone, only the dog Cassady watching over me. On the way back to the Ramada, I found a large speckled hawk feather, and it remains in my straw cowboy hat to this day.